First World War
and Army of Occupation
War Diary
France, Belgium and Germany

6 DIVISION
Headquarters, Branches and Services
General Staff
3 August 1914 - 31 December 1915

WO95/1581

The Naval & Military Press Ltd
www.nmarchive.com
Published in association with The National Archives

Published by

The Naval & Military Press Ltd

Unit 10 Ridgewood Industrial Park,
Uckfield, East Sussex,
TN22 5QE England
Tel: +44 (0) 1825 749494

www.naval-military-press.com
www.nmarchive.com

This diary has been reprinted in facsimile from the original. Any imperfections are inevitably reproduced and the quality may fall short of modern type and cartographic standards.

© Crown Copyright
Images reproduced by permission of The National Archives, London, England, 2015.

Contents

Document type	Place/Title	Date From	Date To
Heading	General Staff Aug 1914-Dec 1915		
Heading	General Staff 6th Division August & September 1914		
Heading	6th Division From 3rd August 1914 To 30th September 1914 Vol 1		
War Diary		03/08/1914	16/08/1914
War Diary	Villemontoire	16/09/1914	16/09/1914
War Diary	Villeblain	17/09/1914	20/09/1914
War Diary	Bazoches	20/09/1914	21/09/1914
War Diary	State Of 6th Division At Midday	21/09/1914	21/09/1914
War Diary	Bazoches	21/09/1914	30/09/1914
War Diary	Bazoches Midday	30/09/1914	30/09/1914
Heading	General Staff 6th Division November 1914		
Heading	War Diary of General Staff 6th Division From 1st To 30th Nov 1914		
War Diary		01/11/1914	30/11/1914
Miscellaneous	C Form (Duplicate). Messages And Signals.		
Miscellaneous	C Form (Original). Messages And Signals.		
Miscellaneous	C Form (Duplicate). Messages And Signals.		
Heading	General Staff 6th Division December 1914		
Heading	War Diary of General Staff, 6th Division From 1.12.14 To 31.12.14 Vol IV		
War Diary		01/12/1914	31/12/1914
Heading	War Diary General Staff 6th Division January 1915		
War Diary		01/01/1915	31/01/1915
Heading	War Diary General Staff 6th Division February 1915		
Heading	War Diary of G.S. 6th Division From 1.2.15 To 28.2.15		
War Diary		01/02/1915	28/02/1915
Heading	War Diary of General Staff 6th Division March 1915		
Heading	War Diary of General Staff 6th Division From 1-3-15 To 31-3-15 Vol VII		
War Diary		01/03/1915	31/03/1915
Heading	Appendix I		
Operation(al) Order(s)	6th Division Operation Order No.22 Appendix I	09/03/1915	09/03/1915
Heading	Appendix II		
Operation(al) Order(s)	17th Brigade Operation Order No.11	11/03/1915	11/03/1915
Map			
Diagram etc	Sketch Shewing Positions Of House In Epinette		
Heading	Appendix III		
Operation(al) Order(s)	17th Infantry Brigade Report On The Operation Carried Out	13/03/1915	13/03/1915
Miscellaneous	17th I.B.		
Operation(al) Order(s)	17th Bde Operation Order No.11	11/03/1915	11/03/1915
Operation(al) Order(s)	1st March Staffordshire Regt Operation Order No.1 1915 Dt. 11.3.15	11/03/1915	11/03/1915
Miscellaneous	O.C. 2nd Crimsted Regt.		
Map	Attach On L'epinette		
Map	Artillery Support Before 12 Midnight		
Map	Artillery Support after 12 Midnight		
Map			
Diagram etc	Sketch Shewing Positions Of Hose In Epinette		

Type	Description	Start	End
Miscellaneous	Appendix IV		
Miscellaneous	A Form Messages And Signals		
Miscellaneous	A Form. Messages And Signals.		
Miscellaneous	C Form (Duplicate). Messages And Signals.		
Heading	War Diary General Staff 6th Division April 1915		
Heading	War Diary of General Staff 6th Division From 1.4.15 To 30.4.15		
War Diary		01/04/1915	30/04/1915
Heading	War Diary General Staff 6th Division May 1915		
Heading	War Diary of General Staff 6th Division From 1.5.15 To 31.5.15		
War Diary		01/05/1915	31/05/1915
Heading	Appendix I		
Operation(al) Order(s)	6th Division Operation Order No.23 Appendix I	31/05/1915	31/05/1915
Heading	War Diary General Staff 6th Division June 1915		
Heading	War Diary of General Staff 6th Division From 1.6.15 To 30.6.15 Vol X		
War Diary		01/06/1915	30/06/1915
Heading	Appendix I II & III		
Operation(al) Order(s)	VI Corps Operation Order No.3 Appendix I		
Operation(al) Order(s)	6th Division Operation Order No.24 Appendix II	15/06/1915	15/06/1915
Map	Zillebeke		
Miscellaneous	Appendix III		
Heading	War Diary General Staff 6th Division July 1915		
Heading	War Diary of General Staff 6th Division From 1.7.15 To 31.7.15		
War Diary		01/08/1915	31/08/1915
Heading	Appendix I (missing)		
Heading	War Diary General Staff 6th Division August 1915		
Heading	War Diary of General Staff 6th Division From 1.8.15 To 31.8.15		
War Diary		01/08/1915	31/08/1915
Miscellaneous	6th Corps H.Q. G.X. 190 mentioned in diary of 1st August As Being Attached Is Missing		
Miscellaneous	Reports On Operations At Hooge On 9th August		
Miscellaneous	16th Infantry Brigade Report On The Operations At Hooge 9th August, 1915	13/08/1915	13/08/1915
Miscellaneous	2nd Sherwood Foresters Report On Operations At Hooge 9th August 1915	11/08/1915	11/08/1915
Miscellaneous	18th Infantry Brigade Report On Operations At Hooge 9th August, 1915	09/08/1915	09/08/1915
Miscellaneous	Report On Operations Near Hooge On 9th August, 1915 2nd Durham Light Infantry	09/08/1915	09/08/1915
Miscellaneous	1st East Yorkshire Regiment Report On Operation At Hooge 9th August, 1915	11/08/1915	11/08/1915
Miscellaneous	Headquarters 6th Division		
Miscellaneous	The B.M.G.O. 18.1.B 6 Division	15/08/1915	15/08/1915
Miscellaneous	6th Div No. 6/6/22	14/08/1915	14/08/1915
Miscellaneous	6th Div. No. 6/6/24	23/08/1915	23/08/1915
Miscellaneous	Operation Orders In Connection With Operations At Hooge On 9th August		
Miscellaneous	Observation Placks		
Miscellaneous	Notes For Conferences	02/08/1915	02/08/1915
Operation(al) Order(s)	6th Division Operation Order No.27	05/08/1915	05/08/1915
Map	G Section		

Operation(al) Order(s)	VI Divisional Artillery Operation Order (on O.O. No.27 Of VIth Division)	05/08/1915	05/08/1915
Miscellaneous	16th Infantry Brigade		
Miscellaneous	6th Divisional Artillery Appendix I		
Miscellaneous	First List Appendix 2		
Miscellaneous	Second Lift Appendix 3		
Operation(al) Order(s)	6th Divisional Artillery Operation Order No,2	06/08/1915	06/08/1915
Miscellaneous	6th Divisional Artillery Operations 8/8/15 Bombardment	08/08/1915	08/08/1915
Miscellaneous	First Lift Appendix 2		
Miscellaneous	Second Lift Appendix		
Miscellaneous	No.2 Group Heavy Artillery Reserve Amended Time Table In Connections With Operations Of 6th Division 9th August, 1915	09/08/1915	09/08/1915
Miscellaneous	No.2 Group Heavy Artillery Reserve		
Miscellaneous	No.2 Group Heavy Reserve Artillery		
Miscellaneous	No.2 Group Heavy Artillery Reserve		
Operation(al) Order(s)	Operation Order No.3 by Lt. Colonel, F.W. Towsey, Commanding 18th Infantry Brigade	06/08/1915	06/08/1915
Miscellaneous	16th Infantry Brigade	06/08/1915	06/08/1915
Miscellaneous	16th Infantry Brigade Operation Order No.	06/08/1915	06/08/1915
Miscellaneous	Notes Regarding Country And Trenches About Hooge		
Miscellaneous	Additional Notes On Hooge		
Operation(al) Order(s)	Divisional Operation Orders Nos. 28,29,30 & 31		
Operation(al) Order(s)	16th Divisional Operation Order No.28	18/08/1915	18/08/1915
Operation(al) Order(s)	6 Division Operation Order No.29	20/08/1915	20/08/1915
Operation(al) Order(s)	6th Divisional Operation Order No.30	21/08/1915	21/08/1915
Operation(al) Order(s)	6th Division Operation Order No.31	01/09/1915	01/09/1915
Heading	Summary Of Information		
Miscellaneous	Summary Of Information No.70	22/08/1915	22/08/1915
Miscellaneous	1st Echelon Coy RE		
Heading	War Diary General Staff 6th Division September 1915		
Heading	War Diary of General Staff 6th Division From 1.9.15 To 30.9.15 Vol XIII		
War Diary		01/09/1915	30/09/1915
Miscellaneous	Divisional Operation Orders Nos. 32,33,34,35 & 36		
Operation(al) Order(s)	6th Divisional Operation Order No.32	07/09/1915	07/09/1915
Operation(al) Order(s)	6th Division Operation Order No.33	13/09/1915	13/09/1915
Operation(al) Order(s)	6th Division Operation Order No.34	14/09/1915	14/09/1915
Operation(al) Order(s)	6th Division Operation Order No.35	19/09/1915	19/09/1915
Operation(al) Order(s)	6th Division Operation Order No.36	23/09/1915	23/09/1915
Miscellaneous	Paper G/6/4		
Miscellaneous	17th Infantry Brigade 18th Infantry Brigade		
Miscellaneous	Points On The Operations At Hooge		
Miscellaneous	Extract From Report By 6 O.C. 6th Division. In Reply To Questions Asked By 2nd Army		
Miscellaneous	6th Corps		
Miscellaneous	16th Infantry Brigade Extract From Report On The Operations At Noose 9th Aug 1915	09/08/1915	09/08/1915
Miscellaneous	Extract From 16th Infantry Brigade Operations Orders Of 6th August 1915		
Miscellaneous	Last paragraph		
Miscellaneous	The Following notes from the experience gained by 6th Division at Hooge are forwareded continuation of this office G/435		
Miscellaneous	Summaries Of Information		
Miscellaneous	Summary Of Information No.69	02/09/1915	02/09/1915

Miscellaneous	Summary Of Information No.90	03/09/1915	03/09/1915
Miscellaneous	Summary Of Information No.91	04/09/1915	04/09/1915
Miscellaneous	Summary Of Information No.92	05/09/1915	05/09/1915
Miscellaneous	Summary Of Information No.93	06/09/1915	06/09/1915
Miscellaneous	Summary Of Information No.94	07/09/1915	07/09/1915
Miscellaneous	6th Division		
Miscellaneous	1st London Cay RF		
Miscellaneous	Summary Of Information No.95	08/09/1915	08/09/1915
Miscellaneous	Summary Of Information No.96	09/09/1915	09/09/1915
Miscellaneous	6th Division		
Miscellaneous	Summary Of Information No.97	10/09/1915	10/09/1915
Miscellaneous	6th Division		
Miscellaneous	Summary Of Information No.98	11/09/1915	11/09/1915
Miscellaneous	6th Division News Sheet (By Wireless)		
Miscellaneous	1st Ln Coy R.E.		
Miscellaneous	Summary Of Information No.99	12/09/1915	12/09/1915
Miscellaneous	6th Division News Sheet (By Wireless)		
Miscellaneous	1st Ln Coy R.E.		
Miscellaneous	Summary Of Information No.100	13/09/1915	13/09/1915
Miscellaneous	6th Division News Sheet (By Wireless)		
Operation(al) Order(s)	Summary Of Information No.101	14/09/1915	14/09/1915
Miscellaneous	Flammenwerfer In Action		
Miscellaneous	6th Division News Sheet (By Wireless)		
Miscellaneous	From "Frankfurter Zeitung". Sunday August 15th	15/09/1915	15/09/1915
Miscellaneous	1st Ln Coy R.E.		
Miscellaneous	Summary Of Information No.102	15/09/1915	15/09/1915
Miscellaneous	6th Division News Sheet (By Wireless)	17/09/1915	17/09/1915
Miscellaneous	1st Ln Coy		
Miscellaneous	Summary Of Information No.104	17/09/1915	17/09/1915
Miscellaneous	Summary Of Information No.103	16/09/1915	16/09/1915
Miscellaneous	6th Division News Sheet (By Wireless)	18/09/1915	18/09/1915
Miscellaneous	1st Ln Coy R.E.		
Miscellaneous	Summary Of Information No.105	18/09/1915	18/09/1915
Miscellaneous	6th Division News Sheet (By Wireless)	19/09/1915	19/09/1915
Miscellaneous	1st Ln Coy		
Miscellaneous	6th Division Poldhu Press (By Wireless)	20/09/1915	20/09/1915
Miscellaneous	1st Ln Coy		
Miscellaneous	Summary Of Information No.107	20/09/1915	20/09/1915
Miscellaneous	Summary Of Information No.108	21/09/1915	21/09/1915
Miscellaneous	6th Division Poldhu Press (By Wireless)	21/09/1915	21/09/1915
Miscellaneous	6th Division Poldhu Press (By Wireless)	22/09/1915	22/09/1915
Miscellaneous	1st Ln Coy		
Miscellaneous	Summary Of Information No.109	22/09/1915	22/09/1915
Miscellaneous	Summary Of Information No.110	23/09/1915	23/09/1915
Miscellaneous	6th Division Poldhu Press (By Wireless)	23/09/1915	23/09/1915
Miscellaneous	1st Ln Coy		
Miscellaneous	6th Division News Sheet By Wireless		
Miscellaneous	1st Ln Coy		
Miscellaneous	Summary Of Information No.111	24/09/1915	24/09/1915
Miscellaneous	Summary Of Information		
Miscellaneous	Summary Of Information No.114	27/09/1915	27/09/1915
Miscellaneous	News Sheet (By Wireless)		
Miscellaneous	1st Ln Coy		
Miscellaneous	News Sheet (By Sheet)		
Miscellaneous	Summary Of Information No.116	29/09/1915	29/09/1915
Miscellaneous	1st Ln Coy		

Miscellaneous	News Sheet (by Wireless)		
Miscellaneous	1st London Field Coy RE		
Miscellaneous	Mr. Lloyd George has accepted invitation to address Congress on Munitions in rolation to war profits and labour.		
Miscellaneous	1st Ln Fd Coy R.E.		
Miscellaneous	Calendar For September 1915		
Miscellaneous	1st London Coy R.E.		
Heading	War Diary General Staff 6th Division October 1915		
Heading	War Diary of General Staff 6th Division From 1st October 1915 To 31st October 1915 Vol XIV		
War Diary		01/10/1915	31/10/1915
Miscellaneous	Divisional Operation Orders Nos. 38, 39 40 41 42 & 43		
Operation(al) Order(s)	6th Divisional Operation Order No.38	05/10/1915	05/10/1915
Operation(al) Order(s)	6th Divisional Operation Order No.39	06/10/1915	06/10/1915
Operation(al) Order(s)	6th Division Operation Order No.40	09/10/1915	09/10/1915
Miscellaneous			
Operation(al) Order(s)	6th Division Operation Order No.41	12/10/1915	12/10/1915
Operation(al) Order(s)	6th Division Operation Order No.42	20/10/1915	20/10/1915
Operation(al) Order(s)	6th Division Operation Order No.43	23/10/1915	23/10/1915
Heading	War Diary General Staff 6th Division November 1915		
Heading	War Diary of General Staff 6th Division From 1.11.15 To 30.11.15 Vol XVI		
War Diary		01/11/1915	30/11/1915
Miscellaneous	Divisional Operation Orders Nos. 44 45 & 46		
Operation(al) Order(s)	6th Division Operation Order No.44	07/09/1915	07/09/1915
Operation(al) Order(s)	6th Division Operation Order No.45	09/09/1915	09/09/1915
Operation(al) Order(s)	6th Division Operation Order No.46	16/09/1915	16/09/1915
Heading	War Diary General Staff 6th Division December 1915		
Heading	War Diary of General Staff 6th Division From 1-12-15 To 31-12-15 Vol XVI		
War Diary		01/12/1915	31/12/1915
Miscellaneous	Paper G/44/7		
Miscellaneous	16th Infantry Brigade 18th Infantry Brigade 71st Infantry Brigade G.O.C. R.A. C.R.E. A.D.M.S. "Q". 14th Division		
Miscellaneous	Divisional Operation Order No.47		
Operation(al) Order(s)	6th Division Operation Order No.47	05/12/1915	05/12/1915
Miscellaneous			

6TH DIVISION

GENERAL STAFF
AUG 1914-DEC 1915

Division disembarked ST NAZAIRE 10.9.14.

GENERAL STAFF

6th DIVISION.

AUGUST & SEPTEMBER 1914.

121/1084

CONFIDENTIAL

WAR DIARY
of the
6th Division.

From 3rd August 1914 to 30th September 1914.

Vol I

Army Form C. 2118.

WAR DIARY
or
INTELLIGENCE SUMMARY
(Erase heading not required.)

Instructions regarding War Diaries and Intelligence Summaries are contained in F. S. Regs., Part II. and the Staff Manual respectively. Title pages will be prepared in manuscript.

Hour, Date, Place	Summary of Events and Information	Remarks and References to Appendices
11pm. 3rd August. 1914	War declared with Germany.	
4·50pm. 4th "	Mobilization order despatched from War Office.	
15th "	6th Division commenced move to England, sailing from CORK and QUEENSTOWN.	
10am. 18th "	Head quarters arrived at CAMBRIDGE.	
18th August to 7th September.	6th Division in camps at CAMBRIDGE & NEWMARKET.	
7th September.	The Division commenced entrainment.	
9·20am. 8th "	Headquarters entrained. detrained at SOUTHAMPTON. and embarked in the "ACHIMEDES".	
9pm. "	Sailed	
9th "	At sea.	
10th "	Arrived at St NAZAIRE. Headquarters disembarked.	
1·45am. 11th "	Entrained.	
11th "	In train.	
2am. 12th "	Headquarters detrained at MARLES. Division into billets COULOMMIERS - MONTCERF - MARLES - CHAUME.	
13th "	Division marched to COULOMMIERS (H.Q).	
14th "	" " - CHATEAU CHARNESSEUIL. (H.Q).	
15th "	" " - ROCOURT (H.Q)	
16th "	" " - VILLEMONTOIRE (H.Q)	

WAR DIARY
or
INTELLIGENCE SUMMARY.
(Erase heading not required.)

Army Form C. 2118.

Instructions regarding War Diaries and Intelligence Summaries are contained in F. S. Regs., Part II. and the Staff Manual respectively. Title pages will be prepared in manuscript.

Hour, Date, Place	Summary of Events and Information	Remarks and references to Appendices
4.40 pm. 16.9.14. VILLEMONTOIRE	Aircraft reconnaissance of German position. Bivouacs of large bodies of troops in rear of Selman position opposite 6 British. Trenches in possession of the 61st Nouveau - Moisan.	G.H.Q. (1)
6 pm. " " "	2 German Corps moving S.S.E. from Peronne.	Received from Lt. Col. Davidson.
9.33 pm. 17.9.14. VILLEBLAIN	Little change - slow progression on the left by the French - on the right the French occupied AILLES - and CRAONNE.	Intelligence 3rd Corps.
18.9.14	French on our left advanced towards PERRIERE FE.	Operation Order 3rd Corps 17.9.14
19.9.14	18th Infantry Brigade ordered to join 1st Corps.	G.H.Q. A.Q. 32
20.9.14	6th Battalion West Riding Rifles from Brixton Cavalry Barracks joined 8 am. 1st Corps.	G.705.
	18th Infantry Brigade join 1st Corps and placed in position	
2.15 pm. 20.9.14. BAZOCHES	1 Bn: (R.B.) 17th I. B. ordered to ST. MARD - 3 remaining Bns. to VIEIL ARCY - intention to replace 5th Infantry Brigade in firing line - marched at 2.30 pm from COURCELLES Orders received from G.H.Q. to await 17th I. B. k.	K.A. 57.
3.20 pm. " "	COURCELLES - there to await orders - Bn marched at 4 pm. 1st Corps report heavy attack all along front - and some troops driven in.	1st Corps No. 717.
3.40 pm. " "	All reserves of 7th and 9th Brigade used up to repel attack which continues - 2nd Corps not for 2 Bns. to relieve tonight some of those in trenches.	2nd Corps No. 358.
3.50 pm. " "	1st Division attacked. West Yorks driven in. 18th Brigade Reserve Coys. attacked - Hostile infantry in wood to front of 5th and 6th Brigades, who have been ordered to turn them out -	G.H.Q. O.C. 64.
4.20 pm. " "	4th Brigade between to have fallen back to CHAVONNE-VAILLY.	

WAR DIARY
or
INTELLIGENCE SUMMARY.

(Erase heading not required.)

Army Form C. 2118.

Hour, Date, Place	Summary of Events and Information	Remarks and references to Appendices
3.35.pm. 20.9.14. BAZOCHES.	The 17th Infantry Bde were directed from VIEILLE ARCY on CHAVONNE to assist the left of the 2nd Division. The 19wn Mounted troops received the same order.	By Col. Furse
5.23.pm. "	Situation 6th Division. Mounted Troops moving on S.t NARD and CHAVONNE. 17th J.B. to VIEILLE ARCY (General Reserve) 16th J.B. arriving at COURCELLES. 18th J.B. on right of the 1st Army Corps. Artillery in Action - 2nd - PAARS - 38th BAZOCHES - 2nd near QUINCEY. 38th Field Coy PAARS. 17th Field Ambulance PAARS. 18th BAZOCHES. 16th MONT NOTRE DAME.	G.H.Q. O.a.70
5.40.pm. "	16th Infantry Brigade placed under orders of 2nd Corps.	G.H.Q. O.a.70 (4)
7.20.pm. "	Situation much improved - all attacks repulsed. French on our right and left have done well.	G.H.Q. O.a.74. (4)
10.30.pm. "	Report from 1st Corps that 18th J.B. had been heavily attacked during afternoon - a confused fight - but Brigade held position. 3rd Dvn asked for 16th Field Ambulance to join 3rd Dvn. H.Q. BRAINE.	1st Corps. G.737 (5)
11.55.pm. "		
7.56.am. 21.9.1914.	3rd Dvn report that Yorkshires and Buffs (16th) had taken 3rd Dvn. G.H.637 over some of his trenches at 3am. without opposition.	3rd Dvn. G.H.637 (1)
8.30.am. "	1st Dvn report loss of about 600 and several officers during yesterdays operations - a portion of W.Yorks Regt Captured. D.L.I. and E.Yorks suffered most. 12th Field Coy rejoined 6th Division.	1st Corps. G.743 (2) (10)

WAR DIARY
or
INTELLIGENCE SUMMARY
(Erase heading not required.)

Army Form C. 2118.

Hour, Date, Place	Summary of Events and Information	Remarks and references to Appendices
21.9.14 11.10am. BAZOCHES.	G. H.Q. ordered 2 Inf. Bdes. (relieved by the 3. 6th Bns. 1st Div.) to form a General Reserve, allotted to I & II Corps. Permanent situation 1 at DHUIZEL, 1 at BRAINE.	O.A. 82 (L)
11.10am. 21.9.14 "	16th Field Amb. to BRAINE to H.Q. 3rd Div. - marched after dinner.	6th Div: G. 154.
11.30am. "	All I.a.a. Carts of 38th Bde. R.G.A. a. b. to BRAINE to 40th Bde. - after dinner.	6th Div: G. 156.
11.45am. "	38th Field Coy. R.E. to join 2nd Div: temporarily.	6th Div: G. 158.

__State of 6th Division at H.Q. at BAZOCHES:__
__midday - 21.9.14__

16th Brigade. (under orders of 2nd Corps). - 2 Bns. in firing line N.E. of VAILLY

17th Brigade. - VIEILLE ARCY. (?) to take up trenches to right of 2 Bns. at COURCELLES 1st Corps G. 747. the 6th Infantry Brigade.

18th Brigade - On right of Army (i.e. N. of PAISSY).
II Bde. R.F.A. - in fields BRUYERE FARM.
XII Bde. R.F.A. - attached 4th Division
XXIV Bde. R.F.A. - PAARS.
XXVIII/38 R.F.A. [less I.a.a. Carts A.C.] which is to join 40th Bde. at Braine] - PAARS.

Heavies - with 4th Division
12th Field Co. R.E. on route to join Division
38th Field Co. R.E. - PAARS. but about to join 2nd Div: temporarily.

P.T.O

Army Form C. 2118.

WAR DIARY
or
INTELLIGENCE SUMMARY.
(Erase heading not required.)

Instructions regarding War Diaries and Intelligence Summaries are contained in F. S. Regs., Part II. and the Staff Manual respectively. Title pages will be prepared in manuscript.

State of 6th Division on 21.9.14. (Continued)

Hour, Date, Place	Summary of Events and Information	Remarks and references to Appendices
3 pm. 21.9.14. BAZOCHES	16th Field Ambce. - to join H.Q. 3rd Divn. 17th Field Ambce. - PAARS. 18th Field Ambce. - BAZOCHES. 6th Brigade at DHUIZEL and 9th Bde at COURCELLES ordered to come under orders of G.O.C. 6th Divn. 5th Brigade at BOURG - General Reserve.	G.H.Q. O.a. 89
9 pm. "	Situation unaltered.	
11.10 pm. 22.9.14.	16th and 17th Inf. Bde. took up position in the firing line.	G.H.Q. O.a. 95
" "	17th Co. R.E. placed at disposal of the 2nd Corps. Situation unaltered.	G.H.Q. O.a. 112.
7.25 am. "	5th Brigade instead of 6th Bde attached to 6th Divn. and billeted at DHUIZEL.	1st Corps. E.966
7.53 pm. 23.9.14.	Situation unchanged. Heavy shelling on PAISSY. French 18th Corps little progress.	G.H.Q. O.A. 139 1st Corps. E 828.
9.10 pm. "	17th Bde. report quiet day but considerable shelling yesterday. Casualties :- 5 men killed 4 Officer and 34 men wounded. 3 missing	17th Bat. Z. Q. 112
9 pm. "	16th Bde.- Killed Capt Hawe. 8 N.C.O. men wounded 10.	16th Bde. 174

Army Form C. 2118.

WAR DIARY
or
INTELLIGENCE SUMMARY.
(Erase heading not required.)

Instructions regarding War Diaries and Intelligence Summaries are contained in F. S. Regs., Part II. and the Staff Manual respectively. Title pages will be prepared in manuscript.

Hour, Date, Place	Summary of Events and Information	Remarks and references to Appendices
9 a.m. 24.9.14. BAZOCHES.	18th Bde report heavy shelling on 23rd but fewer casualties than on 22nd, when the total losses were about 50 - an officer killed on 22nd and 23rd.	Z.R. 24.
12.5 p.m. "	5th Bde lent to 1st Corps for purpose of preparing a position near DHUIZEL.	1st Corps. 836 G.H.Q. O.A. 149.
3.10 p.m. "	16th Bde report situation normal, the right less shelled today than heretofore.	16th I.B. Z.R. 11.
5.5 p.m. "	2nd & 38th Bde R.F.A detailed to report to the 5th Division at SERCHES on morning of 25th to be in action with 5th Division to be controlled by Br. Gen. R.A. 5th Divn. but to revert to 6th Divn. in event of General Reserve being required elsewhere - not to cross AISNE without orders from G.H.Q.	O.A. 151
5.55 p.m. "	16th Bde Casualties:- Other ranks killed 1. Wounded Officer 2, other ranks 2.	16. I.B. Z. P. 192.

WAR DIARY
or
INTELLIGENCE SUMMARY.
(Erase heading not required.)

Army Form C. 2118.

Hour, Date, Place	Summary of Events and Information	Remarks and references to Appendices
10.30 am. 25.9.14. BAZOCHES.	H.Q. remained at BAZOCHES. 1 Coy. 3rd Rifle Bde. (17th Bde) attacked German trenches at dawn - attack unsuccessful. Casualties:- Killed 5. Wounded 1 Officer & 28th others, missing 2 Officers (wounded) and 18 others.	I.Q. 136.
1 pm. " "	2 Bns. of the 9th Brigade relieve 2 Bns. of the 8th Brigade at VAILLY.	O.A. 166.
8.50 pm. " "	Situation unchanged, but greatest vigilance to be observed. 38th Bde. R.F.A. joined the 5th Division. Casualties: 16.I.B. 1 killed - 1 officer & 3 O.R. wounded.	O.A. 168.
8.15 pm. " "	1st Corps ask for a major from H.L. Inf. to command Cameron Highrs. who have no officer qualified to command.	1st Corps. A. 787.
10.2 pm. " "	9th Bde. to relieve 8th Bde which come under command of 6th Division in General Reserve from 10 pm. 26th.	2nd Corps. G.a. 67.
10.50 pm. " "	Situation unchanged. French constructed by enemy about Point 197, east of OSTELL, running N.E - S.W. - Activity in CHIVY Valley and along BEAULNE spur about 7 pm. PAISSY spur heavily shelled.	1st Corps. E. 870.

Army Form C. 2118.

WAR DIARY
or
INTELLIGENCE SUMMARY
(Erase heading not required.)

Instructions regarding War Diaries and Intelligence Summaries are contained in F. S. Regs., Part II. and the Staff Manual respectively. Title pages will be prepared in manuscript.

Hour, Date, Place	Summary of Events and Information	Remarks and references to Appendices
7.30am. 26.9.14. BAZOCHES	Quiet night - attack on right of 1st Corps and French left. 3.30 am. General attack on 1st D. Division 5 am.	1st Corps. 874.
11.45 am. " "	5th I.B. placed at disposal of 1st Corps - only to be used if absolutely necessary.	O.A. 171.
12.30pm. " "	2nd Bde. R.F.A. report being in action.	2nd R.F.A. Bde. B.1.
12.50 p.m. " "	L.a.a. Carts of 24th Bde. R.F.A. replace 38th Bde. carts with 40th Brigade.	3rd Dn. G.C. 878
8.5 p.m. " "	Situation unchanged.	G.H.Q. O.A. 180.
9.30 p.m. " "	During the day an attack was delivered at the south edge of the CHIVY VALLEY - repulsed with difficulty enemy suffered severely. afternoon quiet.	1st Corps. G. 896
4 am. 27.9.14. BAZOCHES	Enemy reported to be crossing CONDE bridge in large numbers - this report late on appeared to be wrong.	2nd Corps. G. 606. " - G. 611.
5.53 am. " "	All quiet along front of 2nd Corps.	" - G. 610.
8.26 am. " "	" " " " " 16.I.B. except for shelling of St. Prind.	I.P. 44
10am. " "	Certain amount of movement along front of 1st Corps - not known whether to front of rear - some German trenches evacuated.	1st Corps. G. 901.

Army Form C. 2118.

WAR DIARY
or
INTELLIGENCE SUMMARY.
(Erase heading not required.)

Instructions regarding War Diaries and Intelligence Summaries are contained in F. S. Regs., Part II. and the Staff Manual respectively. Title pages will be prepared in manuscript.

Hour, Date, Place	Summary of Events and Information	Remarks and references to Appendices
7.30 p.m. 27.9.14. BAZOCHES.	Situation unchanged.	O.A. 189.
8.50 p.m. "	Attack delivered on 2nd, 3rd, & 6th Bdes. Enemy using a projectile emitting dense black smoke and breaking into small bits fired at a range of 800 yards. Attack repulsed.	1st Corps. G.925.
6.20 a.m. 28.9.14. "	Several attacks to date made last night 7 p.m. and 11.30 p.m. on right of our 1st Corps. and on left of French – apparently increasing pressure coming on our right.	1st Corps. G.928.
9.45 a.m. "	Brigade at DHUIZEL in reserve placed at disposal of 1st Corps – the Brigade at COURCELLES may be moved North should 1st Corps so desire.	O.A. 195.
12.5 p.m. "	18th I.B. in reserve at between BOURG and VENDRESSE. with 2 Battalions – two other battalion N of VENDRESSE. Major Green. D/o major of 17th Inf / Bde. killed by sniper.	18th Bde. Z.R.3. 2nd Dn. A.B.39.
12.30 p.m. "	1st Corps H.Q. moved to MONT HUSSART FARM. 2 miles North of COURCELLES.	1st Corps. G.934.
6.45 p.m. "	7th Inf. Brigade report nothing important to communicate. Situation unchanged.	17.I.B. Z.Q. 204. O.A. 204.
8.7 p.m. "		
6.30 p.m. "	Leicester Trenches heavily shelled 1.30-2 p.m. Lt RUND Killed 3 p.m. German entrenching in front of Buffs.	16.I.B. Z.P. 67.
11.5 p.m. "	Enemy attacked Leicester at 9.50 p.m. but repulsed.	16.I.B. Z.P. 71.

Army Form C. 2118.

WAR DIARY
or
INTELLIGENCE SUMMARY

(Erase heading not required.)

Instructions regarding War Diaries and Intelligence Summaries are contained in F. S. Regs., Part II. and the Staff Manual respectively. Title pages will be prepared in manuscript.

Hour, Date, Place		Summary of Events and Information	Remarks and references to Appendices
11.28 p.m.	28.9.14 BAZOCHES	Naval attack on French - all quiet in front of 1st Corps.	1st Corps. G.939.
7 a.m.	29.9.14. "	Situation unchanged.	
7.10 a.m.	"	2nd attack on French at 1.a.m. - 2.15 a.m. attack along whole front of 1st Division - Dead Germans found in empty trenches.	16.1.B. Z.P.62. 1st Corps. G.940
1.2 p.m.	"	18th I.B. East York and Durham L.I. at VENDRESSE in Reserve to 1st Inf. Bde. - H.B. and Sherwood Foresters MOULINS supporting right of 2nd Infantry Bde.	18th I.B. Z.R.2.
7 p.m.	"	Situation unchanged.	O.A. 218.
8.25 p.m.	"	17th I.B. Quiet day. no casualties. Capt. Meade Waldo. 3rd Rifle Bde to be 6.Bde major.	17.I.B. Z.Q.219.
9.7 p.m.	"	16th I.B. Situation unchanged.	16.I.B. Z.P.76.
10.4 p.m.	"	All quiet. no change.	1st Corps. G.963.
7.20 a.m.	30.9.1914 BAZOCHES	16th I.B. Situation unchanged.	Z.P.78
3.40 p.m.	"	18th I.B. No change - East Yorks had 4 killed and 10 wounded yesterday.	18.I.B. R.10.

P.T.O.

Army Form C. 2118.

WAR DIARY
or
INTELLIGENCE SUMMARY
(Erase heading not required.)

Instructions regarding War Diaries and Intelligence Summaries are contained in F. S. Regs., Part II. and the Staff Manual respectively. Title pages will be prepared in manuscript.

Hour, Date, Place	Summary of Events and Information	Remarks and references to Appendices
	6th Division Casualties (Approximately.) Reported up to noon 30th September 1914.	For details see telegrams forwarded with War Diary of the A.A. & Q.M.G. 6th Division.

UNIT.	Officers			Other Ranks.			Remarks.
	Killed	Wounded	Missing	K.	W.	M.	
6th Signal Coy					1.		
17th Inft. Bde. H.Q	1.						Major Green. Bde Major.
16th I.B. { E. Kent Regt.		2.			17		
Leicester Regt.	1.	2.		1.	22		
K.S.L.I.		1*.		1.	4		*Died in hospital.
York & Lancs.		1.		1.	98		[Also [?] WB & Yst say 30 of]
17th I.B. { 1st Bn: Rl. Fusrs:		1.					
N. Staffords. Regt	1.	1.			18		
Leinster Regt.		1.			7.		
3rd Rifle Bde.		2.	2.	3.	46.	18	
18th I.B. { West Yorks Regt.	17. K.W.M.			600. K.W.M.			Not yet confirmed.
East Yorks	9. " "			90 " "			
Sherwood Foresters	14 " "			220 " "			
Durham. L. Inf	12 " "			132 K/2 W/4 M/1			
24th Heavy Batty:							

Army Form C. 2118.

WAR DIARY
or
INTELLIGENCE SUMMARY
(Erase heading not required.)

Instructions regarding War Diaries and Intelligence Summaries are contained in F. S. Regs., Part II. and the Staff Manual respectively. Title pages will be prepared in manuscript.

Hour, Date, Place	Summary of Events and Information	Remarks and references to Appendices
BAZOCHES. Midday. 30.9.1914.	Positions of Units of 6th Division. Head Quarters — BAZOCHES. Mounted Troops — VAUXTIN. Divnl R.A. Hd. Qrs: — BAZOCHES. 2nd Bde. R.F.A. — SERCHES attached 5th Division. 12th " " — VENIZEL " 4th Division. 24th " " — PAARS. 38th " " — SERCHES " 5th Division. Heavy Battery R.G.A. — LE PAVILLON " 5th Division. 12th Company R.E. — VAILLY. 38th " " — BOURG. 16th Infantry Brigade — VAILLY " 3rd Division. 17th " " — SOUPIR " 2nd Division. 18th " " — MOULINS-VENDRESSE. 1st Division. 16th Field Ambulance. — BRAINE & VAILLY. att: 3rd Division. 17th " " — PAARS. 18th " " — BAZOCHES. No.4 Section: Div: Ammn: Col: — CHACRISE Remainder " " — JOUAIGNE.	

GENERAL STAFF

6th DIVIWION

NOVEMBER 1914.

CONFIDENTIAL

WAR DIARY

of

General Staff 6th Division

From 1st To 30th Novr 1914

Army Form C. 2118.

WAR DIARY
or
INTELLIGENCE SUMMARY.
(Erase heading not required.)

Instructions regarding War Diaries and Intelligence Summaries are contained in F. S. Regs., Part II. and the Staff Manual respectively. Title pages will be prepared in manuscript.

Hour, Date, Place	Summary of Events and Information	Remarks and references to Appendices
1. Nov.	A quiet night. Reports received that during the night troops & transport could be heard moving from S. to N. A. & S. Highlanders sent to ERQUINGHEM. Section of heavy battery ordered to LE BIZET to join 4th Division. Quiet day but some shelling.	A, A1, A2.
2. Nov.	Quiet day with some shelling of enemy.	
3. Nov.	Quiet day.	
4. Nov.	Foggy in morning. Slight attacks on 19th Brigade. Leicesters relieved Somers (12th Bn), Inniskillings both retaken posn in trench. Some took Inniskilling place.	
5. Nov.	All quiet.	

WAR DIARY
or
INTELLIGENCE SUMMARY.

(Erase heading not required.)

Army Form C. 2118.

Hour, Date, Place	Summary of Events and Information	Remarks and references to Appendices
6 Nov	Quiet day along whole front, but little shelling. Very foggy day.	
7 Nov. 12 noon	No change during night. Heavy engagement about PLOEGSTREET WOOD. Dept of 4th Div. A.S. Highlanders moved to PLOEGSTREET to assist.	
5.0	The batt? 12" How at CHAPEL D'ARMENTIERS moved to LE BIZET. The W.YORKS The W.YORKS relieve from L'ARMEE to CHAPEL D'ARMENTIERS. Some attacks all along the line to the south, but none serious. Enemy's aircraft very active tonight.	
8 Nov.	Situation unchanged. Rather more shelling opposite 19th Brigade.	
9 Nov.	The usual shelling. West Yorks relieve Leicesters in trenches.	

WAR DIARY
or
INTELLIGENCE SUMMARY.

(Erase heading not required.)

Army Form C. 2118.

Hour, Date, Place	Summary of Events and Information	Remarks and references to Appendices
10 Nov.	Situation unchanged. It was reported that the enemy had established a search light opposite 18th Inf. Bde.	B. B1.
11 Nov.	Shelling exceptionally heavy along most of our front. Shrapnel and high-explosive. J.19. 18th Inf Bde moved to L'ARMÉE. 17th Bde moves L.H.C. Chapel d'Armentières. 1st Bde " to the Ferme Buterne. Queen Westminsters arrived at ERQUINGHEM. Siege Battery knocked out 2 guns and blew up a wagon in an enemy's Battery.	C
12th Nov.	Situation unchanged.	
13th Nov.	Argyll & Sutherland Highrs returned to 19th Bde about noon. Fusiliers relieved Essex in reserve, who were relieved by Seaforths. Leicesters took over from R. Fusiliers by 10.30pm. Situation unchanged.	

Army Form C. 2118.

WAR DIARY
or
INTELLIGENCE SUMMARY.
(Erase heading not required.)

Instructions regarding War Diaries and Intelligence Summaries are contained in F. S. Regs., Part II. and the Staff Manual respectively. Title pages will be prepared in manuscript.

Hour, Date, Place	Summary of Events and Information	Remarks and references to Appendices
14th Nov.	HQ 1/7th Div. Patrol thro' Croix du Bac 10.30am. 19th Bde withdrawn from trenches relieved by 7th Div.	
15th Nov.	No change in situation. No change situation.	
16th Nov.	Leicesters relieve the R. Bde. Weather(?) relieve(?) N. Staffs. All quiet. No change.	
17th Nov.	No change in situation. 19th Bde relieved 10th Bde.	
18th Nov.	Leinsters relieved Warwicks. No change in situation.	
19th Nov.	No change in situation. 5th Bn Scottish Rifles arrived.	
20th Nov.	No change in situation. Germans apparently moving South. Movement by motor + rail reported.	D
21st Nov.	No change in situation. Large draft for Notts + Derbys. Royal Fusiliers relieve by Rifle Bde.	
22nd Nov.	No change in situation. Further movement reported at Perenchies. SW. E, E1, E2.	
23rd Nov.	No change in situation. 19th Bde reports hostile hostile(?) moving NW & SE F continually all day.	
24th Nov.	No change in situation. K.S.L.I. relieved B.W/R in daylight. Bn/ts relieve Yorkshires in Div Reserve.	

Army Form C. 2118.

WAR DIARY
or
INTELLIGENCE SUMMARY.
(Erase heading not required.)

Instructions regarding War Diaries and Intelligence Summaries are contained in F. S. Regs., Part II. and the Staff Manual respectively. Title pages will be prepared in manuscript.

Hour, Date, Place	Summary of Events and Information	Remarks and references to Appendices
25th Nov.	Welsh Fusiliers relieved by Middlesex. Situation unchanged.	
26 Nov.	No change in situation. Fusilighni Bosg destroyed by Our Shells	
27 Nov.	No change in situation. HMS Kenly relieves Dr. 1.	
28 Nov.	No change in situation. Leinsters relieves Rifle Bde	
29 Nov.	No change in situation. (Yorkshires relieves Leicesters)	
30 Nov.	No change in situation. " "	

W S Anson Col. G.S.

1.12.14.

"C" Form (Duplicate).   Army Form C. 2128
MESSAGES AND SIGNALS.

Service Instructions: M ADP W/C Tw

Handed in at the 19 AB Office, at 1/10 p.m. Received here at 1/12 p.m.

TO: 6th Div

A

Sender's Number.	Day of Month.	In reply to Number.	AAA
G.193	1st		
An	officer	of	~~the~~ The
Welch	fusiliers	states	that
from	his	position	in
the	trenches	he	is
of	opinion	that	the
movements	of	transport	last
night	was	in	a Southerly
direction			
			1.14 pm

FROM: 19 J B. 1 Pm
PLACE:
TIME:

"C" Form (Duplicate).
MESSAGES AND SIGNALS.

Army Form C. 2123.
No. of Message

	Z WDW	Charges to Pay £ s. d.	Office Stamp
Service Instructions.			

Handed in at the 18 I 13 Office, at 6.30 A.m. Received here at 6.54 A.m.

TO	6 Div	**A1**
Sender's Number.	Day of Month.	In reply to Number.	AAA
2R1	First		

A quiet night aaa enemys transport heard moving at 6 pm 2 am and 6 am

7am (circled)

FROM	18 I 13
PLACE	
TIME	6.45 am

W. 5375—123.   75,000 Pads—12/12—B. & F.—Forms/C.2123/1.

"C" Form (Original).
MESSAGES AND SIGNALS.   Army Form C. 2123.

Prefix ___ Code ___ Words ___   Received 56 From ___ By ___   Sent, or sent out At ___ To ___ By ___   Office Stamp

Charges to collect ___
Service Instructions ___

Handed in at the 19 L.M. Office, at ___ m. Received here at ___ m.

TO   6 Div   A2

Sender's Number: 7184   Day of Month: 1st   In reply to Number: ___   AAA

A quiet night in front of 19th Inf Bde except in front of Welch Fus where a good deal of firing but no attempt to push home. Are reported from Middlesex and Welch Fus that a continual stream of traffic was passing during night in rear of enemy's lines but impossible to

FROM / PLACE / TIME:
state in which direction it was moving now this may have some connection with your 9776

19th Inf Bde
6 am

"C" Form (Duplicate).
MESSAGES AND SIGNALS.

Army Form C. 2123

Sm 9a ZR morrison

No. of Message

Charges to Pay. £ s. d.

Office Stamp. **B**

Service Instructions.

Handed in at the 15 9B Office, at 9·5 p.m. Received here at 9·15 p.m.

TO: 6 Div

Sender's Number.	Day of Month.	In reply to Number.	
ZR 274	10		AAA
Our	cup	is	now
full	aaa	not	only
are	we	ordered	to
leave	our	home	but
there	is	no	bread
and	no	bacon	aaa
By	the	waters	of
BABYLON	OR	the	LYS
we	shall	sit	down
and	weep	aaa	all
quiet	here	aaa	The
enemy	have	a	searchlight
somewhere	near	the	factory

FROM
PLACE
TIME

"C" Form (Duplicate).
MESSAGES AND SIGNALS.

Army Form C. 2123

B1

aaa They are also wiring themselves in opposite the buffs and rifle brig

9.20 pm

FROM 18 9B
PLACE
TIME 9 pm

"C" Form (Duplicate).
MESSAGES AND SIGNALS.
Army Form C. 2123.

No. of Message

ZR
9

Charges to Pay. £ s. d.

Office Stamp.

C

Service Instructions.

Handed in at the 18 C.B. Office, at 7.10 p.m. Received here at 7.15 p.m.

TO 6th Div

Sender's Number.	Day of Month.	In reply to Number.	
T.14	12	G260	AAA

Regret message not earlier aaa siege battery report they have knocked out top gun enemys battery blown but a wagon and nothing but darkness over the rest aaa otherwise all quiet

7.22 pm

FROM 18th I Bde
PLACE
TIME 7 pm

"C" Form (Duplicate).   Army Form C. 2123.
MESSAGES AND SIGNALS.

KD
LS
Currie

Office Stamp.
D

Handed in at the 19.9.15 Office, at 10-28 Received here at 10-26 a.m.

TO 6th Divn,

Sender's Number: G 26   Day of Month: 20th Nov

AAA Welsh Fusrs report sounds of movement of transport both horse and motor across their front from NW to SE aaa This has been going on since 7 am. this morning aaa Will report later if any further information is obtainable on this subject

FROM 19th Infy Bde
PLACE
TIME 10.30 am

"C" Form (Duplicate).
MESSAGES AND SIGNALS.
Army Form C. 2123.

Service Instructions.	ZQ

Handed in at the 17 I.B. Office, at 11.10 p.m. Received here at 11.11 p.m.

TO: 6 Divn

Sender's Number.	Day of Month.	In reply to Number.
ZQ 2072	22nd	

AAA

Leinsters report movement of trains near PERENCHIES Station at 10.15 pm tonight aaa Have informed 2nd Bde R.F.A.

11.30 pm

FROM: 17 Bde
PLACE:
TIME: 10 pm

"C" Form (Duplicate).
MESSAGES AND SIGNALS.

Army Form C. 2123.

No. of Message

GDS

Charges to Pay. £ s. d.

Office Stamp.

E1

Service Instructions. Priority

Handed in at the 19 IB Office, at 7.37 a.m. Received here at 7.50 a.m.

TO 6th Div

Sender's Number.	Day of Month.	In reply to Number.	AAA
310	22nd		
wither	reports	place	it
beyond	doubt	that	a
movement	of	enemys	wheeled
vehicles	on	a	large
scale	took	place	yesterday
practically	all	day	and
Began	about	six	am
was	still	in	progress
till	after	seven pm	
It	is	suspected that	
these	columns	were	passing
along	the	road	leading
from	DEULEMONT	and	GUESNOY

FROM
PLACE
TIME 8.10 am

W. 5375—423. 75,000 Pads—12/12—B. & F.—Forms/C.2123/1.

"C" Form (Duplicate).   Army Form C. 2123.
MESSAGES AND SIGNALS.
No. of Message

	Charges to Pay.	Office Stamp.
Service Instructions.	£ s. d.	

Handed in at the _____ Office, at _____.m. Received here at _____.m.

TO   **E2**

Sender's Number.	Day of Month.	In reply to Number.	AAA
towards	LILLE		

FROM PLACE: 19/2/13.
TIME: 7.30 p

W. 5375—423. 75,000 Pads—12/12—B. & F.—Forms/C. 2123/1.

"C" Form (Duplicate).   Army Form C. 2123.
MESSAGES AND SIGNALS.   No. of Message

99

T.S. Currie

Charges to Pay.   Office Stamp. **F**

Service Instructions. 19 9 Bde 9.30 P 9.42 P

Handed in at the _____ Office, 6th Divn _____ m. Received here at _____ m.

TO

Sender's Number   Day of Month 25th   In reply to Number.   **AAA**

No movement of hostile transport across our front has been continuous all day and still continues aaa movement is from NW to SE

9.45 pm

FROM   19th Inf Bde
PLACE
TIME   9.30 pm

GENERAL STAFF

6th DIVISION

DECEMBER 1914.

— Confidential —

War Diary
of
General Staff, 6th Division

from 1.12.14 to 31.12.14

Vol IV.

Army Form C. 2118.

WAR DIARY
or
INTELLIGENCE SUMMARY.
(Erase heading not required.)

Instructions regarding War Diaries and Intelligence Summaries are contained in F. S. Regs., Part II. and the Staff Manual respectively. Title pages will be prepared in manuscript.

Hour, Date, Place	Summary of Events and Information	Remarks and references to Appendices
1st Dec.	Two men of the 179th Saxon Regt. captured by the Queens Westminsters. Sent into 9/7/9 by Minister	
2nd Dec	No change in the situation. King George visited the Division, presented 5 Distinguished Conduct Medals and afterwards proceeded to the 4th Div	
3rd Dec	Linisters relieves 1st N. Staffs. Welsh Fusiliers relieves Cameronians.	
4th Dec	No change in situation. Queens West ministers relieved by Q.V.R.	
5th Dec	No change in situation.	
6th Dec.	No change in situation. East Yorks relieves Northants. R.B. relieves R.Fusiliers	
7th Dec	No change in situation.	
8th Dec	No change in situation.	
9th Dec	Three men of the 139th Saxon Regt. captured by 1st Q.L.Highrs. Partial attack delivered by this Regt. against 1st Rede 19 Bde. Not pushed home + Casualties in this Bde. 5 killed and 10 wounded. Situation unchanged	
10th Dec	Linister relieves 1st N.Stafford. Queens Westminster relieves Q.R.R.1. No change in situation.	

WAR DIARY
or
INTELLIGENCE SUMMARY.

(Erase heading not required.)

Army Form C. 2118.

Instructions regarding War Diaries and Intelligence Summaries are contained in F. S. Regs., Part II. and the Staff Manual respectively. Title pages will be prepared in manuscript.

Hour, Date, Place	Summary of Events and Information	Remarks and references to Appendices
11th Dec	18th Bde withdrawn from the line East & west of & going into billets in southern portion of ARMENTIERES. This was made up of Hampshires, Royal Leicester, N. Stafford, Queens Westminster, R. Bde, Leinster, Cameronians, Middlesex, West Riders. Divided into 3 Reserves.	
12th Dec	No change in situation.	
13th Dec	No change in situation.	
14th Dec	The line held by the Div is as before will use orders from 3rd Corps, worried the enemy & showed activity in every way to induce occupying him in his present position, while the operations further north were developing.	
15th Dec	During the night of 14th/15th ARMENTIERES HOUPLINES were bombarded by the Germans. About 50 shells in all fell in the town, a very large proportion being "duds" mostly from the captured French guns. Casualties almost nil – 3 wounded. The Milliverts W. Yorks & civilian killed & wounded in fire.	
16th Dec	No change in situation.	

Army Form C. 2118.

WAR DIARY
or
INTELLIGENCE SUMMARY.
(Erase heading not required.)

Instructions regarding War Diaries and Intelligence Summaries are contained in F. S. Regs., Part II. and the Staff Manual respectively. Title pages will be prepared in manuscript.

Hour, Date, Place	Summary of Events and Information	Remarks and references to Appendices
17th Dec	No change in situation. 4th relieved by K.S.L.I.	
18th Dec	Queens Westminsters relieved by the Royal Fusiliers. Order received from 3rd Corps that a vigorous attack all along the line was to be carried out commencing at 10 am on the 18th. Chief Staff Officer to hold himself in readiness to attend at Corps Hdq. 3rd Corps Operation Order No. 49 dated 18th. 3rd Corps to demonstrate & seize any favourable opportunity to attack enemy's trenches. 6th Div been ordered to continue to attack as ordered in Operation Order No. 47 and to harass the enemy. Support from our Rt. from our Rt guns and the regt of 16th Bde given to the attack of 4th Divn.	
19th Dec	No change in situation. Attitude as before to support operation from our own left.	
20th Dec	No change in situation. Attitude as before.	
21st Dec	No change in situation. Attitude as before.	
22nd Dec	Orders received to carry out some active operations while the French operations at YPRES were proceeding. Point of this operations to be fixed verbally between Corps & Divisional Commanders	

Army Form C. 2118.

WAR DIARY
or
INTELLIGENCE SUMMARY.
(*Erase heading not required.*)

Instructions regarding War Diaries and Intelligence Summaries are contained in F. S. Regs., Part II. and the Staff Manual respectively. Title pages will be prepared in manuscript.

Hour, Date, Place	Summary of Events and Information	Remarks and references to Appendices
23rd Dec	Counter-order received from — to discontinue all preparations and carry out the defensive in future.	
24th Dec.	No change in situation	
25th Dec.	Germans celebrated Christmas. Two men of No. 179th Regt. captured in a slightly intoxicated state. Unofficial truce. No guns fired	
26th Dec.	19th Bde relieved by 18th Bde. K.S.L.I. relieved the Buffs. No change in situation	
27th Dec	No change in situation	
28th Dec	No change in situation	
29th Dec	No change in situation	
30th Dec	No change in situation	
31st Dec	No change in situation	

Elwinde
Major S.S.
1/1/15

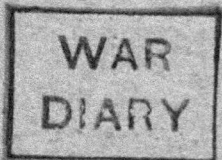

GENERAL STAFF

6th DIVISION

JANUARY

1915

Army Form C. 2118.

WAR DIARY
or
INTELLIGENCE SUMMARY.
(Erase heading not required.)

Instructions regarding War Diaries and Intelligence Summaries are contained in F. S. Regs., Part II. and the Staff Manual respectively. Title pages will be prepared in manuscript.

GENERAL STAFF · 1 - FEB. 1915 · 6TH DIVISION

Hour, Date, Place	Summary of Events and Information	Remarks and references to Appendices
1st Jan.	The Commander 2nd Army orders that informal understanding with the enemy are not to take place. Situation unchanged	
2nd Jan.	Hq. 16th Inf Bde moved to PONT DE NIEPPE at 4.30 pm this day. Nothing to report.	
3rd Jan.	16th Inf Bde was relieved in right section by his during the night 2/3rd by 19th Inf Bde. Relief carried out successfully but Capt. Stuhlrie short immediately after the Relief.	
4th Jan.	N. Staffs relieved the Rifle Bde in the evening. River has fallen about a foot. Nothing of Interest.	
5th Jan.	Two six-inch guns left for 1st to 1st Army 6 orders from 3rd Corps. Wire entanglements cutting scheme at St Omer. One officer from each Bde was present.	

WAR DIARY
or
INTELLIGENCE SUMMARY.
(Erase heading not required.)

Army Form C. 2118.

Hour, Date, Place	Summary of Events and Information	Remarks and references to Appendices
6th Jan.	Situation unchanged.	
7th Jan	Situation unchanged. Our batteries and H Steamer were unmasked on a trench near WEZ MACQUART. Effect good. Enemy shelled Centre of 17thBde wounding 6 men.	
8th Jan.	Order received from 3rd Corps dispensing with Corps Reserve. Line now to be held by four sections as before	
9th Jan.	Situation unchanged. Change to 4 sections successfully carried out	
10th Jan.	No change in situation. Fine day.	
11th Jan.	No change in situation. Fine day. Little rain.	
12th Jan.	No change in situation. Fine day.	
13th Jan.	No change in situation. Breastwork built.	
14th Jan	No change in situation. Ryl.Bde relieved by Jemadar + N. Staff by R.Fus.	
15th Jan	No change in situation.	relief this evening (shelled).

Army Form C. 2118.

WAR DIARY
or
INTELLIGENCE SUMMARY.
(Erase heading not required.)

Instructions regarding War Diaries and Intelligence Summaries are contained in F. S. Regs., Part II. and the Staff Manual respectively. Title pages will be prepared in manuscript.

Hour, Date, Place	Summary of Events and Information	Remarks and references to Appendices
16ᵗʰ Jan	No change in situation. Leicesters relieved Buffs.	
17ᵗʰ Jan	Staffords relieved Lincolns. Artillery Observation Officer in left section of 17ᵗʰ Bde reports that enemy have men wearing R.W.S. Enemy shelled CHAPELLE D'ARMENTIERES heavily both morning + evening.	
18ᵗʰ Jan.	No change in situation.	
19ᵗʰ Jan	Shropshires relieved Yr & 2 Coy Scottish Rifle go into the trenches. No change in situation.	
20 Jan.	Leicesters relieved by Buffs in 16ᵗʰ Bde R.F. relieved by R.S. in 17ᵗʰ Bde. No change in situation.	
21 Jan.	Lincolns relieved Staffords. No change in situation.	
22 Jan.	Enemy shelled FLAMINGERIE FM and Marie at HOUPLINES + FORT EGAL FM. Considerable concentration of German Troops at MENIN and LILLE. No change in situation.	

WAR DIARY
or
INTELLIGENCE SUMMARY.
(Erase heading not required.)

Army Form C. 2118.

Hour, Date, Place	Summary of Events and Information	Remarks and references to Appendices
23rd Jan	K.S.L.I. relieved by York in 16 T.B. Movement of considerable amount of transport in FRELINGHIEN heard. Enemy put 12 shew into FLAMINGERIE Fm. South in right section of 17 Bde throughout the day. Two Germans in khaki. No change in situation.	
24 Jan.	Buffs relieved by Leicesters in 16 Bde. Middlesex relieved Argt. Highrs. No change in situation. Several of enemy aeroplanes flew over us.	
25 Jan.	One 13pdr. Anti-aircraft gun arrived from 4 Div. Placed in 19 Bde area. No change in situation.	
26. Jan	No change in situation.	
27 Jan	No change in situation	

Army Form C. 2118.

WAR DIARY
or
INTELLIGENCE SUMMARY.
(Erase heading not required.)

Instructions regarding War Diaries and Intelligence Summaries are contained in F. S. Regs., Part II. and the Staff Manual respectively. Title pages will be prepared in manuscript.

Hour, Date, Place	Summary of Events and Information	Remarks and references to Appendices
28th Jan.	Leicesters relieved by Bantts. No change in situation	
29th Jan.	Leinsters relieved Staffs. Cameronians relieved Welch Fusiliers. Great deal of fire at our aeroplanes. Commander Little John of Armoured cars came to see the C.O. He was not thought that the 4.7" guns he was well to use to us. Small ridge near destroyed Felinhévrides defiantly located today.	
30th Jan.	No change in situation.	
31st Jan.	Yorks have relieved Shropshires. Intermittent shelling at Hoplines against the 17th Bde lines.	

E.J. Ronaldo
Major &c.

31/1/15

WAR DIARY

GENERAL STAFF

6th DIVISION.

FEBRUARY

1915

Confidential

War Diary

of

G.S. 6th Division

From 1.2.15 To 28.2.15

WAR DIARY
or
INTELLIGENCE SUMMARY.
(Erase heading not required.)

Army Form C. 118.

Hour, Date, Place	Summary of Events and Information	Remarks and references to Appendices
1st Feb.	No change in situation, Rifle Bde relieved Royal Fusiliers in trenches.	
2nd Feb	Anti Aircraft Section No 14 (4pm) left us after a visit of 48 hours. We are to be supplied by 4 Corps. Staff relieved the Ministers. Good deal of sniping at RUE DU BOIS. Eight H.E. fired into A.H.Q. Win no casualties. Armoured Train ordered to join 6th Div. Mitrailleur relieved A.H.Q. Highrs. 18th Bde think that everyhn. near changes opposite them 17 Bde report having seen Germans wearing dark blue uniforms at WEZ MACQUART.	
3rd Feb	No change in situation	
4th Feb	The enemy opened a heavy bombardment against our trench Bois GRENIER line upon which work was being done by civilians. They then shifted to 19th Bde front line & opened heavy musketry against our trenches, but did not leave their trenches. At the same time a slight attack was developed against the 16 Bde at RUE DU BOIS where a few men left their trenches	

Army Form C. 2118.

WAR DIARY
or
INTELLIGENCE SUMMARY.
(Erase heading not required.)

Instructions regarding War Diaries and Intelligence Summaries are contained in F. S. Regs., Part II. and the Staff Manual respectively. Title pages will be prepared in manuscript.

Hour, Date, Place	Summary of Events and Information	Remarks and references to Appendices
5th Feb.	Enemy were driven back by our M.G. fire and artillery fire. Nothing else on the remainder of the line.	
6th Feb	No change in Situation	
7th Feb	Leinsters relieved Staffs. Appearance of enemy registering on the MCZ MACQUART line	
8th Feb	No change in situation	
9th Feb.	A good deal of movement observed from Quesnoy. N. of Trelinghien. Enemy shelled Rue du Bois this morning. Only damage to houses. Connemaras relieve Welsh Fusiliers. Butts relieved Leinsters. 17 Bde billets slightly shelled. Snipers active. No change in situation.	
10th Feb.	N. Staffs relieved Leinsters. A movement of transport moving in direction of TRELINGHIEN. Enemy shelled N. of 17 Bde. No change in situation.	

WAR DIARY
or
INTELLIGENCE SUMMARY.
(Erase heading not required.)

Army Form C. 2118.

Instructions regarding War Diaries and Intelligence Summaries are contained in F. S. Regs., Part II. and the Staff Manual respectively. Title pages will be prepared in manuscript.

Hour, Date, Place	Summary of Events and Information	Remarks and references to Appendices
11th Feb	No change in situation.	
12th Feb	Enemy shelled left of Middlesex trenches and also neighbourhood of CULVERT Fm. One casualty in 19th Bde. Enemy of their 18th Bde reported as wearing a greyish-green uniform, and hats like an English postman.	
13th Feb	Four rockets were fired by enemy near FLEURBAIX at 7.15pm. Nothing known. Enemy shelled BOIS GRENIER and road junction at L'ARMÉE, vicinity of DUBIE, Southern outskirts of ARMENTIERES. Welsh Fusiliers relieved Cameronians. Alterations have been made in barrier and wire in the vicinity of RUEZ MACQUART & its Cemetery.	
14th Feb	L Sinister relieved M. Staffs. Two Aeroplanes exhibited French 9" Corps report general attack on 15th or 16th. K.S.L.I. relieved by Yorkshires. Enemy shelled left of 19th Bde — no casualties. About 50 shell near left of Suffolks trench by 19th Bde 2 hours crossing over level crossing. No change in situation.	

WAR DIARY
or
INTELLIGENCE SUMMARY.
(Erase heading not required.)

Army Form C. 2118.

Hour, Date, Place	Summary of Events and Information	Remarks and references to Appendices

15th Feb. — No change in situation.

16th Feb. — Some shelling in neighbourhood of Artillery and on Rly. near left of 19th Bde. 12 shells between Road & Rly. Barriers at Rue du Bois. No casualties reported. No change in situation.

17th Feb. — Leicestershires relieved Buffs Staffords. Rifle Brigade relieved Royal Fusiliers. Section 4th Siege Bty. rejoined 4th Div. Rue Du Bois Rly barrier shelled in the afternoon.

18th Feb. — Sherwood Foresters relieved Durh. L.I.. A.&S. Haighrs relieved Middlesex. About six shells near cross-roads BAC ST MAUR. 3 Fried who ERQUINGHEM killing 4 horses.

19th Feb. — N. Staffords relieved LEINSTERS. Connaughts relieved Welsh Fus. BOIS GRENIER, left battalion 19.2.15, L'ARMEE, breastworks at RUE DU BOIS, and reserve billets I 3 c shelled by day. 2 casualties reported. Rifle grenades fired into trenches of right battalion 19th S.B caused 4 casualties.

WAR DIARY
~~INTELLIGENCE SUMMARY~~.
(Erase heading not required.)

Army Form C. 2118.

Hour, Date, Place	Summary of Events and Information	Remarks and references to Appendices
1915 20th Feb.	No change in situation.	
21st Feb.	Shropshire L.I. relieved York and Lancs. R. Fus. relieved 3rd R.I.B. Foggy day, quiet.	
22nd Feb.	Buffs relieved Leicestershires. A quiet day. No change in situation. Sounds of rejoicings reported in LILLE.	
23rd Feb.	Seaforths relieved N. Staffords. Middlesex relieved Argyll + Sutherlands. Left trenches 19th Bde. and Louies at RUE DU BOIS received a few shells. Indications that the enemy troops in front of RUE DU BOIS have been changed of that there are some Bavarians in the neighbourhood of DES 4 HALLOTS FME.	
24th Feb.	East Yorks relieved W. Yorks. R. Welsh Fus. relieved (1st Cameronians). A few shells into left trenches 19th I.B. + RUE DU BOIS; three into entrainment at DES PLATNAUE Crossing. Enemy in silver-grey [hune?] cap with blue band seen in WEZ MACQUART trenches + those opposite W. section 17th I.B. reported to be wearing bluish – grey uniform	

WAR DIARY
INTELLIGENCE SUMMARY.
(Erase heading not required.)

Army Form C. 2118.

Hour, Date, Place	Summary of Events and Information	Remarks and references to Appendices
25th Feb.	and cap with red band and number. 3rd R.B. relieved Royal Fus., Sherwood Foresters relieved D.L.I.	
26th Feb.	Enemy shelled farm just behind left centre of right company 17th I.B. Some rifle grenades and 3 shells were fired at RUE DU BOIS. Shropshire L.I. relieved by York & Lancs, Lincolns by N. Staffords. A few shells fired in neighbourhood of H.Q. 16th +17th 132m. Sound of Heavy transport on guns heard in direction of ENNETIERES between 4.0 p.m. + 5.30 p.m.	
27th Feb.	Buffs relieved by Leicestershires, Middlesex by A&S Highrs, East Yorks by W. Yorks. S. H.E. shells fired at breastworks at RUE DU BOIS. A few shells fired at left trenches of left Battalion, a some rifle grenades at trenches in front of FLAMENGRIE FARM. A few shells into CHAPELLE D'ARMENTIERES.	
28th Feb.	Cameronians relieved Welsh Fusiliers, Royal Fus. relieved 3rd R.B. CHAPELLE D'ARMENTIERES, BOIS GRENIER, neighbourhood of 16th.	

Army Form C. 2118.

WAR DIARY
INTELLIGENCE SUMMARY.
(Erase heading not required.)

Instructions regarding War Diaries and Intelligence Summaries are contained in F. S. Regs., Part II. and the Staff Manual respectively. Title pages will be prepared in manuscript.

Hour, Date, Place	Summary of Events and Information	Remarks and references to Appendices
	Field Amb., Mairie at HOUPLINES, + right company 18/4/9/15. Slightly shelled. Our guns made good shooting on FRELINGHIEN  J.M. Snowden? J.O. General Staff.	

WAR DIARY

GENERAL STAFF

6th DIVISION

MARCH

1915

Attached:

Appendices I, II, III, & IV.

— Confidential —

121/4872

War Diary

of

General Staff 6th Division

From 1-3-15 To 31-3-15

Vol VII

WAR DIARY
INTELLIGENCE SUMMARY.
(Erase heading not required.)

Army Form C. 21.

1915

Hour, Date, Place	Summary of Events and Information	Remarks and references to Appendices

March 1st
D.L.I. relieved Sherwood Foresters.
During day enemy shelled ARMENTIERES, RUE DU BOIS & put 6 heavy shells close to L'ARMEE & six shells close to H.Q. left section 17th N.G.B.

March 2nd
Leinsters relieved N. Staffs.
Enemy shelled CHAPELLE D'ARMENTIERES & H.Q. left section 17th I.B.

March 3rd
6" Howitzers in cooperation with Heavy Batty and Field guns bombarded enemy's salient in front of RUE DU BOIS and houses at LA HOUSSOIE, WEZ MACQUART & L'EPINETTE with good effect. Enemy's guns replied on billets of L. North Lancs, DES PLANQUE FARM and 24th Bty, the ORCHARD & parapet of left centre Co. Left Battalion. 16th S.G.. H.M.A.T. Churchill engaged & silenced battery firing at 24th Bty. HOUPLINES mairie & farm in right section 17th I.B. shelled.
K.S.L.I. relieved Y.& L., E. Yorks relieved W. Yorks, Middlesex relieved A. & S. Highrs.

March 4th
BOIS GRENIER & WATER FARM behind it. section 19th I.B., & WHITE FARM behind left section 17th I.B.

March 5th
Buffs relieved Leicestershires, 2nd R.B. relieved R. Fus, Sherwood Foresters relieved Durham L.I., R. Welsh Fus. relieved 1st Cameronians.

WAR DIARY
INTELLIGENCE SUMMARY.
(Erase heading not required.)

Army Form C. 2118.

Instructions regarding War Diaries and Intelligence Summaries are contained in F.S. Regs., Part II. and the Staff Manual respectively. Title pages will be prepared in manuscript.

Hour, Date, Place	Summary of Events and Information	Remarks and references to Appendices
March 6th.	6" Howitzers engaged lorries at LE QUESNE but did not do a great deal of damage. Heavies bombarded FRELINGHEN successfully. Enemy shelled breastworks of left section 19th S.B., LA VESEE, 17th L.B., 2nd Line breastworks, ARMENTIERES Asylum, and Leinster billets. N. Staffords relieved Leinsters. Few shells into BOIS GRENIER. Orders received for departure of armoured train.	
March 7th.	Few shells into BOIS GRENIER. Situation unchanged.	
March 8th.	W. Yorks relieved E. Yorks. Artillery fired on enemy's trenches & support trenches in O.2.A. Enemy replied with few shells. Movement in direction of LA PREVOTE of heavy transport heard at 4.20 a.m. D.C.L.I. relieved Sherwood Foresters 2/A.& S. Highlrs relieved Middlesex.	
March 9th.	Quiet day.	
6.0 p.m.	Received 3rd Operation Order No. 44	
7.30 p.m.	O.O. No. 22 issued.	
March 10th.	Yorks Lancs relieved Shropshires, Leinsters relieved N.Staffs, & 1st Connaughts R.W. Fus. Brisk fire fight against hostile trenches carried on throughout	App. I

WAR DIARY
or
INTELLIGENCE SUMMARY.
(Erase heading not required.)

Army Form C. 2118.

Hour, Date, Place	Summary of Events and Information	Remarks and references to Appendices
11th March	All day, Infantry fired bursts at intervals. Artillery cooperated with infantry in bursts on enemy's Salient at RUE DU BOIS, also trenches at PONT BALLOT and south of FRELINGHIEN, also trenches N. of LILLE road. Guns also engaged hostile guns + shelled houses in FRELINGHIEN and at LA HOUSSOIE. Enemy made very little reply. Leicestershires relieved Buffs.	
12th March	Fire fight continued throughout day. Enemy shelled WATER FARM in 19th I.B. area, 7 DESPLANQUE FARM and CHAPELLE D'ARMENTIERES. At 12 midnight, 11 3/12 – 17th Inf. Bde occupied line of houses along the L'EPINETTE road. Operation very successfully carried out by 1st N. Staffs. Resistance of enemy slight & their fire hurried & high. Casualties not heavy. The enemy succeeded in withdrawing whilst the attack was getting through the wire. During day the position was consolidated being shelled at intervals by hostile artillery which caused	App. II 17th Bde Opn Orders App. III Report on operation

WAR DIARY
INTELLIGENCE SUMMARY.
(Erase heading not required.)

Army Form C. 2118.

Instructions regarding War Diaries and Intelligence Summaries are contained in F. S. Regs., Part II. and the Staff Manual respectively. Title pages will be prepared in manuscript.

Hour, Date, Place	Summary of Events and Information	Remarks and references to Appendices
	Some casualties. Result of operation an advance of 300" over a front of ½ a mile. + The object of the manoeuvre was to gain & fortify a position closer the enemy, with a view to pinning him to his ground & prevent his reinforcing other parts of his front, & to being in a better position to attack his main line when ordered to do so. + The operations consisted of two phases, the first being the rapid occupation & placing in a state of defence of the position ×4 of the front (vide sketch with App II) This phase was timed to end at 11·45 when the working parties were to be withdrawn so as to avoid confusion &corbes from hostile fire if the enemy should open fire along his whole front. The phase was duly carried out The 2nd phase, which involved the capture of houses known to be occupied as hostile advanced posts, strongly fortified, protected by wire entanglements & provided with communications to the main line, was timed to commence at midnight. They had been constantly shelled but were still occupied by the enemy.	

WAR DIARY
INTELLIGENCE SUMMARY.
(Erase heading not required.)

Army Form C. 2118.

Instructions regarding War Diaries and Intelligence Summaries are contained in F. S. Regs., Part II. and the Staff Manual respectively. Title pages will be prepared in manuscript.

Hour, Date, Place	Summary of Events and Information	Remarks and references to Appendices

It was therefore decided to take them by night as far as possible by surprise & to cut off the retreat by the communication trenches. The attack was entrusted to the 1/North Staffs.

Lieut V. Pope 1/N Staffs commanded the company which had the chief duty of dealing with communication trenches and defended houses. This officer was specially mentioned by O.C. 1/N Staffs & by Brigadier General 17th I.B. who reported "the success of the operation was mainly due to the skillful leading of Lieut. Pope."

12th Company R.E. was distributed among the attacking columns and by their efforts the whole front was placed in such a state of defence by daylight that the troops were able to hold their position under a most severe artillery bombardment.

The artillery arrangements were carried out by Lt.-Col. C.C. Laurie D.S.O., R.A.. Owing to nature of defences & to secure surprise there was no preliminary bombardment but all guns were ready laid on their targets in case the enemy should show too great activity.

At dawn a heavy bombardment of the enemy trenches took place

WAR DIARY

INTELLIGENCE SUMMARY.

(Erase heading not required.)

Army Form C. 2118.

Hour, Date, Place	Summary of Events and Information	Remarks and references to Appendices
13th March.	as it was anticipated that an attempt might be made to counter-attack before the troops were fully established. The new position was subjected to a heavy bombardment at intervals throughout the day & night, causing a considerable number of casualties. Counter-attacks delivered up the communication trenches by night were delivered and one party of twenty was caught in the open by machine gun fire on the night of the 12th/13th & left several of its number dead. Three prisoners, two belonging to the 133rd regiment, & one to the 22nd Pioneer Battalion were taken. During the night of the 12th/13th several Recon enterprises were carried out. The 19th, 16th, & 17th Inf. Bdes sending out patrols which attacked the enemy's works & trenches with bomber. 1st N. Staffords remained in new trenches, E. Yorks relieved W. Yorks. Rifle Bde relieved York & Lancs, 1st Middlesex relieved Leicestershires, Sherwood Forester relieved Durham L.I. All these reliefs took place during night 13th/14th.	

WAR DIARY
INTELLIGENCE SUMMARY
(Erase heading not required.)

Army Form C. 2118.

Hour, Date, Place	Summary of Events and Information	Remarks and References to Appendices
14th March.	The policy of harassing the enemy throughout the day by bursts of rifle fire & by rifling fire was continued with evident success as the enemy sent up far more flares than usual during the night. The new line of trenches was again shelled during the afternoon. There are signs both from the enemy's attitude, from statements of prisoners, from evidence contained in papers on enemy's dead that the line in front of us is strongly held & that the enemy is more than usually nervous. Orders received from 3rd Corps for readjustment of front by which 18th Bde is to be relieved on night of 16th/17 by 10th Bde, 16th Bde is to relieve Canadian Bde next to 19th Bde on night of 16th/17th & 18th Bde is to take over portion of our new front on the night of 16th 17th Bdes new line. Two companies 2nd London Regt went into trenches of left Section 17th I.B. to assist Leinster Regt. German working parties were located by patrols along at various points along our front in the small hours of the morning. These working parties were attacked with m.g. & rifle fire with it is believed good effect.	* at L'EPINETTE.

Army Form C. 2118.

WAR DIARY
INTELLIGENCE SUMMARY
(Erase heading not required.)

Hour, Date, Place	Summary of Events and Information	Remarks and References to Appendices
	A good deal of sniping by day on front of 16th & 19th Bdes. New trenches at L'EPINETTE shelled in morning and heavily in the afternoon. An amendment to Corps order just received defines view front of 6th Div as from B.8 N.8 to LILLE railway exclusive.	
8.58 p.m.	Message received definitely cancelling all relief for night of 14th/15th.	
14th/15th. About midnight orders were received by telephone from 3rd Corps for 16th I.B. (less Territorial battalion) to be despatched at once by train from Gare Annexe ARMENTIERES to VLAMER= TINGHE. Brigadier to proceed at once by car to report to 5th Corps H.Q. at POPERINGHE, 1st line transport to proceed by road via BAILLEUL-LOCRE to RENINGHELST. Entrainment commenced at 2.30 p.m and trains left as follows:—	
15th March	1st train Shropshire Light Inf. 2.59 a.m. 2nd train The Buffs 4.19 a.m.	

Army Form C. 2118.

WAR DIARY
INTELLIGENCE SUMMARY
(Erase heading not required.)

Instructions regarding War Diaries and Intelligence Summaries are contained in F. S. Regs., Part II. and the Staff Manual respectively. Title pages will be prepared in manuscript.

Hour, Date, Place	Summary of Events and Information	Remarks and References to Appendices
METEREN.	3rd train Leicesters 5.9 a.m. 4th train York + Lancs 6.9 a.m. Sniping persistent at RUE DU BOIS, Right co. of centre section of left co. of right section shelled. 16th Inf. Bde returned to ARMENTIERES during night of 15th/16th. Three Horse artillery batteries came in in relief of right Bde of Canadian F.A. One F.A. Bde and one Heavy Battery from N. Midland Division came into 6th Div: area under orders of G.O.C. R.A. 6th Div.	Copy of instructions APP. IV.
16th March.	W. Yorks relieved E. Yorks.	
12.20 p.m.	Orders received from 3rd Corps that no further relief will take place at present but preliminary arrangements to be proceeded with.	
4.42 p.m.	Further order received cancelling order for readjustment of line. Corps to return to their original fronts. Artillery redistribution arrangements also cancelled.	

WAR DIARY

INTELLIGENCE SUMMARY

(Erase heading not required.)

Army Form C. 2118.

Hour, Date, Place	Summary of Events and Information	Remarks and References to Appendices
10.5 p.m.	RUE DUBOIS, WATER FARM, and new trenches at L'EPINETTE shelled during the day. Order received for 16 & 17.3.15. to take over from 17th Inf. Bde. & Bde. in former trenches. During the night the 3 Horse Artillery batteries left, returning to 3rd Cav. Bde.	
17th March	Leicestershires relieved Middlesex, York & Lancs relieved 3rd R.B. 2nd R.I. relieved Sherwood Foresters, R Welsh Fus: relieved 2/A.r.S.H. N.Midland Bde F.A. & Heavy Battery left in the morning. 17th I.B. trenches & RUE DU BOIS shelled. Our guns replied. Enemy active in front of 18th I.B. Left. Three loud explosions were heard in WEZ MACQUART at 10.45 a.m., 11.20 & 11.25 a.m.	
18th March	A.S.Highrs relieved 1st Cameronians. The enemy bombarded Q. Westminsters with grenades inflicting several casualties. The fire was returned. Rifle Brigade relieved R.Fus, N.Staffs relieved Leinsters.	
19th March	FLAMENGRIE & WATER Farms, billets in CHAPELLE D'ARMENTIERES, & right of L'EPINETTE trenches shelled. Otherwise quiet day.	

WAR DIARY

INTELLIGENCE SUMMARY

(Erase heading not required.)

Army Form C. 2118.

Hour, Date, Place	Summary of Events and Information	Remarks and References to Appendices
20th March.	Right section 18th I.B. caught a German working-party with rifle fire & produced cries & groans. Indications of a relief in front of W. Yorks. At 2.20 a.m. 18th/19th a selected party from 16th I.B. went out to investigate suspected German Sap but no work was found to be in progress. A patrol with bombs also went out from left section; neither party found any German patrols. Shropshires relieved York & Lancs. E.Yorks relieved W.Yorks. Active sniping opposite 19th I.B.. Heavy Battery got direct hits on WEZ MACQUART church, demolishing it, and on observing station & Sniper's house, causing much damage. Enemy's armoured train appeared at FOURNES and bombarded TOUQUET trenches. Patrols went out during night 20/21st from Shropshires & Leicestershires to examine reported German saps. Rifle Bde. sent out patrols to bomb enemy's working party, which was unsuccessful, and one patrol bombed a listening post.	
21st March.	Buffs relieved Leicestershires, Sherwood Foresters relieved Durham L.I., Middlesex relieved R. Welsh Fus.	

WAR DIARY
or
INTELLIGENCE SUMMARY

(Erase heading not required.)

Army Form C. 2118.

Hour, Date, Place	Summary of Events and Information	Remarks and References to Appendices

ARMENTIERES Asylum, near 16th 4 I.B. H.Q.

Germans shelled between BOIS GRENIER and CULVERT Farm. During the night 21st/22nd a patrol of 1st Shropshires examined new German wire work.

22nd March

Enemy shelled BOIS GRENIER and CULVERT FARM & left section 17th I.B. Effective rifle grenade fire by Buffs & Wellingtons. Sniping active opposite left of 17th I.B. 28th Heavy (4.7") Bde R.G.A. left for 5th Corps. One gun No. 12 Siege Battery Co. arrived. Shropshires & 2nd London Regt. patrolled to German trenches during night.

23rd March

1st Connaughts relieved A. & S. Highrs.
BOIS GRENIER GAS POT – 16th S.B. trenches shelled. Shropshires' patrol went out by night located two German machine guns.
West Yorks relieved E. Yorks.
Trenches of 17th & 19th Bdes shelled, otherwise a quiet day.

24th March

Patrols went out at night all along front of 19th Bde from 16th + 17th Bdes. No Germans came outside their wire.

Army Form C. 2118.

WAR DIARY
INTELLIGENCE SUMMARY
(Erase heading not required.)

Instructions regarding War Diaries and Intelligence Summaries are contained in F. S. Regs., Part II. and the Staff Manual respectively. Title pages will be prepared in manuscript.

Hour, Date, Place	Summary of Events and Information	Remarks and References to Appendices
25th March	Leinsters relieved N. Staffs, Dunham L.I. relieved Sherwood Foresters. Enemy shelled near Crashrooks in centre of left battalion 19th I.B.; otherwise quiet. 3/B Batteries + 1 Heavy Bty N. Midland division marched out at 8.0 p.m.	
26th March	York & Lancs relieved Sherps, R. Fus. relieved R.B., R Welsh Fus. relieved Middlesex. Enemy shelled near DESPLANQUE FARM + Bde H.Q., DU BIE farm and EDMEADS' farm. 3/2 Btns N Midland Division marched in 5.30 p.m.	
27th March	Leicestershires relieved Buffs. Edmeads' + HOBBS farms shelled. Leavies reported one direct hit on enemy's anti-aircraft guns.	
28th March	E. Yorks relieved W. Yorks, A.s.S. Highrs relieved Camerons. 3 pdr gun on armoured motor car shelled snipers' house + German Salient opposite RUE DU BOIS in the early morning with success. Very quiet day.	

Army Form C. 2118.

WAR DIARY
INTELLIGENCE SUMMARY
(Erase heading not required.)

Hour, Date, Place	Summary of Events and Information	Remarks and References to Appendices
29th March.	Sherwood Foresters relieved Durham L.I. Bois GRENIER and L'EPINETTE trenches shelled. Sniping active.	
30th March.	Enemy shelled left Bttn 14th I.B. and fired 20 or 30 shells at aeroplane which came down behind our lines. H.Q. + 2 guns No. 12 Siege Co. arrived in our area.	
31st March.	N. Staffs. relieved Leinsters, Middlesex relieved R. Welsh Fus. 20 shells near 19th Inf. Bde HQ., RUE DU BOIS and trenches of 17th Inf. Bde. Otherwise quiet.	

6th Div
2.4.15

J. O. Trost
Captain
General Staff.

APPENDIX I.

War Diary Appendix I.

SECRET.

Copy No. 17

6th DIVISION OPERATION ORDER No. 22.

Reference Map Sheet 36, scale 1/40,000.

Headquarters 6th Division.
9th March, 1915.

1. The 1st and 2nd Armies will assume the offensive on March 10th and on subsequent days.

2. The role of the 2nd Army will be to prevent the enemy from withdrawing from his front any troops for employment against the 1st Army.

3. With this object the troops of the Division will act as follows:-

    (a). Artillery bombardment will commence at 7.30 am, principally directed on FRELINGHIEN, and also on
    (i) the new German trench East of PONT BALLOT
    (ii) the salient in I.21.a/b.

    (b). G.O.C's brigades will organise fire attacks against the enemy's line by day and night, and maintain a state of activity.

    (c). Sapping and mining operations will be pushed forward vigourously.

4. Reports will be forwarded to 6th Division Headquarters every two hours from 7.30 am.

    Important reports will be forwarded irrespective of the hours named above.

J.S.SHEA, Lieut. Colonel,
General Staff.

Copies issued through Signal Service at 7.30 pm as follows:-

Copy No. 1 to 16th Inf. Bde.
" 2 " 17th Inf. Bde.
" 3 " 18th Inf. Bde.
" 4 " 19th Inf. Bde.
" 5 " G.O.C. R.A.
" 6 to 9 to 4 Brigades R.F.A.
" 10 " C.R.E.
" 11 " A.A. & Q.M.G.
" 12 " A.D.M.S.
" 13 " Mounted Troops.
" 14 " 3rd Corps.
" 15 " 4th Division.
" 16 and 17 Office.

A P P E N D I X II.

SECRET

Copy No
WAR DIARY
APP II

17th Brigade Operation Order No 11.

ARMENTIERES
11th March 1915

Reference:-
Attached Sketch.

1. The 17th Infantry Brigade will during the hours of darkness tonight seize and make good the line W. X. Y and Z on the accompanying map.

2. The line from W to X will be held by 1 company D/Leinster Regt under Capt. E. H. Murphy.
   Separate instructions have been issued to D/London Regt who will provide working parties under Lieut E. F. Tickell R.E. All work in this line will cease at 11.45 pm. when working parties will be withdrawn.

3. At 12 midnight the 1st North Staffs Regt will seize and make good the line X (exclusive) Y.Z.
   106 Co R.E. and 1 Coy D/Leinster Regt is placed under O.C. 1st N. Staffs for this purpose.

4. Artillery support will be furnished under arrangements made by Lieut Col C.E. Lawrie D.S.O. R.A.
   Artillery fire will not be opened during the night unless the enemy prevents the carrying out of the work.
   A prolonged Bombardment of the hostile L'EPINETTE re-entrant will be carried out at dawn.

5. D/Leinster Regt will man their trenches by night and be prepared to support the 1st N. Staff Regt by fire from their trenches.

6. All Troops detailed to occupy the advanced line will take with them 2 days Rations 250 Rounds S.A.A.

7. Reports to B.H.Q at usual place

Copy No 1 Tickall   8 1st B
       2 1 R.F.   9 2 R.B
       3 3 R.B   10 16 Co RE
       4 1 A.S.R.   11 War Diary
       5 1 W/Surrey
       6 N. Staff Regt
       7 D/Leinster Regt

E. Shave
Capt
Bde Major 17 Inf Bde

Issued at 4.45 pm.

SKETCH SHOWING POSITIONS OF HOUSES IN ÉPINETTE.

A P P E N D I X   III.

17th Infantry Brigade.

Report on the Operations carried out 11th/12th March

1. The object of the operations which were undertaken by the 17th Infantry Brigade on the night 11/12 March 1915 was to gain and fortify a line in closer proximity to the enemy than that which had hitherto been held with a view to pin the enemy to his ground and to prevent his reinforcing other portions of his front, and capture his main defence when ordered to do so.

2. The operations were divided into two phases, the first a rapid occupation and defence of portion of the line W.X.Y. which was expected to be carried out without encountering the enemy except as regards one house, which was occupied as a snipers house. On this occasion it was empty.

    This phase was to last to 11.45 p.m. when it was considered advisable to have the working parties withdrawn to avoid confusion and losses from hostile fire from the parapet in the event of any serious resistance to the completion of the remainder of the work, and the enemy resorting to a general fusilade along the whole front.

    This work was duly carried out.

The

(Capture of front XYZ)

The Second phase, which involved the capture of hostile advanced posts was to commence at midnight. Certain of the houses in the L'EPINETTE salient were known to be occupied, strongly fortified and protected by wire entanglements, especially the two largest farms from which communications ran back to the main hostile line.

The houses had been continually shelled by us, but this had not prevented their occupation by the enemy.

It was decided therefore to capture all houses during the night, as far as possible by surprise, and to cut off the enemy's retreat by the communication trenches.

3. To avoid confusion, every detail was as far as possible thought out beforehand and difficulties foreseen.

4. The attack on the Houses was entrusted to the 1st North Stafford Regt.

The Routes taken are shown on the accompanying sketch (A)

5. Lieut V. Pope, 1st North Staff Regt. commanded the company which had the chief duty of dealing with the communication trenches and the defended Houses.

Each.

Each column arrived at its destination without confusion.

As a matter of fact, the enemy made a miserable resistance, and after firing away for some time decided to retreat on appreciating that their communications might be cut.

The Barbed wire entanglements caused some delay to the attacking columns and it was this alone which prevented Lieut Pope from cutting off the enemy.

6. The 12th Field Co R.E. was distributed according to orders, among the attacking columns and it was mainly due to their efforts that by daylight the whole front had been placed in a state of defence sufficiently to enable the troops to hold their position under a most severe Artillery Bombardment. Three counter-attacks were made up the Communication trenches and were successfully repulsed.

7. The Artillery arrangements were carried out by Lieut Col. C.E. Lawrie D.S.O. R.A., as shown in accompanying sketch maps C & D.

Owing to the nature of the defences and to the fact that surprise was to be an important element, it was thought best not to have a previous Artillery Bombardment, but the guns were all laid on their

various

various objectives, telephone arrangements were perfected with Forward Observation Officer in trenches so as to be able to deal with the enemy, in the event of his showing too great activity from the trenches.

It was decided to have a heavy Bombardment at dawn when it was thought most probable that a counter-attack would take place before our troops were properly established. This was duly carried out.

7. The nett result of the operation is that the defensive front of the northern portion of the 17th Brigade has been advanced some 200 to 300 yards for a length of about ½ mile.

The success of the operation is mainly due to the skillful leading of Lieut Roffe and the fact that the enemy put up such a miserable fight does not appear to detract from the merits of the performance.

8. Copies of orders etc issued are attached - also a report from Lt Col de Falbe Comdg 1st N. Staff Regt which I can thoroughly endorse.

G M Harper Brig Genl
17th Infy Bde

13.3.15.

Copy.

17th I.B.

Patrols in early evening did good work & brought back valuable information. I will bring some names to notice later.

Lieut. Pope led his company in the attack with great skill and dash to which I attribute his small losses - and to the success of the whole operation. I recommend him for immediate reward.

Lieut Gordon also led his company most successfully until he was wounded when his duties were taken over promptly and most efficiently by Lieut. de la Mare. Considering the latter officer's youth and inexperience I think he did remarkably well and is deserving of mention. He joined about 2 months ago. I should like to mention the great help given me by the Royal Engineers.

(signed) V. de Falbe
Lieut. Col.
Comdg 1st R. Staff Regt

12.3.15

Copy N°

17th Bde Operation Order N° 11.

ARMENTIERES.
11th March 1915

Reference:-
Attached Sketch.

1. The 17th Infantry Brigade will during the hours of darkness tonight, seize and make good the line W. X. Y and Z on the accompanying map.

2. The line from W to X will be held by 1 company of Leinster Regt under Capt. E.H. Murphy.
   Separate instructions have been issued to 2 London Regt who will provide working parties under Lieut. C.F. Tickell R.E. All work in this line will cease at 11.45 pm when working parties will be withdrawn.

3. At 12 midnight the 1st North Staffs Regt will seize and make good the line X (exclusive) Y, Z.
   136 Co R.E. and one Company of London Regt is placed under O.C 1st N. Staffs for this purpose.

4. Artillery support will be furnished under arrangements made by Lieut. Col. C.E. Lawrie D.S.O. R.A.
   Artillery fire will not be opened during the night unless the enemy prevents the carrying out of the work.
   A prolonged Bombardment of the hostile L'EPINETTE re-entrant will be carried out at dawn.

5. Leinster Regt will man their trenches by night and be prepared to support the 1st North Staffs Regt by fire from their trenches.

6. All troops detailed to occupy the advanced line will take with them 2 days Rations 230 Rounds S.A.A. All ranks will wear a loose white band round the neck as a distinguishing mark.

7. Reports to Bde H.Q. at usual place.

E. Levene
Capt.
Bde Major 17 Inf Bde

Issued at 4.45 pm

Copy N° 1 Lt Tickell
       2 1 R.F.
       3 3 R.B
       4 1 N. Staff
       5 Lt Col Lawrie
       6 2 London Regt
       7 Leinster Regt   11. War Diary
       8 16 I.B   12. Col SHEA
       9 18 I.B
      10 136 Co R.E

1st North Staffordshire Regt.

Operation Orders No 1. 1915 d/- 11-3-15.

1. The Battn. will attack and hold the EPINETTE Houses tonight.
    Attack to commence at 12 midnight and will start from trenches

2. Fall in at the Asylum 7.30 pm.

3. Great Coats will be worn.

4. Water bottles to be filled and 2 days rations carried on the man.

5. Ammunition 220 rounds per man.

6. Patrols will go out at 8 pm as follows:-
    "C" Company will find 3 patrols to reconnoitre the front and flanks of Houses in Western bend of Epinette Road and the Water-wheel house & house in front of it.

7. "C" Company will attack the above houses, taking them by surprise if possible, but if not then by assault.
    Distribution - Patrols. 3.
    1 Bomb party - 1 N.C.O & 3 men provided with spades and wire cutters
    Assaulting Parties 2 - each of 1 platoon 3 Sections. The 3 Sections will carry 15 spades and 15 picks, and 6 sandbags each man. 15 wire cutters, 4 hand axes, and 8 bill-hooks will also be carried, to be distributed by O. C. Company.

8. "D" Company will be in support of "C" Company. Two platoons will be detailed as

follows; to occupy & place in a state of defence the 3 houses on left of road leading from Left Company's Barrier to Epinette:-

Distribution.

(1.) 2 Sections (one Section working party)
(2.) 3 Sections (one   "   "   ")
(3.) 3 Sections (one   "   "   ")

Working parties equipped as in 7.

These houses must be defended from N.E & S.E. and defiladed from S.W.

The party for house No.3. will also deal with the Barrier (German)

Remainder of "D" Coy - in support in Left trenches.

9. "B" Company. Two platoons starting from Chicken Farm will make good house on N.W. side of Road, standing in small oblong enclosure, and leaving 3 Sections there (one of which a working party) will advance and take the remaining house on both sides of the road S.W. of the water wheel house. This party consisting of 1 platoon 1 section will have 2 sections as working party.

Remainder of "B" Coy will be in support at Chicken Farm. A patrol will be sent out at 8pm. to reconnoitre the route and houses.

10. "A" Company will be in support of "B" Coy in the left platoon trench of Centre Company.

11. "A" & "D" Coys will each take 20 spades and 10 picks, in addition to those carried by working parties. Each man in the Battn. will carry 2 sandbags except the men of working parties who will carry 6 each.

3.

12. As soon as the new line is established, each house party will work to establish a trench connecting it with the next house on the right.

13. <u>Machine Guns.</u> Two machine guns will accompany "C" Company and will act under orders of O.C. Company.
"D" Company will detail a carrying party for extra ammunition to each gun. 6 men each to report to O.C. M.Gs. in the Asylum at 7 p.m. 3 for ammunition, 3 for sandbags and spades.

The Two remaining M.Gs go with A. Coy.

14. R.E. parties will be detailed as follows:-
2 parties of 1 officer and 10 men to "C" Coy.
3 parties of 1 N.C.O. & 10 men to "D" Coy.
3 parties of 1 N.C.O. & 10 men to "B" Coy.

Battalion H.Q. will be at Left Companys telephone.

2nd in Command will be at Centre Coy's H.Q.

11.3.15.

(sgd) V. de Falbe Lieut. Col.
Commdg. 1st Bn. N. Staffs R.

Ref. attached
sketch map.

O.C.,
    2nd Leinster Regt.

(1.)   Your Battalion will find a covering party of one Company tonight from your Reserve Company.
    220 rounds a man and two days Rations will be carried.
    This covering party will be in position by 8 pm.

(2.)   Two Platoons 2nd London Regt will relieve your two Platoons at WHITE FARM at 7pm, and will come under your orders.

(3.)   The Machine Gun at present with your Centre Company will be moved forward to house A and will be placed under the orders of the O.C. Covering party.

(4.)   The Covering Party will remain in occupation of the houses and will hold the line House E to road junction by House R inclusive.

(5.)   They will take over the tools of the working party at 11.45 pm when it withdraws. The working party will leave these in the houses.

11/3/15.

(Sgd) E. R. Meade Waldo. Capt.
    Bde. M.G. Offr.

C1

ARTILLERY SUPPORT before 12 midnight.

ⓒ

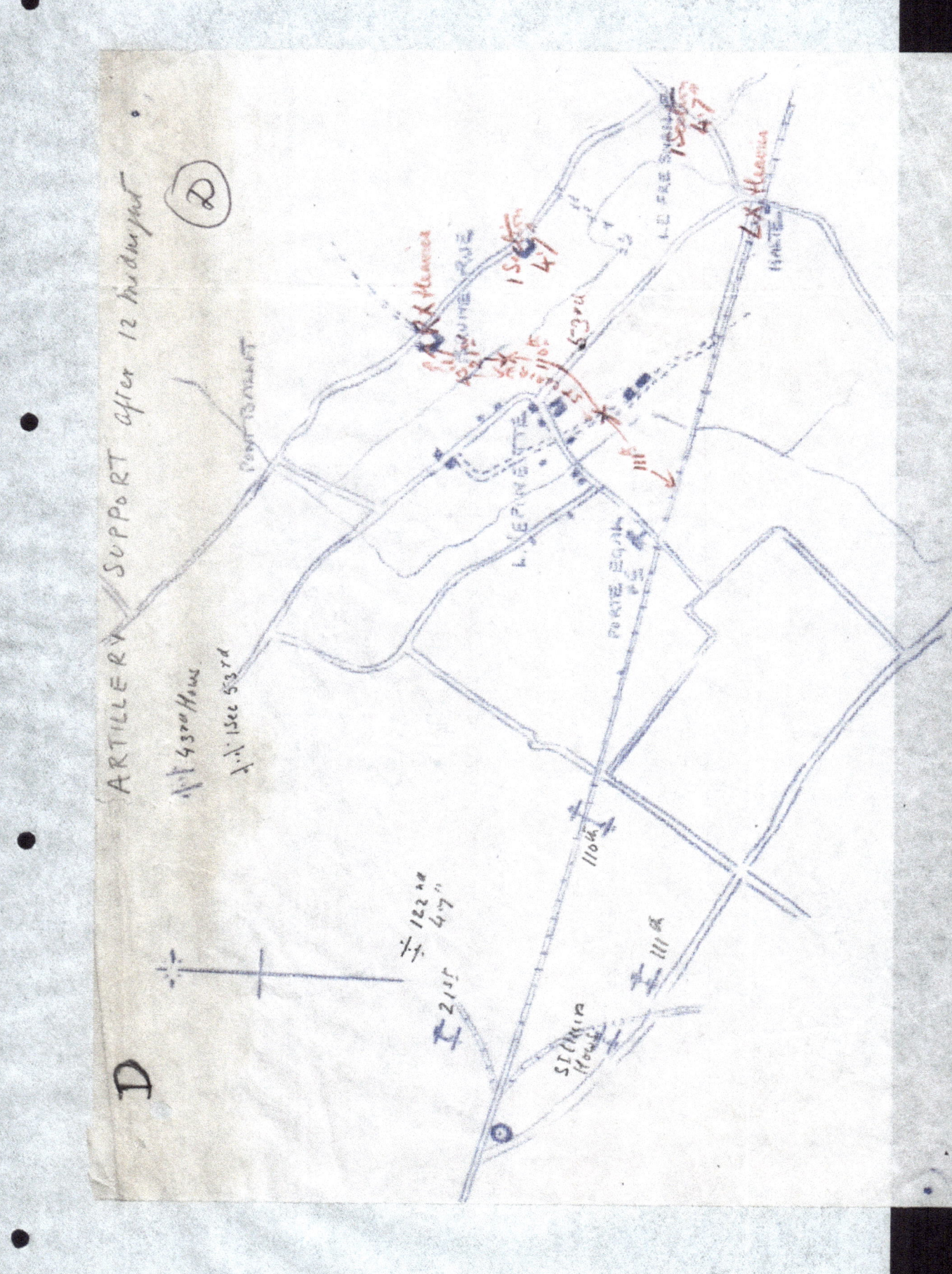

LEFT SECTION

HQ

L'EPINETTE

STREAM

STREAM

To PERENCHIES

Scale 1/5000
(1" = about 135 yds)

WAR DIARY
APP VII

SKETCH SHEWING POSITIONS OF HOUSES
IN EPINETTE.

1 to 8 chupet
Entrance

Front ½ mile
300 yds aso.

Whole no do travel
cover tych

A P P E N D I X   IV.

"A" Form.
MESSAGES AND SIGNALS.
Army Form C. 2121.

Prefix	Code	m.	Words	Charge	This message is on a/c of:	Recd. at	m.
Office of Origin and Service Instructions.			Sent		War Diary	Date	
			At	m.	Service.	From	
			To		App IV	By	
			By		(Signature of "Franking Officer.")		

APP IV

TO 6th Division

Sender's Number	Day of Month	In reply to Number	AAA
G 362	15th		

Copy of instructions received from 2nd Army for move of 16th Inf Bde (less territorial Bn) is forwarded in confirmation of telephone messages. Please inform 3rd Corps when the first train has left, what time the following trains are expected to leave and when the last train has actually left. What time the will 1st line transport reach RENINGHELST

From
Place
Time 1.25 am.

"A" Form. Army Form C. 2121.
MESSAGES AND SIGNALS.

Prefix____ Code____ m.	Words.	Charge.	This message is on a/c of:	Recd. at____ m.
Office of Origin and Service Instructions.				Date____
	Sent		APP IV	From____
	At____ m.		Service.	
	To____			
	By____	(Signature of "Franking Officer.")		By____

TO { Sixth Div.   War Diary App IV

| Sender's Number | Day of Month | In reply to Number | AAA |
| G 362 | 15th | | |

Following received from Second Army begins G54 the sixteenth brigade now at ARMENTIERES will move by rail from the ANNEXE station to the neighbourhood of VLAMERTINGHE tonight aaa the hour of the first train will be communicated as soon as it is known and the intervals at which they will move AAA the brigade commander will be sent by motor to fifth corps headquarters at POPERINGHE to report for instructions aaa should the fifth corps require the detrainment to take place at POPERINGHE they will make arrangements to stop the trains there aaa The transport of this

From
Place
Time

"A" Form.   Army Form C. 2121.
MESSAGES AND SIGNALS.

Prefix	Code	m.	Words.	Charge.	This message is on a/c of:	Rec'd at	m.
Office of Origin and Service Instructions.			Sent			Date	
			At	m.	*appd* Service.	From	
			To				
			By		(Signature of "Franking Officer.")	By	

TO { 2

| Sender's Number | Day of Month | In reply to Number | AAA |

brigade will move via BAILLEUL-
LOCRE to REMINGHELST and from
that point will be directed by
the fifth corps aaa

Following also received begins G55
In continuation of my G54 third corps
will inform fifth corps and second
army of the hour of departure of
first and last trains from
ARMENTIERES aaa The journey will
probably occupy two and a half
hours aaa As no transport can
be taken on the train fifth corps
must make arrangements for
feeding and ammunition supply of this
bde. until its own transport arrives

From			
Place			
Time			

The above may be forwarded as now corrected. (Z)

Censor.   Signature of Addressor or person authorised to telegraph in his name
* This line should be erased if not required.
(24473). M.R.Co.,Ltd. Wt.W4843/541. 50,000. 9/14. Forms C2121/10.

"C" Form (Duplicate). Army Form C. 2123.
MESSAGES AND SIGNALS.

		Charges to Pay	Office Stamp.

Service Instructions: Priority

Handed in at ___ Office 1.30 a.m. Received 1.30 a.m.

TO 1st Division

Sender's Number	Day of Month	In reply to Number	AAA
G 515	15th	—	

16th Brigade will detrain at VLAMERTINGHE aaa what hour will 1st Line transport reach RENINGHELST

Col. Shea.
This has just arrived —
Transport will arrive about
7 p.m. H.H. Headlam

FROM PLACE & TIME: 3rd Corps
                    1.30 am

WAR DIARY

GENERAL STAFF

6th DIVISION

APRIL

1915

- Confidential -

War Diary

of

General Staff 6th Division

From 1.4.15 To 30.4.15.

WARDIARY
INTELLIGENCE SUMMARY.
(Erase heading not required.)

Army Form C. 2118.

Hour, Date, Place	Summary of Events and Information	Remarks and references to Appendices
1st April	Leicesters relieved by 1st Cameronians, York & Lancs by 3rd Rifle Bde, E. Yorks by W. Yorks. 16th Lg Bde then all out of the front line. H.Q. 19th I.B. moved on account of shelling. Enemy's guns active in afternoon against BOIS GRENIER and H 17 c. 18th Bde reports nothing a difference in the sound of the enemy's rifles.	
2nd April	Durham L.I. relieved Sherwood Foresters. Quiet day. No occurrence of interest.	
3rd April	DESPLANQUE Farm & GRAND FLAMENGRIE farm & their neigh. bourhood shelled. Several H.E. shells fired into CHAPELLE D'ARMENTIERES. 3 pdr motor gun fired 20 rounds at farm + 20 rounds at enemy trenches at dawn. Result not observed. R. Welsh Fus: relieved A.&S. High[rs]	
4th April	Quiet day. Une hair observed in FOURNE STATION in afternoon. Warwickshire F.A. Bde & S. Midland Heavy Bty arrived, also 1 Section 7th Siege Bty R.G.A. not to fire till receipt of orders. Rifle Bde relieved by Sharps. L.I., W. Yorks by E. Yorks	
5th April	Quiet day. No change in situation	

Army Form C. 2118.

WAR DIARY
INTELLIGENCE SUMMARY.
(Erase heading not required.)

Instructions regarding War Diaries and Intelligence Summaries are contained in F.S. Regs., Part II. and the Staff Manual respectively. Title pages will be prepared in manuscript.

Hour, Date, Place	Summary of Events and Information	Remarks and references to Appendices
April 6th	Buffs relieved 1st Canadians, Leinsters relieved N. Staffs, Durham L.I. relieved Sherwood Foresters. Second line breastworks near DESPLANQUE FARM & LILLE post + houses near it shelled by enemy.	
April 7th	Very quiet day. DESPLANQUE FARM shelled. 38th Field Company left the division to join 28th Div.	
April 8th	Rifle Bde relieved R. Fusiliers, A. & S. Highrs relieved 1st Middlesex. A few shells behind centre of 14.9.13. & some on PONT BALLOT road near HOUPLINES. Otherwise quiet. 16th Infy Bde took over part of the line N. of the LILLE road & rearranged it distribution accordingly. It now has 2 companies S.L. North Lancs in on its left, 2 Co. + 1 platoon K.S.L.I. in reserve.	
April 9th	W. Yorks relieved E. Yorks. 20 shells fell close to ARMENTIERES – ERQUINGHEM road. DESPLANQUE FARM and RUE DU BOIS railway shelled.	
April 10th	Durham L.I. relieved Sherwood Foresters, 1st Canadians relieved R Welsh Horses + KENTISH farms shelled. Two French Howitzers ordered to go to 4th Div.	

Army Form C. 2118.

WAR DIARY
INTELLIGENCE SUMMARY.
(Erase heading not required.)

Instructions regarding War Diaries and Intelligence Summaries are contained in F. S. Regs., Part II. and the Staff Manual respectively. Title pages will be prepared in manuscript.

Hour, Date, Place	Summary of Events and Information	Remarks and references to Appendices
April 11th	York & Lancs. relieved K.S.L.I. &	
April 12th	Few shells near CULVERT FARM and EDMONDS farm. Right battalion 16th I.B. had a rifle grenade engagement with enemy opposite them. Lincolnshires relieved Buffs. N. Staffs relieved Leinsters. Sniping more active opposite 16th I.B. otherwise a quiet day. Reported that Saxons have been replaced by Bavarians opposite 19th I.B.	
April 13th	E. Yorks relieved W. Yorks. 1st Middlesex relieved 2nd Arg. Highrs. Neighbourhood of GRANDE FLAMENGRIE farm shelled. Otherwise quiet. R. Fus. relieved Rifle Bde. Sherwood Foresters relieved Durham L.I.	
April 14th	Very quiet day, nothing to report. Squadron 19th Hussars left division. "C" Sqn. Northamptonshire Yeomanry replaces them as Div M.H. troops. R. Welsh Fus. relieved 1st Cameronians.	
April 15th	Quiet day, no occurence of interest.	
April 16th	During night 15/16th a patrol of York & Lancs located German working parties on both sides of the LILLE road. These were effectively engaged by our machine-guns. WATER FARM I 25 d, 1, 9th. Bde new communication trench and RUE DU BOIS area shelled.	
April 17th	K.S.L.I. relieved York & Lancs, W. Yorks relieved E. Yorks.	

WAR DIARY
INTELLIGENCE SUMMARY.

(Erase heading not required.)

Army Form C. 2118.

Hour, Date, Place	Summary of Events and Information	Remarks and references to Appendices
18th April	Patrols out from York & Lancs & R. Welsh Fusiliers during night 16/17th. 19th Bde left communication trench & farm in C.22.a. shelled. 18th Inf Bde. 1/Londn 7?Co, 2nd F.A. Bde (Can 1 Bty), 12th F.A. (How) Bde (Can 1 Bty), 7th Siege Bty, ?section 12th Siege Bty remaining in 6th Div area (H.Q. & 1 sec moved out on night 16/17th) came under orders of 4th Div. 2nd Heavy Bty marched out to join No 1 H.A.R. & 87th & ST CLAIRS Btés (How) moved into 4th Div area. 30th Co R.E. was placed under orders of 6th Div.	
19th April	Buffs relieved Leinsters/Lewis, Leinsters relieved N. Staffs, Dublins L.I. relieved Sherwood Foresters, R.I.S. Highrs relieved Middlesex R. Farm X , DESPLANQUE & DE LA HAIZERIE Farms, & centre of 16th. G.B. breastworks shelled.	
20th April	Quiet day. Very little shelling. Patrols out night of 18th/19th from K.S.L.I. & L.N. Lancs. Rifle Bde relieved R. Fus., Cameronians relieved R. Welsh Fus.: Enemy artillery more active farms in T.31.c.9.4., T.15.c.8.10, T.14.b. bombarded, also breastworks in rear of farm in T.16.a.3.9. Patrols out night of 19/20th from Buffs & K.S.L.I. Lieut BABER machine-gun officer Queens Westminsters successfully carried out a special reconnaissance.	

WAR DIARY
INTELLIGENCE SUMMARY.
(Erase heading not required.)

Army Form C. 2118.

Instructions regarding War Diaries and Intelligence Summaries are contained in F. S. Regs., Part II. and the Staff Manual respectively. Title pages will be prepared in manuscript.

Hour, Date, Place	Summary of Events and Information	Remarks and references to Appendices
21st April	E. Yorks relieved W. Yorks. Active grenade firing by both sides at RUE DU BOIS. Raised in I 31 c 3.10, centre section 19 G 13 – RUE DU BOIS area shelled. Slight shelling in area of 18.d.g.13. Patrols out on night 20/21st. from Buffs + K.S.L.I. Sherwood Foresters relieved Dunham L.I.	
22nd April	Very quiet day. Four shells fired at 19 G 13. Trenches near FERME ENERIE Farm. Patrols out from Buffs + Cameronians. Cameronian patrol took a flag. Two officers of Rifle Bde went out 30 yards in front of trenches + successfully engaged a German working party with rifle-grenades. These patrols were busy during night 21/22nd. Yorks + Lancs relieved K.S.L.I. Middlesex relieved A. + S. Highrs. 16th J.B. made good shooting with trench mortar to which enemy replied by shelling RUE DU BOIS. In the afternoon the 16 Y & L. night headquarters by DESPLANQUE level crossing were heavily shelled. 16 J.B. report enemy continues to work actively on his defences. On the night 22nd/23rd a patrol of the Buffs obtained useful information about enemy's defences + Captain BLIGH and one Sergt from Rifle Bde went out about 80 x up a dyke in a special boat designed + made by Captain BLIGH + silenced with wife- grenade poise a machine gun which had been interfering with one of our working parties.
23rd April		

Army Form C. 2118.

Instructions regarding War Diaries and Intelligence Summaries are contained in F.S. Regs., Part II. and the Staff Manual respectively. Title pages will be prepared in manuscript.

WAR DIARY
INTELLIGENCE SUMMARY.
(Erase heading not required.)

Hour, Date, Place	Summary of Events and Information	Remarks and references to Appendices
24th April.	Leicestershires relieved Buffs N. Staffs relieved Lincolns. In view of the fighting in progress in the north the Corps commander allotted an extra 10 rounds of shrapnel per gun for 18 pdrs with a view to making a demonstration by fire to hold the enemy in front of us. This demonstration was carried out in cooperation between the infantry & artillery along the whole front of the 16th, 17th, & 4th Bdes.	
2.0 p.m.	At 2.0 p.m. the infantry of the 16th increased the intensity of its sniping.	
3.15 p.m.	Bursts of rifle fire delivered on RUE DU BOIS salient & SNIPER'S HOUSE briskly answered by enemy.	
3.30 p.m.	18 Pounders opened fire along the whole front as follows :- opposite 19th Line for 8 minutes distributed along 1st line trenches particularly on heads of communication trenches; opposite 16th & B. on the Garden near SNIPER'S House to cut enemy's wire here; opposite 17th & B. concentrated fire for five minutes or two points in enemy's front line. The 18 pndrs. co-operated along the whole front by bursts of rifle fire & machine gun fire & by trench-mortar bombs & rifle grenades.	
3.35 p.m.	Guns in 17th Bde zone ceased fire. Infantry fire also suspended.	
3.38 p.m.	Guns in 19th Bde Zone ceased fire. Infantry fire also suspended.	
3.40 p.m.	Guns in 19th Bde zone opened again for 2 minutes on loophole trenches, & infantry opened slow fire particularly on known machine gun positions.	

WAR DIARY
INTELLIGENCE SUMMARY.
(Erase heading not required.)

Army Form C. 2118.

Instructions regarding War Diaries and Intelligence Summaries are contained in F.S. Regs., Part II. and the Staff Manual respectively. Title pages will be prepared in manuscript.

Hour, Date, Place	Summary of Events and Information	Remarks and references to Appendices
3.45 p.m.	Infantry of 18th Bde opened rapid fire all along the line for five minutes. Guns in 7th Bde opened again on the same two points doing considerable damage to enemy wire & breastworks.	
3.50 p.m.	5 minutes rapid fire by infantry of 18th Bde. The demonstration lasted from 3.30 p.m. to 4.05 p.m. The enemy's artillery replied concentrating most of their fire on positions where supporting troops might be likely to be collected or approaches. 13 different hostile batteries were identified as firing and were located, 4 others unlocated also fired. The enemy's guns included field guns, 4.2", 5.9" Hows. The success of the demonstration is established by the fact that German Official reports announced that their artillery fire had checked an intended attack West of D 4.11.15. During night 23rd/24th Patrol from The Buffs & 1/Royal W. Yorks relieved 2/Yorks R. Welsh Fus. relieved Cameronians. During night 24th/25th a rifle grenade party under 2/Lt S.H. SETCHTON and a machine gun party under Captain CHANCE went out from the Sherwood Foresters trenches & engaged a German working party shelling it to Festubert work.	
25th April.		

Confidential. Forms/C. 2118/10

WAR DIARY
INTELLIGENCE SUMMARY
(Erase heading not required.)

Army Form C. 2118.

Instructions regarding War Diaries and Intelligence Summaries are contained in F.S. Regs., Part II. and the Staff Manual respectively. Title pages will be prepared in manuscript.

Hour, Date, Place	Summary of Events and Information	Remarks and references to Appendices
26th April.	Quiet day. Enemy shelled FERME DE LA HALLEBIE. Royal Fusiliers relieved Rifle Bde. Durham L.I. relieved Sherwood Foresters. During night of 25th/26th a patrol from the Middlesex Regt. took a large German flag which had attached to it a newspaper of WERZEN of the 15th April. It appears that 179th Regt. has relieved 9th Bav. Reserve just S. of WAVRIN line. Captain Beigh & two other officers of Rifle Bde. were out & fired rifle grenades into German trenches & N. Staffs. had two patrols out to reconnoitre hostile line.	
27th April	Quiet day. During night of 26th/27th a patrol of Middlesex regiment went out to try & capture a reported hostile patrol. They failed to meet it but went on & bombed a German Sap-head, driving some enemy who occupied it back into their main line. 17th Inf. Bde. area shelled more than usual, otherwise a quiet day.	
28th April.	A.& S. Highrs. relieved Middlesex Regt. LA VESÉE Farm in I 19 ℅ 10·5 & left section 16th F.B. shelled. This morning news was received of the death of Brigadier-General HASLER, lately commanding the Buffs. In him the Service has lost a very fine & gallant soldier, whose energy & soldierly qualities all had	

WAR DIARY
or
INTELLIGENCE SUMMARY.
(Erase heading not required.)

Army Form C. 2118.

Hour, Date, Place	Summary of Events and Information	Remarks and references to Appendices
	all had learnt to admire during the time he was serving in this division. In him many of the division have lost a charming companion, & a noble example.	
	During the night of the 28th/29th the following alterations were carried out under orders of the Corps acting on instructions from G.H.Q.	
	18th 6th Div: took over a portion of 4th Div's line N. of R. Lys at LE TOUQUET. 18th-9.13 relieved a battalion and a half of 12 4 I.B. E. Yorks 1½ Queen's Westminsters going into the new trenches. The left of our line is now on the RNTB=CLUES shown just west of the LE TOUQUET rly. 1st London 7° Company returned to 6th Div. 2nd & 12th F.A. BDes returned to 6th Div. and 4th F.A. B2 C. and one section 2nd Mountain Bty came under orders of 6th Div. Heavy artillery in 6th & South Midland areas placed into a group under Colonel CURRIE, R.G.A.	
	½ 2/Lond Regt. Wildham from trenches.	
29th April	K.S.L.I. relieved York Lanes. 2/Lond R. relieved W. Yorks 17K.7.0. After extending to left to relieve 1 Bn of 18 7.0. Enemy shelled BOIS GRENIER, GRANDE FLAMENGRIE farm, CHAPELLE D'ARMENTIERES, houses in left section 17 9.B. and HOUPLINES church tower. 24th Bty R.F.A heavily shelled by S.I."	

Army Form C. 2118.

WAR DIARY
INTELLIGENCE SUMMARY.
(Erase heading not required.)

Hour, Date, Place	Summary of Events and Information	Remarks and references to Appendices
30th April	Hows. three guns being damaged one so badly as to have to be sent back for repair. Owing to new arrangements regarding heavy arty in our area & communication with Group Comd' wonder of having been satisfactorily established there was delay in engaging the hostile howitzers which were shelling the 2nd F.A. Bde. Buffs relieved Leicestershires, Leicestershires relieved N. Staffs, Cameronians relieved R Welsh Fus. A quiet day. 6th Division 2nd May 1915	

J. Thro? Captain
General Staff

GENERAL STAFF · 2 MAY 1915 · 6TH DIVISION

WAR DIARY

GENERAL STAFF

6th DIVISION

MAY

1915

Attached:
Appendix I.

— Confidential —

War Diary.

of

General Staff 6th Division

From 1.5.15 To 31.5.15.

Army Form C. 2118.

WAR DIARY
INTELLIGENCE SUMMARY.
(Erase heading not required.)

Instructions regarding War Diaries and Intelligence Summaries are contained in F. S. Regs., Part II. and the Staff Manual respectively. Title pages will be prepared in manuscript.

Hour, Date, Place	Summary of Events and Information	Remarks and references to Appendices
1st May	Sherwood Foresters relieved Queens Westminsters. Left section 16th K.R.B. and neighbourhood of HOBBS' FARM (C23a 5.9) shelled. Enemy reported by 16th K.R.B. to be very busy strengthening back defences. Patrol from 2nd Lond. R. went out during night 30/1st to dishoy waggon suspected of being used by enemy as a listening-post.	
2nd May	Rifle Bde relieved Royal Fus. W. Yorks relieved Durh. L.I. A quiet day. A few shells into BOIS GRENIER and four into L'Ar- MEE billets. On the night of 1st/2nd a patrol from 18th I.B. got as far as WHITE HOUSE C20d 3.3.	
3rd May	Middlesex relieved A. & S. Highrs. At 8.30 a.m., owing to reports that the enemy was working forward in our gallery & was only 3 ft distant the mine which was being driven on the Barricade at FRELINGHIEN had to be fired, about 40 feet short of its objective. A large crater was formed between the CHICKEN RUN and the barricade and two hostile covered communications opened up. Gun and rifle-fire was opened by us on the surrounding area and Germans seen leaving	

WAR DIARY
or
INTELLIGENCE SUMMARY.

(Erase heading not required.)

Army Form C. 2118.

Hour, Date, Place	Summary of Events and Information	Remarks and references to Appendices

4th May.

in three allotees were sniped. The enemy replied by a more than usually heavy bombardment of HOUPLINES in which 5.9" howitzers participated. The breastwork in I21a 8.2 and in front of DESPLANQUE Farm, the right section 17 J.B. L'EPINETTE Salient and LE BIZET were also shelled during the day. During night 2/3 a patrol of the 1/Buffs was out for two hours close to the enemy's line

H.M.S. "PET" left during the day for DUNKIRK.

A few shells at night were @ 17 & J.B. L'ARMÉE & GRIS POT. About 100 field-gun shells & howitzer drawn in afternoon & part of adjoining farm blown in. Also HOUPLINES Lock-bridge & neighbouring farm replied with 5.9" in evening. Enemy occupied our mine crater. During night 3/4 two patrols from K.S.L.I. went out close to German wire & returned with some very useful information.

Royal Welsh Fus relieved A.T.S. Knylies.

5th May.

A few shells at CHARD'S FARM (I 16a 9.3) & HOUPLINES shelled in the morning. During night circulars & N.S.L.I. had patrols out to listening line

WAR DIARY
or
INTELLIGENCE SUMMARY.
(Erase heading not required.)

Army Form C. 2118.

Instructions regarding War Diaries and Intelligence Summaries are contained in F.S. Regs., Part II. and the Staff Manual respectively. Title pages will be prepared in manuscript.

Hour, Date, Place	Summary of Events and Information	Remarks and references to Appendices
6th May	N Seaforths relieved Leinsters. Dark. L.I. relieved E. Yorks. From 5.30 a.m. to 6.45 a.m. enemy shelled ARMENTIERES with shells of various sizes, largely French ammunition. About 4.00 shells but very few casualties. A few shells behind Centre Battalion (9th I.B.) at Left Battalion 16th 9.13. Gtterrine Chiet. On the night of 5th/6th a patrol of the Buffs reconnoitred area work near the German Salient at RUE DU BOIS. A patrol of the 3rd R.B. also reconnoitred battle works & locating a working party bombed them with good effect. Leinsters relieved Buffs. York & Lancs relieved 2/Lond Regt. During the night 6th/7th own patrols were very active. A patrol from 55 Sec. R.E. wanted & fetched in the effects of a man of the 49th Regiment, XIX Saxon Corps shot close to their entering post	
7th May	on the morning of the 6th. The 2nd Lond R. sent out one patrol, Buffs one, KSLI one, and 3rd Rifle Bde several. These all returned with useful information. That of the KSLI made 2 theirs BIRD cut through three lines of the enemy's wire. From the reports of these patrols it appears that though the enemy's front trench is	

Army Form C. 2118.

WAR DIARY
or
INTELLIGENCE SUMMARY.
(Erase heading not required.)

Hour, Date, Place	Summary of Events and Information	Remarks and references to Appendices
	still held it is possible that it is not occupied in great strength. Official 18th G.O. The enemy is reported to be lowering his front line parapets & strengthening second line works. The day was exceptionally quiet, about a dozen shells were fired near FLAMENGRIE FARM. The enemy is reported to be working very diligently on the defences on the PREMESQUES ridge. This afternoon a new pontoon bridge was constructed near HOUP= LINES in Square C.26.6. In connection with projected operations by the 1st Army, the 3rd Corps was ordered to carry out a vigorous demonstra= tion on the 8th with a view to attracting the enemy's attention. Between 8.0 p.m. on 7th & 2.0 a.m. on 8th a train was run into the Gare Annexe at ARMENTIERES six times, left there for half-an-hour and then run out again. Bodies of troops were collected quietly under cover of dark in the station & marched ostentatiously out in connection with the drains & through the town. A constant movement of motor traffic was also kept up throughout the first half of the night.	

WAR DIARY
INTELLIGENCE SUMMARY.
(Erase heading not required.)

Army Form C. 2118.

Instructions regarding War Diaries and Intelligence Summaries are contained in F.S. Regs., Part II. and the Staff Manual respectively. Title pages will be prepared in manuscript.

Hour, Date, Place	Summary of Events and Information	Remarks and references to Appendices
8th May.	Orders were issued in the morning for the confinement to their houses throughout the whole of the 8th of all the civil population of ARMENTIERES, HOUPLINES, & CHAPELLE D'ARMENTIERES. At 2.0 p.m. orders were received postponing the demonstration for twenty-four hours. Royal Fus: relieved Rif. Brig: Queens Washington relieved Sherwood Foresters A & S. Highrs relieved Wiltshire. During the night of 7th/8th Lieut PRICE MAN, K.S.L.I. & one man patrolled to German wire. Both were hit by m.g. fire but succeeded in getting back to our line. Lieut Inskipp & two R. Welsh Fus. patrolled close to German line. Their presence being detected 2 No German picquet set out by doubling back along close under the German parapet they were able to evade their pursuers. Considerable sounds of movement nearly N. to S. heard during night 7/8th. A very quiet day; only a few hostile shells at CULVERT FARM, T.25. C.3.4. & a few at BOIS GRENIER.	

Army Form C. 2118.

WAR DIARY
or
INTELLIGENCE SUMMARY.
(Erase heading not required.)

Instructions regarding War Diaries and Intelligence Summaries are contained in F. S. Regs, Part II. and the Staff Manual respectively. Title pages will be prepared in manuscript.

Hour, Date, Place	Summary of Events and Information	Remarks and references to Appendices
6 May	Patrols during night of 5/6th. One from K.S.L.I., one from York & Lancs. Latter found part of their front line unoccupied. During the night of 6/7 - the Germans fired a mine in front of FR.2 LINGHIEN close to the CHICKEN RUN. It is close to their line than to ours. Our parapet & defenses were uninjured. The demonstration ordered for 8th + postponed was carried out as follows:—	
4.30 a.m.		
	6 guns of 14th F.B. groups shelled enemy's wire for 20 minutes + at	
4.50 a.m.	turned onto enemy's trenches & communication trenches in the same region. Unavailable bursts of rapid rifle-machine-gun fire were delivered on points where communication trenches come into fire-trenches. The guns of the 16th L.B. group opened a sudden bombardment on the enemy's trenches on either side of the LILLE road & then lifted onto the area behind WEZ MACQUART. A.B. with rifle machine gun fire was opened on the enemy's trenches which were shelled, rifle fire was opened along the whole line + a vigorous bombardment with trench mortars & rifle grenades was delivered from ROE DU BOIS.	

Forms/C. 2118/10

WAR DIARY
INTELLIGENCE SUMMARY.
(Erase heading not required.)

Army Form C. 2118.

Instructions regarding War Diaries and Intelligence Summaries are contained in F. S. Regs, Part II. and the Staff Manual respectively. Title pages will be prepared in manuscript.

Hour, Date, Place	Summary of Events and Information	Remarks and references to Appendices
	The guns of the 17th J.B. bombarded the enemy's second line trenches, rapid rifle fire was opened along the whole line & machine-gun fire was directed on road-junction in rear. The 18th J.B. fired a mine near the railway barricade at LE TOUQUET. Immediately it was fired the guns opened on neighbouring trenches & a heavy rifle, machine gun & grenade fire on the crater. The enemy's salient at LE TOUQUET was bombed & south of the river a brisk rifle & m.g. fire was opened from selected points. The mine had to be fired short of its objective & postponed, & little effect on the enemy's defences except to unsettle him. Enemy made very little attempt to retaliation. LE TOUQUET and the trenches of right battalion 19th J.B. were shelled and there was a vigorous exchange of rifle-grenades & trench-mortar bombs at RUE DU BOIS. Throughout the day the machine gun & rifle batteries of 16th J.B. were turned onto roads in rear of the German lines.	

Army Form C. 2118.

WAR DIARY
or
INTELLIGENCE SUMMARY.
(Erase heading not required.)

Instructions regarding War Diaries and Intelligence Summaries are contained in F. S. Regs., Part II. and the Staff Manual respectively. Title pages will be prepared in manuscript.

Hour, Date, Place	Summary of Events and Information	Remarks and references to Appendices
	Brisk sniping was maintained all day along the whole front of the division.	
	During the day enemy shelled BOIS GRENIER road junction in I 19 c, during heavies behind centre of 19th Q.B. & FERME DU BIE	
5.45 p.m	At about 5.45 p.m. the officer in charge of W.Yorks snipers detected the enemy in the act of carrying out a relief. He estimated the range, got his two machine guns trained on a point, firing indirect, & also directed the fire of his platoon, having arranged a code of whistle signals he returned to his look-out post. On the next appearance of the enemy at the marked spot he opened fire successfully. When the next party selected a fresh route he relaid his guns & checked the platoon fire. He was rewarded by catching the enemy in a close column of fours. One officer & 114 men were killed for certain & the estimated casualties were 40 to 50. E.Yorks relieved W.Yorks. Camerenians relieved R.Well.Fus.	
10th May	On the night of 9/10th a patrol of Loyal North Lancs patrolled	

WAR DIARY or INTELLIGENCE SUMMARY.

(Erase heading not required.)

Army Form C. 2118.

Instructions regarding War Diaries and Intelligence Summaries are contained in F.S. Regs., Part II. and the Staff Manual respectively. Title pages will be prepared in manuscript.

Hour, Date, Place	Summary of Events and Information	Remarks and references to Appendices
11th May	close up to the evening. Our returned with useful information. During the day Bers GRANIER, ROE DU BOIS front trenches & Fme DU BOIS communication trench were shelled. Two patrols from K.S.L.I. on night of 9/10th reported the enemy very much on the alert. Our demonstration seems to have brought troops which had been taken out back into the front line. Sherwood Foresters relieved Durham L.I.	
12th May	Quiet day. 11 light field gun shells into Fme DU 5152 9421 Little Willies into I 5 c. Leinsters relieved N. Staffs. On the night of 11th/12th a patrol of 1st R.B. went out to investigate a report that a German patrol was near our lines. They killed a wire-field wind of the 139 Regt (1xx Saxon Corps) & personalis body. A few Little Willies into ROE DU BOIS and five White Hopes into Begium, causing 11 casualties WATER-WHEEL FARM attacked with hand grenades.	

WAR DIARY
INTELLIGENCE SUMMARY.
(Erase heading not required.)

Army Form C. 2118.

Instructions regarding War Diaries and Intelligence Summaries are contained in F.S. Regs., Part II. and the Staff Manual respectively. Title pages will be prepared in manuscript.

Hour, Date, Place	Summary of Events and Information	Remarks and references to Appendices
13th May	½ K.S.L.I. came out of trenches & L.N. Lancs increased to 3 Coys in. Middlesex relieved R.45 Highrs. On night of 12th/13th a patrol of L.N. Lancs located hostile working parties. At 4.25 a.m. enemy opened heavy rifle & shrapnel fire on the left company 18 I.B. on the LE TOUQUET railway. They also throwed communication trenches with machine gun fire & shrapnel. Following this they blew a big mine [crossed out] about half way between their trench & the "fort" on the railway. We had 3 killed & 17 wounded & our listening galleries were blown in. 30 killed Willies at PONT BALLOT and 22 at F^{lle} DE LA BOUTERIE. Enemy has added greatly to his wire on W.2. MACHURET — RUE DU BOIS road.	
14th May	Buffs relieved Leicesters. K.O. Brig: relieved R.I. Rifles 2 Londons relieved York & Lancs. W. Yorks relieved Queens Westminsters. Patrol of L. North Lancs on night 13/14 ascertained that enemy was working in front of & behind his breastwork.	

WAR DIARY
or
INTELLIGENCE SUMMARY.
(Erase heading not required.)

Army Form C. 2118.

Hour, Date, Place	Summary of Events and Information	Remarks and references to Appendices
18th May	20 shells in our trenches of Left Battalion. 19 H.A.B. in reply to bombardment carried out by 49th Div. Four shells Willie H.E. into Left Section 1649 B. 69th + 88th Batteries removed during night to 4.6" + 4.15" + their place taken by Canadian F.A.B.De 3 batteries in action. 1 in reserve. R. Welsh Fusiliers relieved Cameronians.	
19th May 12.15 p.m.	Enemy reported very active at LE TOUQUET railway barricade. Aeroplane occupied their mine craterless. Major DOVE showed Foulon killed. Two guns of Laurel Howitzer battery sent to deal with the situation. A few shells along road in T 19 C. near ESPLANQUE FARM. FOBOs FARM and suspn. Kurew at LE TOUQUET shelled by field guns. Enemy active with grenades + trench mortars opposite Reg. Post at LE TOUQUET. At 9.30 p.m. owing to reports that enemy could be heard withdrawing over our parapet men at LE TOUQUET railway barrier the [illeg.] was talked round. Heavy firing, bombing and MG. went on	

WAR DIARY
INTELLIGENCE SUMMARY.
(Erase heading not required.)

Army Form C. 2118.

Hour, Date, Place	Summary of Events and Information	Remarks and references to Appendices
16th May	Bombardment by both sides resulted. Durham L.I. relieved Sherwood Foresters.	
11.15 a.m.	During night 15th/16th a patrol of 2nd Lent. Regt. examined enemy wire & a patrol of Lincolns threw two bombs into enemy trench. 19th 9 B. bombarded enemy's trenches & fired bursts of rifle fire to which enemy's guns replied against their front line trenches. 17th 9 B. guns bombarded points behind German first line, their infantry fired occasional bursts of fire + m.g. fire was directed on road junctions behind their lines. All brigades were particularly active to shell enemy's attention. During the day enemy shelled support trenches N.of BURNT FARM (I.2.a 27), CHARD'S FARM (I.16.a 9.3), DUBIEZ comm- unication trench, Brig. Hqg. Batt. hqs, head qrs of battalion.	
16.4.13.		
6.0 p.m.	A special grant of 150 rounds 18 pounder shrapnel having been obtained from the corps they were employed to carry out wire cutting in square T 26 b in front of 19th 9. B. Fire was directed	

WAR DIARY or INTELLIGENCE SUMMARY.

Army Form C. 2118.

(Erase heading not required.)

Instructions regarding War Diaries and Intelligence Summaries are contained in F. S. Regs., Part II. and the Staff Manual respectively. Title pages will be prepared in manuscript.

Hour, Date, Place	Summary of Events and Information	Remarks and references to Appendices
17th May	for half an hour on a front of 100 yards. Fifty yards was completely destroyed & a further 20 yards so cut up as to be barely passable. During the night the enemy made several attempts to repair the damage. These were detected by listening posts & patrols & frustrated by gun rifle & m.g. fire. During night 16th/17th a patrol of 3rd R.B. bombed a bivouac in the Germans' trenches where some of them could be heard talking. A very quiet day.	
18th May	N. Staffs. relieved Lincolns. Duneed Westminsters relieved 3. Yorks. Middlesex relieved A.& S. Hydrs. During night of 17th/18th a patrol of North Lancs made unsuccessful reconnaissance. Several attempts on the part of the enemy to mend the wire cut on the 16th were frustrated by our fire. A very quiet day. Nothing of note. During the night 18th/19th the 86th Bty. was withdrawn from action and left the division permanently. Two batteries of the 3rd Bde. action and left the division permanently. 52nd Bde relieved Canadian F.A. Bde. took its place the same night.	

(2 29 6) W 4141—463 100,000 9/14 HWV Forms/C. 2118/10

Army Form C. 2118.

WAR DIARY
INTELLIGENCE SUMMARY.
(Erase heading not required.)

Instructions regarding War Diaries and Intelligence Summaries are contained in F.S. Regs., Part II. and the Staff Manual respectively. Title pages will be prepared in manuscript.

Hour, Date, Place	Summary of Events and Information	Remarks and references to Appendices
19th May.	Area I 11 a I 11 3 and neighbourhood of ARMENTIERES Rly. Station shelled. A few small shells in 1112 a.c.	
20th May	Lucestaghuir relieved Buffs, 2/Kent Regt relieved York & Lancs., R. Fus. relieved Rif. Brig, Sherwood Foresters relieved W. Yorks. Right & centre sections 14th F.B., + 13th N.Z. R.C.V.S. Rif. Bde. relieved. L'EPINETTE trenches bombarded about 4.45 p.m. while 1st Rifle Bde. + 17th search mortar bombs. Two Officers wounded.	
21st May.	Cameronians relieved R. Welsh Fus. On night of 20th/21st. receiving 2 Batteries 53rd (How) Bde. were brought into action. A few shells near CULVERT FARM (I 2 S.c. 3.4.) + near DES = PLANQUE FARM. L. Yorks relieved Queens Westminsters.	
22nd May.	Front line between FLAMENGRIE Farm and Farm in I 2 d.t.7.1. CHAPELLE D'ARMENTIERES LE TOUQUET neighbourhood of ARMENTIERES Station shelled.	
23rd May.	Middlesex Regt. relieve A. & S. Highrs.	

Army Form C. 2118.

WAR DIARY
INTELLIGENCE SUMMARY.
(Erase heading not required.)

Instructions regarding War Diaries and Intelligence Summaries are contained in F.S. Regs., Part II. and the Staff Manual respectively. Title pages will be prepared in manuscript.

Hour, Date, Place	Summary of Events and Information	Remarks and references to Appendices
24th Aug.	A quiet day. Du Briez Farm + Distillery on LILLE road	
1.15 a.m.	w T.S. & slightly shelled. Leicesters relieved N Staffs. W Yorks relieved Park L.I. Report received from 19th S.B. that 49th Bn shorts were lying occupied the advanced trench dug by 148th Bde. Enemy to be turned out with bayonet. Communication to be pushed. Fire research company placed in second line trench + Bde reserve ordered to stand to arms.	
3.30 a.m.	149 Bde report trench occupied with very little opposition. Cooperation of 148 S.B. not required. A few shells at front line trenches at 16th Aug. 4 B. + a few in neighbourhood of FORT ZOMPU, RUE DONOINE + RUE ST MAUR.	
5.50 p.m.	19 I.B. report enemy has enfiladed a sauf mine near FRE- LINGHIEN just west of CHICKEN RUN. No damage to our own.	
8.0 p.m.	Cooperation with operation being carried out by 148 Bde as a demonstration. The 149th Bde would occupy the advanced trench it holding on passing reorganed astride the TOUQUET-BRIDOUX	

WAR DIARY
or
INTELLIGENCE SUMMARY.
(Erase heading not required.)

Army Form C. 2118.

Hour, Date, Place	Summary of Events and Information	Remarks and references to Appendices
	and a ruined house on that road between the two huts. In co-operation with this two batteries of the 12th F.A. Bde. carried out wire cutting in front of 200 yards of the German trench on the east of the road & Cameronians assisted with machine-gun fire from the flank, two extra machine-guns being put into the line to assist. At sunset 18 pdr was dug into the parapet and H.E. at the German parapet opposite particularly at a suspected m.g. emplacement. The results were not of the single gun fire were not actually satisfactory. The suspected m.g. emplacement was destroyed but the enemy's parapet was not apparently breached. High vegetation between the two lines makes it difficult to estimate the extent of the damage but there seem to be some doubt whether H.E. shell at such short range is detonated properly. At Regt H.O. p.m. 12 midnight & 2.0 a.m. on 25th a few minutes bombardment of selected points on roads in rear of the enemy's lines was carried out. The operation of 145th Bde. was satisfactorily carried out. the co-operation of our Guns & of the Cameronians being very	

WAR DIARY
INTELLIGENCE SUMMARY.
(Erase heading not required.)

Army Form C. 2118.

Hour, Date, Place	Summary of Events and Information	Remarks and references to Appendices
25th May	Effective. Enemy made little reply. Buffs relieved Leicestershires.	
	Quiet day; slight shelling of 19th Bde front & support trenches. 4 Sig. Sqq. in 16th I.B. front line. Orders received for relief of 6th Div by 27th Div., 19th I.B. to remain behind in its present line.	
26th May	2nd London Regt. relieved York & Lancs. Rif. Brig. relieved R. Fus., Queens Westminsters relieved E. Yorks, R. Welsh Fus. relieved Camerons. 2nd F.A.B. was relieved on night 26/27th by 30th F.A.B. from 27th Div + marched to 5th Corps area. 2nd F.A.B. marched 11·0 p.m. Germans fired a mine in front of FRELINGHIEN brewery & endeavoured to occupy crater. Quiet day, very little sniping. A few little Willies at Breastworks left of LILLE road.	
27th May	Quiet day. LYS Farm + adjoining farm shelled in morning + burnt down.	
2·0 p.m.	Major-General Sir JOHN KEIR left to take up command of 6th Corps. Major General CONGREVE took up command of the division. General PAGET left to command 6th Corps artillery being succeeded by General HUMPHREYS.	

WAR DIARY
INTELLIGENCE SUMMARY.
(Erase heading not required.)

Army Form C. 2118.

Hour, Date, Place	Summary of Events and Information	Remarks and references to Appendices
28th May.	Officers of 82nd J.B. into trenches of 18th J.B. 38th F.A.B. relieved during night 27th/28th by 18th & 20th F.A.B. from 27th Div & 2 Batteries Colonel PERERO's Bde from 9th Div. 38th F.A.B. into billets at L'HALLOBEAU. Four sections 2nd F.A.B. relieved 4 sections 31st F.A.B. of 29th Div. A.&S. High[rs] relieved Middlesex Regt. 62nd F.Amb. + 2nd Wessex F.Co arrived & took over part of 6th Div front. 18th 7th Aust. + 72. 7.Co withdrawn & marched to billets near BAILLEUL. 18th J.B. relieved in trenches by 82nd J.B. 18th on completion marched to billets in BAILLEUL. Remainder of 2nd F.A.B. relieved rest of 31st F.A.B. L'EPINETTE trenches heavily shelled at 8.30 a.m. considerable damage to parapets and 20 casualties.	
29th May.	Distillery in T[ua] of F[m] DE LA BUTERNE heavily shelled. Cotton partially burnt. Surgeons reported to leave set on fire BLANCHISSERIE in FREELINGHIEN. 81st J.B. Officers into 16th J.B. trenches. 38th F.A.B. relieved & marched on relief, into 5th Corps area.	

WAR DIARY
INTELLIGENCE SUMMARY.
(Erase heading not required.)

Army Form C. 2118.

Hour, Date, Place	Summary of Events and Information	Remarks and references to Appendices
30th May	A quiet day. 18th I.B. with 12th & 7th Co. & 18th & 7th Cav. marched from billets about BATTUE UE to WIPPENHOEK. M/d.tranp.& cyclists marched 12.30 & 12.0 respectively for new area, three of 27th Div. arriving in 6th Div. area. 16th & 2 Arnt. relieved by 81st and marched to neighbourhood of BAILLEUL. before they could move started for billets in 5th Corps area. Div. Arns. 16th marched. Officer 37th F.B. into 16th? 16th F.B. relieved by 81st I.B. Relief completed 11.20 p.m. 16th F.B. marched to billets in BAILLEUL. Officer 18th F.B. into 82nd I.B. trenches. ⅔ 38th F.A.B. arrived 5th Corps area & commenced relief of 146th F.A.B. ½ 1st F.A.B. & 95 Bty of 19th F.A.B. arrived in 6th Div. area. half 2nd F.A.B. marched to 5th Corps area.	
31st May	6th Div. HQ. closed at CROIX DU BAC and opened at CHATEAU DE COUTHOVE on POPERINGHE - PROVEN road at 10.0 a.m. at which hour G.O.C. 27th Div. took over command of front billets held by 6th Div. all tramps remaining in the area. 1st London 7th Co. to billets near BATTUE EVE.	

Army Form C. 2118.

WAR DIARY
INTELLIGENCE SUMMARY.
(Erase heading not required.)

Instructions regarding War Diaries and Intelligence Summaries are contained in F.S. Regs., Part II. and the Staff Manual respectively. Title pages will be prepared in manuscript.

Hour, Date, Place	Summary of Events and Information	Remarks and references to Appendices
9.0 p.m. 6th Division 1st June 1915	Div. Amm Col., Mobile Vety Section, H.Q. & No 1 Section Div. Signal Company moved to new area. Operation orders No 2, 3 issued. Remainder of 2nd F.A.B. relieved & marched to new area. First half went into action in relief of 2nd F.A.B. 18th I.B. relieved 9th & 13th I.B. in trenches, ½ bn in front line, ½ in Second & 2 bns in reserve. Relief completed 12.0 midnight. G.O.C. 6th Div. took over command from this hour. H.S. Croft, Major d. General Staff.	Appendix 1.

APPENDIX I.

Secret   Appendix 1 to War Diary   Copy No.....

6th Division Operation Order No 23

Reference, map sheet 28. 1/40000.   31st May 1915.

1. The 16th Infantry Brigade group will billet and bivouac as follows tomorrow, June 1st:-

   16th Infantry Brigade. Two battalions in huts in H.5.a.b.d.
   Three battalions in A.30. bivouac
   Brigade Headquarters H.5.a

   1st London Field Coy RE — WIPPENHOEK.

   16th Field Ambulance — WIPPENHOEK.

   The brigade will be met by a Staff officer at road junction A.34.d.

2. The 16th Infantry Brigade will take over the line YPRES - VERLORENHOEK road (exclusive) to YPRES - ST JULIEN road (inclusive) from the 11th Infantry Brigade, 4th Division, on the night of June 2nd/3rd. Officers of the battalions (probably 3) who are actually going into the line, will visit the trenches on the nights June 1st/2nd. Buses will be provided to take them to YPRES and they will be at I.I.B.3.Q. at 8pm June 1st.

3. The relief of the 11th Inf Bde 4th Division, by the 16th Inf Bde, will be carried out in direct communication between the brigades concerned.

4. The 16th Infantry Brigade will report when the relief is completed.

5. 6th Divisional HeadQuarters are at CHATEAU COUTHOVE, N.W. of POPERINGHE. A report centre will be opened until further orders, from 10 am to 6.30pm daily at H.5.C.9.8.

                     sd J.S. Shea. Lt Col.
                          General Staff.

Issued at 9 pm.

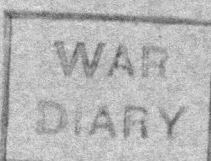

GENERAL STAFF

6th DIVISION

JUNE

1915

Attached:

Appendices I, II & III.

6th Division   121/5991

— Confidential —

—

War Diary.

of

General Staff 6th Division

From :- 1.6.15 To 30.6.15

Vol. X

Army Form C. 2118.

WAR DIARY
INTELLIGENCE SUMMARY.
(Erase heading not required.)

Instructions regarding War Diaries and Intelligence Summaries are contained in F.S. Regs., Part II. and the Staff Manual respectively. Title pages will be prepared in manuscript.

Hour, Date, Place	Summary of Events and Information	Remarks and references to Appendices
1st June	Distribution of 18th I.B. in new line:— Front line. 3 Cos E Yorks on right, 3 Cos Durh. L.I. on left 2nd line 1 Co E Yorks on right, Queens Westminsters, 1 Co Durh. L.I. N. of POTIJZE. In reserve Yorkshires + W Yorks in huts in I 45 (sheet 28) 16th Inf. Bde marched during the morning to WIPPENHOEK. Trenches of Durh. L.I. shelled during day. Officers of 16th I.B. reconnoitred trenches of 11th I.B. during the night. Relief of 3rd F.A.B. by 2nd F.A.B. completed night of 1st/2nd.	
2nd June	Zeppelin dropped bombs on YPRES, night of 1st/2nd.— Distribution of 18th I.B. — Front line as before, 2nd line 1 Co E. Yorks, 3 Cos Q Westminsters, 1 Co Durh. L.I. One Co. Durh Q. Westminsters behind 2nd line. E Yorks trenches + neighbourhood of YPRES shelled. 16th I.B. commenced relief of part of 11th I.B. Relief of 17th I.B. in old line by 80th I.B. completed 11.20 pm. 17th I.B. marched to billets in BAILLEUL	
3rd June. 3.30 am	Relief by 16th I.B. completed. 16th I.B. front extends from VERLOREN HOEK road exclusive to WIELTJE inclusive.	

WAR DIARY
INTELLIGENCE SUMMARY.

(Erase heading not required.)

Army Form C. 2118.

Hour, Date, Place	Summary of Events and Information	Remarks and references to Appendices
4. June. 5.0am	No incidents by day ST JEAN Heavily shelled by heavy guns by night.	
11.30am	17th Inf. Bde, 1/London 7 Co, 117 & 72 Amb. invalided from BAILLEUL. Above units arrived in billets in 6th Bri. area. 16th J.B. trenches shelled all day by little Willie. A party of Germans seen late in the evening to E. of WIELTJE was successfully engaged by machine-guns. During the night the enemy's sap near WIELTJE was successfully bombed and a working party located by a patrol, fired on. During night 4/5th the following reliefs took place:— 16th J.B. 5/L. North Lancs (less 1Co) relieved Somerset L.I. 1 Co. 5/2 ML 9 K.S.L.I less 2 Cos to Canal Bank. 2 Cos K.S.L.I. to huts vacated by Loyal N. Lancs.	
11.0pm	18th J.B. W. Yorks relieved E. Yorks (Distribution W. Yorks, 2 West.-inniskers, Durh. L.I. each 2 Cos in front & 2 in support). Artillery. One section per battery 6th Div guns taken over from 1 Sect. 4th Div. Officers of 17th J.B. reconnoitred 4th Div. trenches.	
5th June. 1.35am	Relief of Somerset L.I. by L. North Lancs completed. Left of 16th J.B. now extends to include WIELTJE farm.	

WAR DIARY
INTELLIGENCE SUMMARY.

(Erase heading not required.)

Army Form C. 2118.

Hour, Date, Place	Summary of Events and Information	Remarks and references to Appendices
2.45 p.m.	A quiet day. 16th I.B. captured a prisoner of 53rd Reserve Regt near WIELTJE. Orders received for transfer of 5th Lingt North Lancs to 157th Bde as soon as possible. During the night 5/6th the 17th I.B. relieved the remainder of the 11th I.B. and the whole of the 10th I.B. This the relief of the 4th Div. Arty was completed. This completes the relief of the 4th Div.	
6th June 2.50 a.m.	Relief of 11th & 10th Inf Bdes by 17th Inf Bde completed. The left of the Divisions front now extends to the cross-roads in C.15.c, east of TURCO Farm. The 17th I.B. had now 2 battns Rifle Bde on right, R. Fus. on left; in 2nd line + at LA BRIQUE & WIELTJE; in reserve on Canal bank N. Staffs. Sherwood Foresters relieved Brad L.I. Distribution from right to left F. Yorks, Q. Westminsters, Sherwood Foresters. During day enemy's artillery was fairly active against our trenches particularly those of the 16th Inf Bde. Artillery Bdes of 50th Div withdrawn during night 6/7th and returned to 5th Corps.	

Army Form C. 2118.

WAR DIARY
INTELLIGENCE SUMMARY.
(Erase heading not required.)

Instructions regarding War Diaries and Intelligence Summaries are contained in F.S. Regs., Part II. and the Staff Manual respectively. Title pages will be prepared in manuscript.

Hour, Date, Place	Summary of Events and Information	Remarks and references to Appendices
7th June.	A good deal of shelling all along line, particularly of 16th I.B. Leicestershires caught a German working party when the fog lifted + engaged them with success. Buffs shelled in Huts in H.S. at 6.30 pm; 1 O/R - 7 O/Rs were killed + some wounded. Div. H.Q. closed at CHATEAU DE COUTHOVE at 10.0 a.m. and opened at VLAMERTINGHE CHATEAU at 2.0 p.m. Whole of Div. H.Q. moved to + billeted or bivouaced in or round latter place.	
8th June.	A normal day. Certain amount of shelling but little damage. Trenches joining up WIELTJE to the salient south of it com- pleted during night of 8th/9th. During the same night fire was opened by 16th I.B. on two small German working-parties located by patrols.	
9th June.	Some shelling during day. An enemy working-party which at- tempted to work in the open by day was stopped by rifle fire. During the night of the 9th/10th the 16th I.B. was withdrawn from the front, its sector being divided between the 18th + 17th I.Bs. Relief completed 11.50 P.M.	

WAR DIARY
INTELLIGENCE SUMMARY.
(Erase heading not required.)

Army Form C. 2118.

Hour, Date, Place	Summary of Events and Information	Remarks and references to Appendices
10th June.	The front is now divided as follows:— Right sector, at present held by 18th I.B., from a point 50 yards N. of the ROULERS Rly to a point at about C 29 a S.W. corner; left sector thence to cross-roads in C 15 c, at present held by 17th I.B. The boundary between the two areas passes through S.W. corner of C 28 d, thence to corner of Arg. log road in I 2 d 6.6, thence along road to southern end of KAAIE (road inclusive to [strikethrough] right sector). The whole of POTIJZE should prove to be in right sector. The distribution of units in the sector is as follows:— Right September W. Yorks, E. Yorks, Sherwood Foresters, Durh. L.I. each with 2 companies in front line + 2 cos in support in second line. 2 Washington in reserve on canal bank. Left Front line N. Staffs, 3 Cos 3/Rifle Bde, R. Fus. 2nd line 2/Leinster Regt. Reserve 1 Co 3/R.B. at LA BRIQUE, 2/Lond Regt on E. bank of canal. 16th I.B. has 1 Bn in huts in H 5 a, remainder in a bout wood in A 30. A quiet day.	

Army Form C. 2118.

WAR DIARY
INTELLIGENCE SUMMARY.
(Erase heading not required.)

Instructions regarding War Diaries and Intelligence Summaries are contained in F.S. Regs., Part II. and the Staff Manual respectively. Title pages will be prepared in manuscript.

Hour, Date, Place	Summary of Events and Information	Remarks and references to Appendices
11th June.	5th Loyal North Lancs marched out in morning to join 50th Div. A quiet day except for some shelling of left battalion.	
12th June.	Only change in dispositions Company 3/R.B. at LA BRIQUE relieved by Co 2/Lond Regt from canal bank. Some shelling right sector. Enemy's artillery less active against left. Huts in H5a shelled intermittently during night 11/12th + again in morning. VLAMERTINGHE and neighbourhood fairly heavily shelled in evening a church set on fire about 9.0 p.m. Church burnt out two houses opposite caught fire but we wereable to prevent the fire from spreading. About 7.0 p.m. right section 17d.9.D. used woolarm – guns effectively against a party of Germans near SHELL-TRAP farm	
13th June.	A quiet day. Nothing of interest.	
14th June.	14th Bde several little Willies at right section. 18th Bde area heavily shelled in evening. 6th Corps Operation order No. 3 received. During night of 14/15th Belgian artillery was withdrawn. Two batteries of 15 pdrs from 50th division arrived took places of Belgian artillery.	Appendix I
8.12 p.m.		

(9 28 6) W 4141—463 100,000 9/14 H W V Forms/C. 2118/10

Army Form C. 2118.

WAR DIARY
INTELLIGENCE SUMMARY
(Erase heading not required.)

Instructions regarding War Diaries and Intelligence Summaries are contained in F. S. Regs., Part II. and the Staff Manual respectively. Title pages will be prepared in manuscript.

Hour, Date, Place	Summary of Events and Information	Remarks and References to Appendices
15th June. 7.0 a.m.	6th Div: Operation Order No 21 issued. Comparatively quiet day. 12th How: Bde arrived went into bivouac in reserve.	Appendix II.
12 midnight	6th Div Adv: H.Q. opened at T.1.Z.3.9.	
16th June.	Between 2.50 a.m. – 3.0 a.m. 2nd F.A. Bde & Section 37th How Bty cooperating with 3rd Div attack carried out a demonstration against enemy front near VERLOREN HOEK. At 3.45 a.m. 2nd F.A. Bde and 2 batteries of 50th Div. demonstrated against HAMPSHIRE FARM and the ridge beyond. 2 Sections 37th How Bty also fired on German trenches at the same time. No active part was taken by any troops of the 6th Div other than artillery. He in Ypres made frequent offers of help to Northern Central Trenches but these were declined. The 37th How Bty & 2nd F.A. Bde twice opened fire effectively on German counter-attacks which were developing. Soon after the attack 37th Bty dispersed about 50 Germans advancing towards RAILWAY WOOD. About noon a party of about 100 was successfully engaged by 37th 4Bty & 2nd Bde. The party was apparently annihilated only one man being seen	

Army Form C. 2118.

WAR DIARY
INTELLIGENCE SUMMARY
(Erase heading not required.)

Instructions regarding War Diaries and Intelligence Summaries are contained in F. S. Regs., Part II. and the Staff Manual respectively. Title pages will be prepared in manuscript.

Hour, Date, Place	Summary of Events and Information	Remarks and References to Appendices
	to go away. At 1.15 enemy observed advancing S. through woods in I.1.C was engaged with effect. A group consisting of 38". Bde R.F.A., 65". How. Bty R.F.A. was formed for the support of the left Zone of the 3rd Div. attack. At 2.50 a.m. this group, known as "B" group commenced by cutting wire + bombarding the enemy's front parapet. The wire cutting was apparently effective + at 4.15 the infantry assaulted successfully. "B" group lifting its fire onto the enemy's communication trenches.	
4.15 a.m.	18th Inf. Bde group of artillery (2nd F.A. Bde 91 sec" 37". How Bty) turned onto trenches just N. of ROULERS Rly. Inf. opened rifle fire on trenches both sides of Rly + grenade fire on Rly barrier. This fire accounted for a good many enemy as they left their trenches.	
4.45 a.m.	B group lifted onto I.12.a.6.4. — I.12.a.4.6.	On operation Sa 1/10,000 map Appendix III
5.43 a.m.	Inf. reported to have taken 3 lines of trenches. Right Battery lifted to I.12 centre. Other batteries watching left flank of attack.	
6.20 a.m.	"B" group formed barrage between Y.12 + Y.9	

WAR DIARY

INTELLIGENCE SUMMARY

(Erase heading not required.)

Army Form C. 2118.

Instructions regarding War Diaries and Intelligence Summaries are contained in F. S. Regs., Part II and the Staff Manual respectively. Title pages will be prepared in manuscript.

Hour, Date, Place	Summary of Events and Information	Remarks and References to Appendices
16th June (cont?)		
6.55 a.m.	Two left batteries of B group left Y9 to Y5 under a slow rate of fire.	
7.0 a.m.	"B" group received report that it was held up by machine gun between Y11 Y8. Howitzer Bty turned onto trench but it g could not be located.	
8.0 a.m.	A group formed barrage between Y12 Y9 to cover infantry consolidating gain. From this time on constant reports were received of enemy collecting on both sides of + in railway cutting. Against these the guns of "B" group of the 18th & of the group did good execution as did also the rifle & m.g. fire of the 19th Inf. Bde. Lt Colonel TOWSEY wire in trenches on both sides of railway with the W.Yorks. supported by Queens Westminsters, the whole under instructions to assist the 9th Bde but noth with an attack against 47 unless 9th Bde was seen to be seriously engaging the attention of its garrison. This trench was not bombarded on the wire cut & the 9th Bde attack does not appear to have turned in its direction. No opportunity therefore arose for any co-operation otherwise than by fire on the part of Lt Col Towse Y's command.	

WAR DIARY
or
INTELLIGENCE SUMMARY
(Erase heading not required.)

Army Form C. 2118.

Instructions regarding War Diaries and Intelligence Summaries are contained in F. S. Regs., Part II. and the Staff Manual respectively. Title pages will be prepared in manuscript.

Hour, Date, Place	Summary of Events and Information	Remarks and References to Appendices
17th June	Quiet day. Durhams unsuccessfully attempts to bombard an outpost of Germans at Collare 250 yds N.E. of Kai left Co. Extra Battalion men sent for support of 3rd Bn was withdrawn. Fine day. N.E. wind	
18th June	Relief of 2 Bns in regt of 18th Bde by 2 Bns 16th Bde completed by midnight 17/18th. Little sniping. A good deal of German aeroplane patrolling. Very quiet day. Weather fine Wind N.E.	
19th June	Relief of 18th Bde completed. Quiet day of much German aeroplane patrolling. Bufs several shells sent over right rite for shells Wind N.E.	

WAR DIARY or INTELLIGENCE SUMMARY

Army Form C. 2118.

Hour, Date, Place	Summary of Events and Information	Remarks and References to Appendices
20th June	During the night gas was let out in front of 165 Bde. Some men had helmets on for 3 hours. Helmets effective. About 5 gas casualties in all. Breeze gentle from North in morning. No indication of reaction of enemy in front of us. German aeroplane brought down in German lines. One of our aeroplanes brought down in ours.	
21st June	Some shelling along the whole of front. Buffs on the right of the line enfiladed by heavy howitzer from right front. Left & centre battalions of right sector report shelling with shells containing chlorogen collosius? No increase received.	
22nd June	New forward trench S. of CRUMP FARM reported completed last night. Capt A.V. JARRETT York Lancs communicating working party wounded on way back & has since died. N° Staffs report one of the m.g. got into a relief or working party at a range of 1600 at dusk last night, with good effect.	

WAR DIARY

INTELLIGENCE SUMMARY

(Erase heading not required.)

Army Form C. 2118.

Instructions regarding War Diaries and Intelligence Summaries are contained in F. S. Regs., Part II. and the Staff Manual respectively. Title pages will be prepared in manuscript.

Hour, Date, Place	Summary of Events and Information	Remarks and References to Appendices
22nd June (cont?)	The right & centre battalions 16th Bde were shelled in the morning by heavy howitzers & had 6 men killed. In the evening the 42nd & 43rd Bde, 14th Division made an attack on enemy's trenches in front of them. The 38th F.A. Bde & 2 guns 87th How Bty R.F.A. cooperated in this attack as follows:—	
7.30 p.m.	Ten minutes bombardment then ten minutes pause, then a further ten minutes bombardment of front trenches. During this phase 24th Bty bombarded German front line Y8 – Y5. 72nd Bty watched Rly. 36th Bty engaged front line trenches N. of Rly. See 87th Bty bombarded Y11 – Y8.	(See 1/1000 map, App III)
8.0 p.m.	Infantry assault. 2nd Bty searched ROULERS Rly. 72nd Bty watched Rly to Y9 & Y10. 36th Continued fire on old target. Hows lifted to Y12 – Y9.	
9.10 p.m.	Attack reported to have been unsuccessful.	
10.0 p.m.	Our right company reports a good deal of shelling of its trenches.	

Army Form C. 2118.

WAR DIARY
INTELLIGENCE SUMMARY
(Erase heading not required.)

Instructions regarding War Diaries and Intelligence Summaries are contained in F. S. Regs., Part II. and the Staff Manual respectively. Title pages will be prepared in manuscript.

Hour, Date, Place	Summary of Events and Information	Remarks and References to Appendices
23rd June.	Right company fired with good effect on a German working party detected at 6.0 a.m. Buffs shelled by heavy howitzers between 10.0 a.m & 11.0 a.m.. 45 shells, 4 casualties.	
24. June.	WIELTJE shelled. Buffs trench again enfiladed by heavy howitzer about 4.30 p.m. Otherwise quiet day.	
25th June.	Very quiet day. Enemy very busy strengthening his defences. 26th French Hour Bty arrived from 4th Div and attached to 16th Inf-Bde. Relief of 17th & 18th Inf Bde by 18th commenced. Brigadier commanding 18th took over command 10.35 p.m.	
26th June.	Relief of 17th by 18th & of 18th Inf Bde completed 1.5 a.m. Sherwood Foresters, Queens Westminsters & W. Yorks in front line, E. Yorks in 2nd line. D.cinl. L.I. on canal bank. 2nd line South of POTIJZE a good deal shelled tonight. Battalion's front line trenches shelled at 5.0 p.m..	

WAR DIARY

INTELLIGENCE SUMMARY

(Erase heading not required.)

Army Form C. 2118.

Hour, Date, Place	Summary of Events and Information	Remarks and References to Appendices
27th June.	Sniping more active during night 26/27th and enemy's guns also fired. Kent trenches in centre of right sector shelled. Quiet day on the left.	
28th June.	During night 27th/28th our trench howitzer battery fired 15 shell at the mound, south of VERLORENHOEK road. A big gap formed disclosed a large iron screen believed to shelter a machine gun. The communication trench to mound mine in front of mound were also damaged by fire of trench howt. The enemy retaliated with 8 heavy shells on our trench opposite the mound. Front trenches in I 5 c & d shelled by heavy howitzers about 1.30 p.m. + Leicestershire second line.	
29th June.	POTIJZE road shelled during morning; and a German machine gun very active opposite WARWICK FARM. Orders received for 26th Trench Hows Bty to be sent to 4th Division.	

Army Form C. 2118.

WAR DIARY
or
INTELLIGENCE SUMMARY

(Erase heading not required.)

Instructions regarding War Diaries and Intelligence Summaries are contained in F. S. Regs., Part II. and the Staff Manual respectively. Title pages will be prepared in manuscript.

Hour, Date, Place	Summary of Events and Information	Remarks and References to Appendices
30. June.	Patrols from 16th Inf Bde to enemy's wire on night 29/30. report no signs of renewal. Wire is being put up. A good deal of hostile shelling during day. Sniping less. A few gas shells fired at 16th Inf Bde without result. Patrols night of 30th/1st report enemy's wire in front of 16th Inf Bde still intact. 6th Division 4 July 1915	J. Young Major General Staff

APPENDICES I, II & III.

SECRET.

Copy No. 4.

VI Corps OPERATION ORDER No. 3.

Appendix I

Reference M.p 1/40,000, Sheet 28.
and special map 1/10,000, ZILLEBEKE Sheet.

1. The Vth Corps intends to attack the BELLEWAARDE FARM ridge on the 16th June with the 3rd Division, their object being to gain the line Y 21 - Y 19 - Y 18 - Y 8 - Y 7, and connect it with our existing trenches.

    The preliminary bombardment will commence at 2.50 am and the infantry assault is timed to commence at 4.15 am.

2. The VI Corps will cooperate as follows:-

    (a). One Brigade R.F.A. and one battery R.F.A. (Howitzer) from 6th Division will be placed under the orders of 3rd Division for the operation.

    The V Corps have allotted ammunition to these batteries as follows

18-pounder.	(High Explosive, 900 rounds.
	(Shrapnel, 2,000 rounds.
4.5" Howitzer.	(High Explosive, ~~2,0~~ 390 rounds.
	(Shrapnel, 390 rounds.

    (b). The 6th Division will move one battalion into the cover trenches, which have been made in rear of their right, on the night of the 15th/16th June. This battalion will seize any opportunity that offers to take the enemy's trench south of the Railway about Y 7. It is not intended that this battalion should attack unless the enemy show signs of retiring or troops of the 3rd Division are seen to be approaching along the trench from the Railway Wood. But on the other hand if any opportunity for assisting the 3rd Division occurs it will be immediately seized.

    (c). The 6th Division will also demonstrate against the German salient South of the farm in C.22.a. and also against VERLORENHOEK. No ammunition beyond the ordinary daily allowance will be allotted for this demonstration.

3. All reports to Corps Headquarters.

    Sd. LOCH. B.G.G.S. VI Corps.

WAR DIARY. Appendix II

Copy No......

6th DIVISION OPERATION ORDER No. 24:-

15th June, 1915.

Reference:-
Special Maps, 1/10,000, SAINT JEAN & ZILLEBEKE Sheets.
1/40,000, Sheet 28.

1. The 3rd Division intends to attack on June 16th, with the object of gaining the line Y.21, Y.19, Y.18, Y.8, Y.7, and of connecting it with the existing trenches.

    This attack will be primarily carried out by the 9th Infantry Brigade (a copy of whose Operation Orders has already been issued to the 18th Infantry Brigade).

    An artillery bombardment of the front to be attacked will last from 2.50 am to 4.15 am, with 3 pauses at 3.10 am, 3.40 am and 4 am.

    The infantry attack will start at 4.15 am.

2. The 6th Division will co-operate with the above attack as follows:-

    (a). <u>18th Infantry Brigade.Group.</u>

    Brigadier General H.S.Ainslie.

    Troops:-   2nd Brigade R.F.A.
    1 Section 37th (How.) Battery.
    12th Field Company R.E.
    18th Infantry Brigade.
    1 battalion 16th Infantry Brigade (This battalion to move to a position in reserve on the Canal, I.1.b.).

    (i). One battalion will be moved into cover trenches (already prepared) on the night of June 15th/16th.

    This battalion will seize any opportunity which offers to take the enemy's trench South of the railway about Y.7.

    It will not attack unless the enemy shows signs of retiring or troops of the 3rd Division are seen to be approaching along the trench from Railway Wood.

    But if any opportunity for assisting the 3rd Division occurs, it will be immediately seized.

(ii).

(ii). By covering fire on the Left of the 9th Infantry Brigade attack.

(iii). By a demonstration <u>by fire only</u> which will be made against the VERLORENHOEK Group of houses in I.5.b.

(b). <u>17th Infantry Brigade Group</u>.

Brigadier General G.M.Harper, C.B. D.S.O.

<u>Troops</u>:- 24th Brigade R.F.A.
2 Sections 37th (How.) Battery.
1 Battery 15-prs (from 5th Corps).
One 18-pr. gun dug in near Garden Villa C.28.c.).

17th Infantry Brigade.

By a demonstration <u>by fire only</u> against the German salient South of HAMPSHIRE FARM, C.22.a.

3. The 38th Brigade R.F.A. and 65th (How.) Battery are placed at the disposal of the G.O.C. 3rd Division for his operations.

4. (a). Advanced Divisional Headquarters will open at 18th Infantry Brigade Headquarters dugout, I.1.b.3.9., at midnight June 15th/16th.

(b). 18th Infantry Brigade Headquarters will be established at Headquarters Dugout near POTIJZE, I.4.c.1.9., from midnight June 15th/16th.

J.S.SHEA. Lieut. Colonel,
General Staff.

Issued at 7 am.

Copies to:-
No. 1 - 6th Corps.
.. 2 - 5th Corps.
.. 3 - 3rd Division.
.. 4 - 4th Division.
.. 5 - 9th Infantry Brigade.
.. 6 - 16th Infantry Brigade.
.. 7 - 17th Infantry Brigade.
.. 8 - 18th Infantry Brigade.
.. 9 - No. 2 Group H.A.R.
.. 10 - G.O.C. R.A.
.. 11 - C.R.E.
.. 12 - Signals.
.. 13 - Office.
.. 14 - Office.

WAR DIARY

GENERAL STAFF

6th DIVISION

JULY

1915

6th Division

— Confidential —

/31/6410

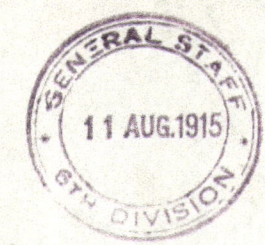

War Diary

of

General Staff 6th Division

From 1.7.15 To 31.7.15

INTELLIGENCE SUMMARY

(Erase heading not required.)

Summaries are contained in F. S. Regs., Part II. and the Staff Manual respectively. Title pages will be prepared in manuscript.

Hour, Date, Place	Summary of Events and Information	Remarks and References to Appendices
1st July.	Enemy shelled second line in right sector with gas shells. Brisk sniping from enemy's salient in C.29.c.9.9 was dealt with by fire of 2½" Bhy on the salient. 111th Bhy got 4 four rounds into a large working party near KULTUR FARM with good effect.	
2nd July.	Very quiet day. Slight shelling. ST JEAN shelled.	
3rd July.	German aeroplanes very active in front of our line, flying low, apparently too low for A.A. guns to deal with. A good deal of shelling particularly of ENGLISH HILLTOP & IRISH FARMS & ZA BRIQUE. Also about 50 small calibre gas-shells into POT & IZE wood. Relief of 16th by 17th Inf. Bde. B.G.C. 17th assumed command 10p.m. Relief completed 11:10 a.m. Distribution: N. Staffs on right with 3 Cos in front 1 in second line; Leinsters in centre 2 & 2; London Regt. 3 Cos in front, one in second; R. Fus. 1 Co attached London Regt. in 2nd line, 3 Cos on Canal Bank; Rifle Bde half in H.11.B. & half in I.7.A.	
4th July.	2 or aeroplane bombs on W Yorks trenches 6.15 a.m. A good many gas shells into right sector. Moderate amount of shelling by heavy guns on left sector.	

INTELLIGENCE SUMMARY

(Erase heading not required.)

Hour, Date, Place	Summary of Events and Information	Remarks and References to Appendices
5th July	About 9.30 a.m. enemy attacked railway barrier on ROULERS Rly. with bombing party, after shelling it heavily. C Company N. Staffs. sent up bombing party at once + retook barricade, whilst their machine-guns prevented Germans from leaving their trenches N. of Rly. The situation was promptly retired. Hostile artillery rather active during day.	
6th July	4th Division on our left carried out a successful operation capturing German trench in C.7. Our 29th F.A.B9c and 87th (How) Bty cooperated carrying out a demonstration between 5.30 a.m. + 6.30 a.m. Targets engaged were trenches from J.11 (I.12.a 4.4) to Y.3 (I.6.c.3.6), Rly barriers at Y.5 (I.6.c.2.0), + Y.6 (I.6.c.6.3) + along ROULERS Rly. A fair amount of shelling by enemy including 17" B2c HQ on canal bank, WIELTJE, + C.T.s near IRISH + HILLTOP FARMS. Canal reported to be falling in. R.E.L.I.	
7th July	An uneventful day on our front. Slight shelling of 17" B2c trenches.	
8th July	Quiet day. Very little shelling. Enemy reported very busy on his defences.	

INTELLIGENCE SUMMARY
(Erase heading not required.)

Hour, Date, Place	Summary of Events and Information	Remarks and References to Appendices
9th July	49th Div. have now relieved 4th Division on our left. One platoon Rifle Bde ordered to occupy POTIJZE. Front line trenches fairly heavily shelled in both sectors, WIETJE especially attended to; somewhat the shells being gas-shells.	
10th July	A good deal of shelling of centre of right sector uy 4 Bn. about 8.55 p.m. enemy rushed centre company of their left sector. A prompt counter-attack drove them out again at once.	
11th July	A quiet day. 18th Inf Bde relieved by 16th Inf Bde. Relief completed 12.35 a.m. 11/12.	
12th July	German bombing patrol anticipated our post at FORWARD COTTAGE but was cleared out by fire of 2nd F.A.B.de at 2.0 a.m. Distribution of 16th Inf Bde Y.TZ. Buffs, R.S.L.I in front, Leicestershires less 1 Co in 2nd line; W.Yorks + 1 Co Leicestershires on Canal bank. Quiet day. A little shelling of left sector.	

INTELLIGENCE SUMMARY

(Erase heading not required.)

Hour, Date, Place	Summary of Events and Information	Remarks and References to Appendices
13th July.	Advanced post at ODER HOUSES I.5.Z 3.10, held by Leinsters rushed by Germans at 10.0 a.m.. 24th & 72nd batteries immediately formed a barrage of fire beyond and to right of ODER HOUSES and LEINSTERS counter-attacked promptly by the two communication trenches. The enemy were turned out without difficulty. Own casualties, chiefly from shell fire, 5 o.r. killed, 2 offs and 20 o.r. wounded. Enemy casualties km fan rifle-fire estimated at 12 to 15, from shell fire unascertained.	
14. July.	Hostile artillery more active than usual during day. Shelling heavy at ODER HOUSES during night 13th/14th. Hostile aircraft very active and a certain amount of shelling of left sector, especially about WIELTJE.	
15th. July.	Some shelling of communication trenches in centre & right sector. About 60 shells on Y.9.d. trenches. One obtained a direct hit on a m.g. which had previously disposed of a German working party.	
16th. July.	A quiet day. Owing to report by German deserter of intended attack on 17th, Reserve Brigade ordered to be ready from 8.0 p.m. to move at an hour's notice.	

INTELLIGENCE SUMMARY.

(Erase heading not required.)

Hour, Date, Place	Summary of Events and Information	Remarks and references to Appendices
17th July.	A quiet day; not much shelling. Enemy busy on his rear lines and communications. POTIJZE garrison increased to two platoons.	
18th July.	Right sector quiet; a good deal of shelling on all parts of left sector. Enemy reported working very hard on rear lines at night.	
19th July.	Enemy still reported to be doing a great deal of work on his defences opposite left sector. An encounter between 16th S.B. patrol & German patrol about FORWARD COTTAGE during night of 18th/19th left us in possession. 18th Inf Bde relieved 17th Inf Bde:- relief completed 2.0 a.m. on 20th.	
20th July.	Distribution of 18th Bde:- In front line E Yorks Westminsters, Durh. L.I.; on canal bank Sherwood Foresters; Hdrs in YPRES and 2nd line W.Yorks. Further fighting between German patrols and our covering party covering work about FORWARD COTTAGE. Our casualties 8. New trench completed and occupied.	
21st July.	A quiet day. Certain amount of shelling. TOBY mortars fired effectively on German barrier on ST JULIEN road.	

INTELLIGENCE SUMMARY.

(Erase heading not required.)

Summaries are contained in F.S. Regs., Part II. and the Staff Manual respectively. Title pages will be prepared in manuscript.

Hour, Date, Place	Summary of Events and Information	Remarks and references to Appendices
22nd July.	Our snipers stopped German working party attempting to work. Any day on trench in front of right of our left sector. Certain amount of shelling especially about WIELTJE, CROSS ROADS & VIEW FARMS shelled.	
23rd July.	Enemy's artillery a little more active against left sector. TOBY mortar again used with effect against enemy's trenches opposite WIELTJE. A quiet day. Intermittent shelling. Our snipers & trench Mor.	
24th July.	A quiet day. Intermittent shelling. Our snipers & trench Mor. tyers did good work. CRUMP FARM set on fire by enemy's artillery.	
25th July.	A quiet day. One of our scout aeroplanes brought down a German machine armed with a machine gun. The German plane was burnt out a fell behind our lines. A patrol of Y.r. shot two Germans who tried to rush them near WIELTJE & recovered the rifle of one of the men. It proved to be marked 233 R.	
26th July.	A quiet day. German sniping less. Our snipers appear to have attained ascendancy over Germans.	

INTELLIGENCE SUMMARY.

(Erase heading not required.)

Summaries are contained in F.S. Regs., part II. and the Staff Manual respectively. Title pages will be prepared in manuscript.

Hour, Date, Place	Summary of Events and Information	Remarks and references to Appendices
27th July	Usual shelling of right sector. Shelling of left sector more than usual. A certain amount of damage to parapet + some casualties. Our trench mortar + M.G. fire from WIELTJE very effective. Germans reported very busy during night 26/27 on trenches opposite left sector. Several of their working parties were dispersed by our artillery + M.G. fire. 16th Bde relieved by 17th in our left sector. Relief completed	
28th July 1.30 a.m.	Distribution of 17th Bde:– 1st East Surrey, Leinsters, Rif. Bde.; R. Fus.; in 2nd line N. Staffs; on canal bank London Regt. A quiet day. Right batt'n of right sector did some effective rifle-grenade shooting.	
29th July	N. Staffs occupied St JEAN defences without relief. Enemy much quieter opposite right sector. Considerable shelling of St JEAN & WIELTJE. Rif. Bde dispersed a carrying party at 5 a.m.	
30th July	14. Division attacked at 3.30 a.m. and driven out of Klein trenches at HOOGE back to the northern edge of ZOUAVE and SANCTUARY WOODS. Our right battalion reports	

INTELLIGENCE SUMMARY.

(Erase heading not required.)

Hour, Date, Place	Summary of Events and Information	Remarks and references to Appendices
3.55 a.m.	at 3.55 a.m. RAILWAY WOOD being heavily shelled & some shells falling in their front. Has appearance of preparation for attack.	
4.27?	Counter-attack took place at 2.45 a.m. but was unsuccessful. Jul. Our 38th FA Bde co-operated by taking over wetting	
Inte.?	B zone between ROULERS Railway and DEAD MAN'S BOTTOM forming a barrage to prevent reinforcements moving down from North.	
4.10 p.m.	16th Inf Bde ordered to hold itself in readiness to move at half an hours notice.	
	All quiet on our front.	
31st July.		
3.0 a.m.	W. Yorks report 2.40 a.m. they are being shelled but no sign of inf. attack. Fighting heard in direction of HOOGE.	
3.20 a.m.	W. Yorks report 3.5 a.m. firing to their right dying down.	
4.18 a.m.	Message from Corps that 14th Div. report everywhere cap= tured N. edge of ZOUAVE wood. 16th Inf Bde to be ordered to move immediately leading battalion to new French works west	

(Erase heading not required.)

Hour, Date, Place	Summary of Events and Information	Remarks and references to Appendices
4:55am.	YPRES, remainder to conc immediately in rear. instr. from Corps:- 14th Div report they have recaptured N edge of ZOUAVE WOOD.	
4:37am.	Ordered 16th Bde to move.	
8:55am.	During the morning the 16th Bde reached its allotted positions with 3 battalions in area HSc and HII a+b. HQ at Chateau H11 central. The corps commander saw G.O.C. 16th Bde personally at 14th Div HQ + arranged that Bde should deliver an attack on morning of 1st August but these	
1:15pm.	instructions were cancelled by wire at 1:15 p.m.	
2:20pm. 2:40pm.	Messages received from 14th Div that enemy were said to be massing. Repeated to Div Arty.	
9:15pm.	Order received from Corps for 16th Bde to stand by at once. two Battalions placed at disposal of 14th Div, two in readiness in Corps reserve.	
9:17pm.	Order to 16th Bde accordingly	
9:20pm.	14th Div reports 8:45 p.m. heavy bombardment of ZOUAVE WOOD & northern edge evacuated but order had been given for its reoccupation.	Appendix I

INTELLIGENCE SUMMARY.

(Erase heading not required.)

Summaries are contained in F.S. Regs., Part II, and the Staff Manual respectively. Title pages will be prepared in manuscript.

Hour, Date, Place	Summary of Events and Information	Remarks and references to Appendices
9.5 pm	By telephone from Corps. Situation at ZOUAVE WOOD critical.	
9.32 pm	Message from corps to 14th Div repeated to us. As it is essential that ZOUAVE wood should be held 14th Div empowered to call on whole of 16th Bde.	
9.35 pm	From 16th Bde. Leicestershires & Y.C. detailed as two battalions at disposal of 14th Div.	
9.45 pm	From 14th Div. Leicestershires ordered to western edge of ZILLEBEKE LAKE in div reserve, understand another battalion 16th Bde being ordered to ramparts.	
2.15 pm	Message from Corps G X 190 received announcing that 6th Division is to be relieved by other troops found by 2nd Army, with a view to undertaking the recapture of HOOGE. During the afternoon G.O.C. & G.S.O.I attended a conference with 5th Corps Commander arranging details.	
7.45 pm	O.O. No 25 regarding relief issued	Appendix I

8th August 1915

V. Crow? Major
General Staff

APPENDIX I.

(Missing)

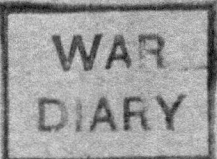

GENERAL STAFF

6th DIVISION

AUGUST

1915

Attached:-

Reports on Hooge
Operations 9th Aug.
Operation Orders in
connection with Hooge.
Div. Operation Orders.
Summary of
      Information.

— Confidential —

War Diary

of

General Staff 6ᵗʰ Division

From 1.8.15   To 31.8.15

G.F.B.

WAR DIARY
or
INTELLIGENCE SUMMARY.

(Erase heading not required.)

Army Form C. 2118.

Hour, Date, Place	Summary of Events and Information	Remarks and references to Appendices
1st Aug.	On the night of the 31st July an order was received from the 6th Corps that the 6th Div. was to be relieved from its line on a future day by a Div. to be provided by the 2nd Army. On being relieved, the 6th Div. was to carry out an attack to regain the HOOGE POSITION. The 14th Div. to strengthen the position they were holding. Orders were issued by 6th Div. for the handing over of their present line to 9th Bde on night of 2/3rd Aug. (18th Bde) and to 7 nth Bde on night of 3/4th Aug. (17th Bde.)	6th Corps HQ. GX190 attached. 6th Div. O.O. No 25 attached.
2nd ⎫ 3rd ⎬ Aug.	Nothing of interest. Relief of 18th Bde quietly carried out.	
4th Aug.	Relief of 17th Bde quietly carried out. Orders were issued for 16th Bde to relieve the 14th Div. from Y wood to BOND STREET and for 18th Bde from BOND STREET to J.13.c.1.6. relieving 14th Div. and a portion of 4 th Div. on night 5/6th Aug.	6th Div. O.O. No 26 attached

WAR DIARY
or
INTELLIGENCE SUMMARY.
(Erase heading not required.)

Army Form C. 2118.

Instructions regarding War Diaries and Intelligence Summaries are contained in F.S. Regs., Part II. and the Staff Manual respectively. Title pages will be prepared in manuscript.

Hour, Date, Place	Summary of Events and Information	Remarks and references to Appendices
5th Aug.	The Artillery of 6th Div supporting front attack by 14th Div from South end of Y wood to Rly. came under C.P.E. 6th Div but supplied 14th Div.	6th Corps O.O. No 9.
6th Aug.	Nothing of interest. Reconnaissance of front line by officers of 16th and 18th Bdes.	
7th Aug.	Relief quietly and successfully completed. Decided afternoon reconnaissance that the actual trenches be carried out on the 9th and not 8th. Bombardment successfully carried out with seeming great effect, night and morning.	
8th Aug.	Bombardment continued night and morning with evident success. One machine gun evidently seen hoisted in the air. Troops all moved up into position. Right 1st S.L.I. Left York & Lancs. 16th Inf. Bde. Support Buffs & 2. Southern Ireland Oxford Street Reserve Leicesters Ramparts of YPRES	

Army Form C. 2118.

WAR DIARY
or
INTELLIGENCE SUMMARY.
(Erase heading not required.)

Instructions regarding War Diaries and Intelligence Summaries are contained in F. S. Regs., Part II. and the Staff Manual respectively. Title pages will be prepared in manuscript.

Hour, Date, Place	Summary of Events and Information	Remarks and references to Appendices

8th Aug.

17th Bde.

HQ & Trench Hon Bty } GOLDFISH CHATEAU
Machine Guns }
ROYAL FUSILIERS   YPRES
RIFLE BRIGADE   VLAMERTINGHE
LONDON REGT   WOOD in A.30.
LEINSTERS   A.30.
N. STAFFORDS   POPERINGHE HUTS

18th Bde.

Front line
D.L.I.   SANCTUARY WOOD
Suffolks
SHERWOODS   SANCTUARY WOOD
E. YORKS   ZOUAVE WOOD
WESTMINSTERS   MAPLE COPSE
WEST YORKS   RAMPARTS

9th Aug.

An intense bombardment of this enemy's line was commenced at 2.45 p.m. after intermittent shelling

WAR DIARY
or
INTELLIGENCE SUMMARY.
(Erase heading not required.)

Army Form C. 2118.

Hour, Date, Place	Summary of Events and Information	Remarks and references to Appendices
9th Aug	During the night the Bombardment lasted until 3.15a.m. in accordance with the artillery programme. Ten minutes before this finish the Infantry got out of their trenches, removed the wire which had been previously prepared, and worked slowly forward towards the enemy's trenches. The artillery fire was very accurate, and only 8 of our men were hit. At 3.15am precisely the men jumped up & dashed into the German trenches which were occupied within two minutes of the start, most of the occupants surrendering or being bayonetted at once. The left attack established itself at once in the enemy deep trenches running from P20 to the Crater and bombers were at once sent up towards P7 & P6 which were blocked. The trench towards H13 was finished on the night of 9th with the help of the 145th. The position lines heavily shelled was consolidated at once. The great difficulty in reversing the parapet was found. We have numbers of German dead buried actually built into the parapets underlying almost everywhere	

WAR DIARY or INTELLIGENCE SUMMARY

Army Form C. 2118.

Hour, Date, Place	Summary of Events and Information	Remarks and references to Appendices
9th Aug	About 400 Germans were lying about, and about 200 in the Crater. Snow is very high state. The right attack did not fare so well. The line G1, G2, G3 is very exposed and suffered heavily by shellfire from the South, which enfilades & took the trench in reverse. Urgent calls for reinforcements from the Dr.1 & Sherwoods caused the Commander of the 1843 Bde to send up more of the E. Yorks covering the line to be too strongly & thickly held. The enemy's fire developing consolidation became heavy. With difficulty the line was gradually thinned in again. At 11.35am the position was a glance:— In the two right Brigades ZOUAVE WOOD 2½ Cos E. YORKS SANCTUARY WOOD 1½ Cos WESTMINSTERS MAPLE COPSE 2 Cos WESTMINSTERS At 4.30pm. the Sherwoods were driven out of G1, G2 & G3 by shellfire, the Durhams still remaining in rather isolated parties in the STAPLES, CRATER (TRENCH)	

G.3.

Hour, Date, Place	Summary of Events and Information	Remarks and references to Appendices
	Losses having been heavy the W. Yorks and R. Fusiliers were ordered up to relieve the Forresters who suffered the Westminsters occupied the line of G1, G2, G3 with parts of the W. Yorks. by evening the whole line of Paris + machine gun in BOND STREET. The battlefield was systematically cleared by the 8th Sherwoods lasting the 139th Bde. the 46th Div. under cover of the Westminsters Posts. The Germans were thoroughly frightened and undertook no counter attacks. On the left except for a little shelling all went well and the position was consolidated. The whole affair was thoroughly successful, due to the cooperation between the arms + the excellent artillery bombardment. Intermittent shelling. Our retaliation has been most successful. Some of the Durham trench mortar posts have come in. Estimates Spoil 11 machine guns and a minenwerfer	See Reg^t Accounts
16th Aug.		

Army Form C. 2118.

WAR DIARY
or
INTELLIGENCE SUMMARY.
(Erase heading not required.)

Instructions regarding War Diaries and Intelligence Summaries are contained in F. S. Regs., Part II. and the Staff Manual respectively. Title pages will be prepared in manuscript.

Hour, Date, Place	Summary of Events and Information	Remarks and references to Appendices
11 Aug.	Enemy active with big guns and Whizbangs. Bufs heavily bombarded by 11 inch and trench mortars. Hostile aeroplanes active. L'inistin relieved Bufs.	
12 Aug.	Bombing duel between L'insters and Boches. German dwarfs canecim.	
13 Aug.	Nothing [?].	
14 Aug.	Boche guns active during the night. Retaliation Excellent. Fusiliers Royal Fusiliers, R.B. Knights, R. Staffords. L'inisters.	
15th Aug.	Attacks of our Bombment. Gen Shute & major drum tooks another visit Division. Casualties heavy in CRATER. Enemy shelling during the early morning but little [?]	

Army Form C. 2118.

WAR DIARY
or
INTELLIGENCE SUMMARY.
(Erase heading not required.)

Instructions regarding War Diaries and Intelligence Summaries are contained in F. S. Regs., Part II. and the Staff Manual respectively. Title pages will be prepared in manuscript.

Hour, Date, Place	Summary of Events and Information	Remarks and references to Appendices
16th Aug.	Good and hot. Bombardment ceased.	
17th Aug.	CRATER, BOND STREET, FLEET STREET Shelled during night. Retaliation good. Station quiet YPRES heavily bombarded with 15" Shells during noon. Afternoon enemy attacks with bombs from P7. Intense bombardment. Emily enough.	
18th Aug.	17th I.B. at HOOGE heavily shelled by 8" Hows. Retaliation good. 16th & 18th Bdes withdrawn in rear.	
19th Aug	16th Bde relieved us 7th Inf. Bde from WIELTJE to the Sap running towards MORTELDJE ESTAMINET. Bde came under temporary orders of G.O. 28. Div (18th)	See G.O. 28.
20 Aug.	Distribution 11th I.B. 7th Right X Lewis Leicesters Centre X Lewis K.S.L.I. Left Buffs.	

WAR DIARY
or
INTELLIGENCE SUMMARY.
(Erase heading not required.)

Army Form C. 2118.

Hour, Date, Place	Summary of Events and Information	Remarks and references to Appendices
17th Bde	R.F. Pipul { 1 Co Leinsters Support RB. Café { 3 Cos Leinsters Ramparts N. Staff left { Londres in H 11 & 12	18 T.B. reserve
21st Aug.	CRATER No 20 heavily shelled. Quiet day.	
22nd Aug.	Hostile Aeroplanes active. 9th patrol shewn German near WIELTJE and Dugouts him in 23.6.4.5. Rest.	
23rd Aug.	18 T.B. relieved 41st B.I. and 115th Territorials in front. Quiet day.	See O.O. Deg. in ord of
24th Aug.	Disposition 18 TB.: Leinsters } Front line M. Yorks } Westminsters 1 Co × 8 1 Co × 5 1 Co POTIJZE	

WAR DIARY
or
INTELLIGENCE SUMMARY.

(Erase heading not required.)

Army Form C. 2118.

Hour, Date, Place	Summary of Events and Information	Remarks and references to Appendices
	1 Co Cadre of H.S. E Yorks (Brielen Road) D.L.I. A.30. 17 F.B. relieved by 7th Bde 2nd Div. Quiet day.	See O.O. No 30.
25th Aug.	Quiet day.	
26th Aug.	Sniping more active. Germans announced by means of a board lit up of BREST LITOVSK.	
27th Aug.	After-shells in A.30. Otherwise quiet.	
28th Aug.	Quiet day.	

Army Form C. 2118.

WAR DIARY
or
INTELLIGENCE SUMMARY.
(Erase heading not required.)

Instructions regarding War Diaries and Intelligence Summaries are contained in F. S. Regs., Part II. and the Staff Manual respectively. Title pages will be prepared in manuscript.

Hour, Date, Place	Summary of Events and Information	Remarks and references to Appendices
29th Aug.	German bombing party near FORWARD COTTAGE dispersed at night. German field guns active. Retaliation good.	
30th Aug.	Distribution 16th B. Buffs with 1 Co Leicesters support 7th with ½ Co " X Line Leicesters less 1½ Cos K.S.L.I. on Canal 18th B: Border } Front line W. Yorks } Northumb. Fus } Close Support 1 Co E. Yorks } 3 Co E. Yorks Canal D.L.I. 1 Co Canal 2 Co B. reserve 1 Co Bourgomastre Fm.	17th B. Coy. Reserve

Army Form C. 2118.

WAR DIARY
or
INTELLIGENCE SUMMARY.

(Erase heading not required.)

Instructions regarding War Diaries and Intelligence Summaries are contained in F. S. Regs., Part II. and the Staff Manual respectively. Title pages will be prepared in manuscript.

Hour, Date, Place	Summary of Events and Information	Remarks and references to Appendices
31st Aug.	Quiet day.	
	E. Inommi de May Lt. 1/9/15	

6th Corps H.Q. G.X.190 mentioned in
diary of 1st August as being attached
is MISSING.

Divisional Operation Orders Nos. 25 & 26
mentioned in diary as being attached are
MISSING.

6th Corps Operation Order No. 9 is
MISSING.

REPORTS ON OPERATIONS AT HOOGE ON 9TH AUGUST.

-:16th INFANTRY BRIGADE:-

REPORT ON THE OPERATIONS AT H O O G E 9th August, 1915.

(1). Preliminary bombardment was all that could be desired. Only 3 or 4 men were hit by our own shells. Germans did not reply on our front line trenches before the advance started, but they almost immediately started on our back line trenches, and on ZOUAVE WOOD. (N.B:- I had purposely cleared all the trenches behind the front line and we had no men in ZOUAVE WOOD). The assembly trenches were not touched and were excellent.

N.B. The assembly trenches for 2nd York & Lancaster Regt were in a hollow and had not been discovered though dug two days before the fight. The assembly trenches for 1st Shropshire L.I. were dug during the night 8th/9th.

(2). Not many Germans in front line. About 50 or 60 were found dead or wounded, and about 15 prisoners were taken.

(3). Very few German Machine Guns were apparently left in front line fit to fire. Two or three were found destroyed, and at least one was destroyed by our own men.

Later, Machine Guns opened from places in BELLEWAARDE WOOD, and from a house at West end of HOOGE - this was knocked out by our Trench Howitzer.

Neither battalions found any difficulty in getting up their Machine Guns. There was a little difficulty in getting the team together on arrival in German lines, and also in finding suitable positions for the guns, but they came into action almost at once. The 2nd York & Lancaster Regt guns got a good target at Germans in the wood.

(4). Germans used bombs in BOND STREET and at ISLAND POST, but not as a means of defence on the main line.

Our own bombs were most effective, and both battalions also picked up and used the German bombs freely.

Our

Our men appear to have used a great many bombs without seeing a good target for them; consequently both battalions ran short at times.

A great many bombs were dropped or fell out of the boxes, which are cumbersome.

It is suggested that bombers should carry nothing but bombs and a slung rifle or a revolver.

The supplying of bombs to the firing line was difficult, and the positions of reserve depots required thinking out. The system of supply of bombs to the firing line required to be more organised.

Very large reserves of bombs are suggested.

Probably what is most required is a better carrying apparatus in order to avoid bombs falling out all over the place; and also more definite superintendence of the throwing of bombs. Undoubtedly large numbers were wasted by being thrown at nothing, and by being used at times when rifle fire would have been more effective.

(5). The Wires between battalions and the Brigade Headquarters were broken at once.

The 2nd York & Lancaster Regt were in touch with all their companies up to 3.15 am. They were in touch with one company again after a quarter of an hour, and kept in communication by telephone with all the front line till 4 pm. Wires got broken, but were mended.

The 1st Shropshire L.I. were unable to keep wire communication, and everything was done by runner.

(6). Both battalions agree as to the efficacy of the shrapnel helmets, which saved several men from nasty wounds.

(7). The 1st Shropshire L.I. report that several Germans pretended to be dead, and then got up and shot our men in the back

after

after they had passed. These men were dealt with.

One man of the 2nd York and Lancaster Regt was set on fire by an explosive bullet. Clips of reversed bullets were found. The morale of German troops was distinctly bad. They were apparently greatly demoralised by the bombardment.

(8). Each battalion employed two companies in front line and two in reserve.

The advance was made in lines of platoons at about 40 yards intervals.

Morale of our men was all that could be desired. They behaved splendidly under very heavy shell fire.

Officers were able to keep good control.

Men got a little out of hand in their desire to get on further, and some who advanced too far were probably killed by our own barrage.

(9). SOME SUGGESTIONS.

(a). A larger supply of water must be stored ready to be sent up at once.

(b). Some special strong dug-outs should be made ready for wounded to crawl back to.

(c). Stretcher parties were very late in arriving. They should be on the spot immediately it is dark.

(d). More Medical Officers are required to each battalion going into action. The 1st Shropshire L.I. had an extra one on this occasion.

It is suggested that one Medical Officer should be up in the firing line, and a second in the Regimental Aid Post.

(e). More runners required - to be posted on relay system. Well buried wires would be a help, but in this case there was no time to do this thoroughly.

(f). Sanitary measures to be taken immediately position is held require to be arranged for.

(10). In conclusion, I submit the following points with regard to which I think valuable experience has been gained:-

(a). The necessity for disposing supporting troops away from the probable areas of enemy shell fire.

As far as this Brigade is concerned, it was recognised beforehand that this area was bounded by the MENIN ROAD - the South edge of ZOUAVE WOOD - OXFORD STREET - and G.H.Q. line back to the MENIN ROAD.

This area was entirely cleared, and the supporting troops disposed in the trench running South from the South arm of OXFORD STREET, in the West end of OXFORD STREET, and in HALFWAY HOUSE, suffered practically no loss.

(b). The absolute necessity for good communication trenches. The existing ones were, in my opinion, badly sited and not nearly deep enough or sufficiently protected. Time did not admit of their improvement, but if it had, the removal of the wounded and the work of the orderlies would have been much facilitated.

(c). Where no natural cover exists for Collecting and Dressing Stations, strong deep dug-outs should be constructed some little way off but connected with recognised communication trenches.

Had time permitted, very good ones could have been constructed in the Railway cutting in I.16.a. combined with a strong barrage of sandbags across the cutting.

(d). Bombing parties should be supplied with bombs by some system of sending them up from reserves at regular intervals to certain points, thus obviating the necessity of sending back for them.

The whole system of bomb carrying equipment requires organisation. The boxes at present in use for certain types of bombs are most unsatisfactory.

(e).

(e). The question of disposal of the dead in a captured trench which it is intended to hold is one which requires careful previous arrangement. Burial parties previously detailed should start work as soon as possible, by day if the situation permits, but in any case as soon as it is dark. Parties should not be too big, each under a selected N.C.O. with an officer to superintend the area. Quicklime should be provided beforehand. Each party should, if possible, be accompanied by a trained R.A.M.C. orderly to minimise the risk of badly wounded men being buried.

                                 Sd. L. NICHOLSON. Br. General,
13th August, 1915.   Commanding 16th Infantry Brigade.

2nd SHERWOOD FORESTERS:-

REPORT ON OPERATIONS AT H O O G E 9th August, 1915.

Orders received:-

(1). To support Durham L.I. in frontal attack, especially providing for protection of their Right flank by occupying and holding G.1, G.2, and G.3 up to and including the MENIN Road.

(2). To open up and improve communication by S.1 and S.2.

2.30 am. Battalion in position as follows:-

2 Companies in G.1 and B.8. Head of leading Company about 50 yards North of saphead.

1 Company in trench originally occupied by Durham L.I. as their front trench.

½ Company in Durham L.I. original Left support trench.

½ Company told off as wiring and carrying parties distributed at 3 dumps at S. ends of G.1, S.1 and S.2, respectively.

2.45 am Our bombardment started.

2.55 am. German retaliation started, shells dropping in and around Durham L.I. original front trench and G.1 and B.8.

3.10 am. Battalion started to advance. The two companies up G.1 and G.2 preceded by strong bombing party apparently met first opposition about 60 yards East of junction of G.2 - S.1, which was quickly overcome by our bombers.

At the same time 2 platoons pushed up S.1 and S.2., S1. being found practically useless as a communication trench, affording no cover, half full of water and dead men and impossible to dig.

German shelling on all these trenches.

3.35 am. Slight lull in German shelling.

3.45 am. Wounded Sergeant of Durham L.I. reported that the front trenches

trenches had been taken and prisoners captured.

4 am. One platoon of my support company pushed up G.1 to join with rear of the two companies on Right flank.

4.10 am. Message from O.C. leading company up G.3 asking for more bombs and bombers. Sent up 12 bombers with bombs from the next company. German shelling continuous on G.2, G.3 and S.2.

4.15 am. Lull in German shelling.

4.20 am. Report from leading company on right that they are in touch with Durham L.I. on their left who are astride of MENIN Road. Sent up 1 Machine Gun and got it into position at junction of G.1 and G.2.

4.30 am. Sent up last platoon of support company to join up my right with 8th Sherwood Foresters in S.8.

4.40 am. Message received from company in G.1 asking for another company to fill up gap between my right and 8th Sherwood Foresters. Sent it on to Brigade Headquarters.

5.0 am. German shelling heavier.

5.30 am. Report from O.C. Company working up S.1 and S.2 that he had supported Durham L.I. by holding G.6 with 2 platoons, but finding men were too thick, was sending some back to work on S.2. Reported that counter-attack was expected on his left, but could see nothing of it.

5.45 am. Received message that communication had been interrupted between my two leading companies about centre of G.2 owing to trench having been blown in for a considerable distance and rifle and machine gun fire sweeping the rear of the trench from direction of Fort 13.

Heavy casualties amongst officers reported in G.2 and G.3.

6.0 am.   Sent my 2nd in command (Captain STREET) up G.2 to report on situation.

6.30 am. O.C. Companies in G.1 and G.2 continually reporting that they are being shelled from direction of YPRES, presumably by our own guns. Asked Headquarters to investigate.

7.15 am. German shelling G.2, G.3 and G.6 very heavily.
Ordered O.C. Company in G.6 to hold line from STRAND on his left to junction of G.3 and G.6 lightly and send all available men into G.3 to connect up the two companies there if possible.

7.55 am. Received report from O.C. my leading company on right that the line was established from the CRATER via the STABLES and joining up with my left. He had sent one subaltern to the CRATER as Durham L.I. were short of officers.

8.40 am. Lull in German bombardment.

9.0 am.   Being unable to get any report from Captain STREET, went up myself to ascertain the situation. Found communication up G.2 and G.3 very difficult owing to heavy and accurate rifle and Machine Gun fire from direction of Fort 15 and Q.5 to G.8. Trenches badly knocked about.
Sent up some more men from the right to cut through communication if possible, and sent another message to O.C. Company in G.6 to send every available man he could spare to G.2 to cut through from that end.

9.45 am. Went down to Brigade Headquarters to report situation personally. Germans shelling G.1 heavily.

10.45 am.	O.C. Company in G.6 reported that communication with G.3 was impossible as trench had been all blown in about the junction of the two trenches. Only about fifty men left in this trench, and none available for G.2.
11.5 am.	Intense German bombardment started, principally on G.1, G.2 and G.3.
11.10 am.	Machine Gun opened fire from direction of Q.5.
11.30 am.	Rough estimates of casualties up to this, 8 officers and 300 Rank and File.
12 noon.	All trenches reported badly blown in, and only held by isolated groups.
12.35 pm.	Bombardment of G.2 and G.1 reported with heavy trench mortar.
1 pm.	Message from G.6 - only 20 men left in that company, which was still being very heavily shelled.
1.30 pm.	Sent messages to O.C. Companies on right to hold on to trenches with as few men as possible to avoid shell casualties
2.0 pm.	The whole of G.2 and G.3 and most of G.6 appeared to have been completely flattened out.
3.0 pm.	Went up G.1 to find out how things were going, and found it impossible to send up further reinforcements to the front by way of G.2. The Durham L.I. having already reported that S.2 was impossible, I decided not to attempt to send any more men forward, but to hold G.1 with as few men as possible.
4.0 pm.	Lower end of G.1 was getting too crowded, so I sent 2 platoons to hold Durham L.I. original front trench with 2 platoons of Queen's Westminster Rifles, and organised G.1 for defence from a point about 50 yards North of saphead, with a Machine Gun

Gun at junction of sap and main trench, which could enfilade front of G.1, thus making certain that no Germans could get into it.

5.0 pm. G.1 heavily bombarded, as well as G.2 and G.3.
German bombardment continued.

5.30 pm. German bombardment slightly slackened, but continued intermittently till 8.10 pm, when a sudden burst was opened all along the line lasting about ten minutes.

No change in situation until the Battalion was relieved by Queen's Westminster Rifles at 9.45 pm, when a patrol was sent up G.2 and G.3 to the CRATER and found no signs of the enemy, but reported the whole of these trenches completely flattened out. 1 officer and about 30 men from these trenches rejoined the battalion after dark - the sole survivors of the original garrison.

R.E. WORK. Lieut. GAMAGE, and his section R.E., were attached to the battalion for the attack.

Two wiring parties of 15 and 25 men, respectively, were organised to work under Lieut. GAMAGE and his sappers in putting out wire entanglements in front of G.1, G.2 and G.3.

Owing to the congestion in the trench in the early stages of the attack, it was found very difficult to get the wiring parties up to the points required, and only a short length of wiring was completed in front of G.1. Lieut. GAMAGE and his sappers subsequently rendered valuable assistance in the trenches, directing the work of clearing out and rebuilding the trenches under very heavy shell fire, until Lieut. GAMAGE was severely wounded.

Sd. C. HOBBS. Major,
11-8-15. Commanding 2nd Sherwood Foresters.

18th INFANTRY BRIGADE

REPORT ON OPERATIONS AT H O O G E 9th August, 1915.

3.55 am.	Durham L.I. reported to be digging in on new position, but not in touch with 16th Infantry Brigade.
4.35 am.	Durham L.I. ask urgently for reinforcements and East Yorks warned to be in readiness to support them.
4.55 am.	Two companies Westminsters moved into SANCTUARY WOOD from MAPLE COPSE.
5.10 am.	One Company East Yorks sent to reinforce Durham L.I.
5.30 am.	One Company Westminsters placed at disposal of Durham L.I., but only to be used in case of great urgency.
5.55 am.	Enemy's fire troublesome from Q.10 and Q.11. Division informed.
6.10 am.	Durham L.I. line established on line CRATER - STABLES, and in touch with 16th Infantry Brigade, but no touch between Durham L.I. Right and Foresters Left where trenches had been entirely blown in.
6. am.	Foresters suffering from fire from Fort 13. Division informed.
7.40 am.	Foresters ask for reinforcements.
8.45 am.	Durham L.I. ask for guns to lift 50 yards. Division informed.
8.55 am.	Durham L.I. using 2 platoons Westminsters for carrying.
10.15 am.	Foresters suffering heavily from guns, mine-throwers, machine guns and rifles.
11.35 am.	Bombardment intensifies on whole front. Previous to this the front line had been gradually thinned by withdrawing men, and at this hour the following were in the hands of the Brigadier:-

2½ companies East Yorks - ZOUAVE WOOD.
1½   ..   Westminsters - SANCTUARY WOOD.
2   ..   Westminsters - MAPLE COPSE.

12.10 pm.   Hostile bombardment very severe.

1.25 pm.   West Yorks warned to move up at dusk.

2.25 pm.   G.3 no longer held by Foresters.

2.30 pm.   Report of hostile counter-attack from direction of Q.10. 6th Division and 2nd F.A.Brigade informed.

3 pm.   Movement of Germans reported near Q.7, Q.10 and Q.9.

3 pm.   Foresters reported to be no longer holding G.2.

4 pm.   East Yorks report their numbers to be considerably reduced.

4.10 pm.   Movement of German Infantry reported along the line Q.9 - Q.10 - Q.12.

4.15 pm.   Division orders that if present line cannot be maintained, the line F.1, S.2 to CRATER must be held.

4.? pm.   Sherwood Foresters compelled to withdraw out of G.3, G.2 and G.1, as far as the edge of the wood.

4.30 pm. and onwards.   There were conversations with the 6th Division, and officers of the West Yorkshire Regt were sent up to reconnoitre G.1, G.2 and G.3 with a view to reconstructing these trenches. Eventually it was decided in consultation with officers of 6th Division Staff who came up to MAPLE COPSE to reconstruct BOND STREET. The remainder of the day was devoted to making arrangements for relieving the Durham L.I., Foresters and East Yorks by the West Yorks, Westminsters and Royal Fusiliers, for holding G.1, G.2 and G.3, and STABLES with patrols from Westminsters; for evacuation of wounded by West Yorks and a battalion of the 139th Infantry Brigade, and for turning BOND STREET into a fire trench and linking it up with the 16th Infantry Brigade.

REPORT ON OPERATIONS NEAR H O O G E ON 9th August, 1915:-

2nd DURHAM LIGHT INFANTRY:-

2.15 am.   The Battalion deployed according to diagram by 2.15 am.

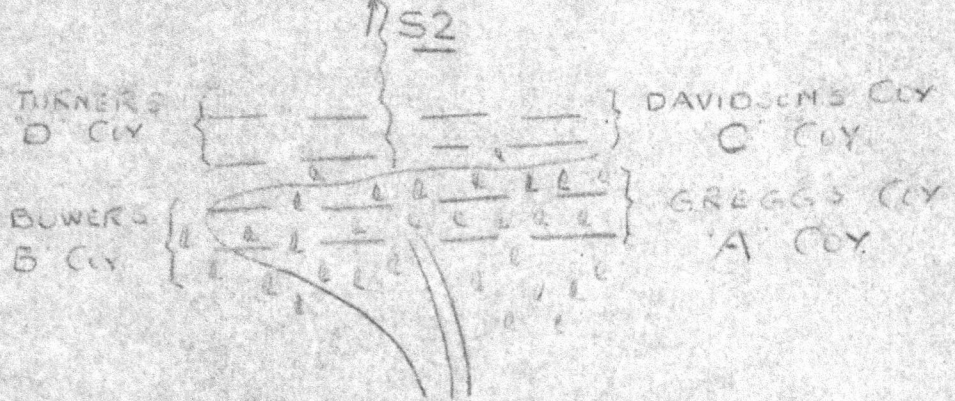

Right of "C" Company resting half way between S.2 and S.1.
Left of "D" Company on THE STRAND.
Right of "D" Company, and left of "C" Company on S.2, which
trench gave the direction for the attack. "D" Company directing.
"A" and "B" Companies followed in the same formation as the
leading Companies, after deploying in the Wood, i.e. 50 yards
distance between platoons, which were deployed to single rank.
No greater distance or interval was possible owing to space
and darkness.

The 2 leading platoons of "C" and "D" Companies carried:-

    120 rounds S.A.A.) per man.
    4 Sandbags.)

Their 2nd line platoons carried:-

    170 rounds S.A.A.)
    6 sandbags.) per man.
    ½ shovel (i.e. 1 shovel)
        to 2 men).)

"A" and "B" Companies carried:-

    220 rounds S.A.A.)
    6 Sandbags.) per man.
    1 Shovel.)

MACHINE GUNS.

3 Machine Guns were sent with the leading line, and 3 with the second line.

Four guns reached their destination. One gun was brought down, but 3 were left up - they were buried more than once

BOMBS.

Bombers of "C" and "D" Companies were to advance with these Companies, and on reaching the line CRATER - STABLES - MENIN ROAD to push forward down communication trenches and block them, whilst the new line was being dug.

3 separate bombing parties under Lieut. STOREY were ordered to advance up the STRAND and to proceed down:-

    BOND STREET,

    G.8,

    G.7,

where they would join hands with the bombing parties of the 16th Infantry Brigade.

A bombing party was sent in advance of the battalion up

    S.2,

    S.1.

The bombers carried out their duties excellently, and displayed activity and initiative.

I suggest that German bombs should be collected and that their manipulation should be explained to all our bombers. There are a number of our bombs lying in S.2 and THE STRAND which could not be got up.

SIGNALLING.

Lines were laid out before 1.30 am to dug-outs at the Southern ends of the STRAND and S.2, down which signallers were sent with the leading attacking platoons in order to lay lines to our objective.

All means of visual communication were arranged for.

The line laid up S.2 succeeded in establishing communication with Captain TURNER.

	At 3.45 am the instrument was broken, taken down to Head Quarters and another taken up.
	After re-establishing communication, the instrument was buried and no further communication was established by telephone.
	Another line was laid up at dusk.
	Orderlies were utilised frequently.
2.45 am.	Artillery Bombardment started.
3.5 am.	Companies advanced as close as possible to the bombarded area.
3.10 am.	Battalion advanced to the attack. The line CRATER - STABLES - MENIN ROAD was reached without much loss. The enemy held the line in some strength, and with Machine Guns at Q.17, FLEET STREET and MENIN ROAD, also at entrance to the CRATER.
	There was a large number of the enemy at the CRATER.
	The 2nd line Companies were ordered to make good G.5 - G.7 whilst the leading Companies dug themselves in on the new line.
	The bombardment appeared to be effective, and the shrapnel curtain well directed.
CARRYING PARTY.	One Company East Yorkshire Regt provided carrying parties. Each party was made to 35 men for carrying bombs, sandbags and S.A.A.. Parties were started at 5 minutes interval to carry to a dump at the top of S.2. First party left at
3.40 am.	3.40 am.
3.55 am.	Captain TURNER reported he was digging in on the line ordered. He was not then in touch with 16th Infantry Brigade and consequently occupied the CRATER.
4.0 am.	Ten prisoners reached Battalion Headquarters from Q.17, and were handed to East Yorkshire Regt.

5.0 am.	About this time several messages were received asking for reinforcements.
5.10 am.	One Company 1st East Yorkshire Regt was ordered by 18th Infantry Brigade to reinforce.
5.35 am.	Two Companies Queen's Westminster Rifles were sent up from 18th Infantry Brigade, but were not utilized. They occupied the trenches from which the battalion started, and remained there throughout the day supplying carrying parties when asked for. Throughout the day it was found exceedingly difficult to send up stores; the upper portion of S.2 was obliterated.
6.0 am.	All officers of 2nd line Companies had been killed or wounded except Lieut SHERIFF - also Captain TURNER.
6.10 am.	Lieut. DAVIDSON ("C" Company) reported "A" and "B" Companies had not been able to make a support trench in rear; also that the trench between the STABLES and MENIN ROAD was practically blown away. At the same time Lieut CARTWRIGHT reported "D" Company in connection with 16th Infantry Brigade.
7.30 am.	On instructions from 18th Infantry Brigade to thin the line to save casualties from shelling, I sent 3 separate messages up to Captain GODSAL, who had gone to the front line. These were not delivered, but Captain GODSAL sent down about 50 men on his own authority. A message sent to Captain GODSAL ordering him to put a working party on S.2 failed to reach him.
12 noon.	A message was received from Captain GODSAL that, at 10.20 am, the front line was a continuous fire trench, in touch on both flanks. That battalions were mixed up - that there was no sign of a counter-attack. The left was on the CRATER

CRATER. The Right at G.4, where it meets the MENIN Road.
The front line was organised in 3 Companies:-

LEFT.	CENTRE.	RIGHT.
Lieut. SHERIFF.	Lieut. SOPWITH.	Lieut. DAVISON.
Lieut. LAYNG.	Lieut. BRIGGS.	Lieut. CARTWRIGHT.

The M.O. reported that 125 men had passed through the battalion dressing station.

2.35 pm. Lieut. BRIGGS reported that the enemy were massing in the woods on our Right front, and that the position seemed rather critical.

2.19 pm. A report was received from O.C. Sherwood Foresters that there was a gap of 200 yards between his Left and my Right - and stating that he would hold G.6, as their former trench no longer existed.

At the same time Lieut. LAYNG reported that the BELLEWAARDE WOOD was full of Germans, and asking for artillery fire and reinforcements.

2.45 pm. I handed over temporarily to Major TYRWHITT, Queen's Westminster Rifles, and proceeded up G.2 to find out the situation, taking all my remaining men with me.

I could see no sign of a counter-attack, and returned to Battalion Headquarters.

From now onwards the situation remained the same until orders were received to withdraw.

Messages to withdraw were sent up in duplicate and also by telephone.

An officer's patrol was sent up THE STRAND and S.2 to communicate with the front line.

Lieut. DAVIDSON came down and reported the ridge clear. Patrols also reported that there were no more of my men on the ridge.

I collected my Battalion (Battalion H.Q. and 132 Other ranks)

and

and marched to YPRES.

Sd. M.D.Goring-Jones, Lt. Colonel,
Commanding 2nd Bn. Durham Light Infy.

-: 1st EAST YORKSHIRE REGIMENT :-

REPORT ON OPERATIONS AT H O O G E   9th August, 1915.

(1). <u>Disposition of Battalion at commencement of operations 2.45 am</u>

    2 companies holding the front edge of ZOUAVE WOOD from BOND STREET to track adjoining SANCTUARY WOOD, I.18.d.5.1.

    ½ company in support trench behind Left front.

    1 platoon in support trench behind Right front.

    1 platoon in Redoubt at Battalion Headquarters.

    4 platoons had been placed at disposal of O.C. Durham L.I. for carrying stores.

    2 machine guns in front line.

    1 machine gun in Left support trench.

    1 machine gun in Redoubt at Battalion Headquarters.

(2). 3 bombing parties were detailed to accompany the assaulting troops; 1 party in support of the grenadiers of the Durham L.I. 2 parties to work up FLEET STREET. These parties assembled at the Southern end of the STRAND, where a Bomb Depot was established. A 4th party was posted at the Depot in reserve and to assist in the supply of bombs up THE STRAND.

(3). 1 platoon from each of the front line companies was detailed to work on THE STRAND as soon as the attack had reached the ridge to open it up as a communication trench.

(4). At 5.10 am a message was received from Brigade Headquarters to send up a company to reinforce the Durham L.I. near the CRATER. The Right front company was ordered to go, and proceeded under Lieut. BRINDLEY, being replaced by a platoon from the Right support company.

(5). Requests for reinforcements kept arriving at the front line, so the O.C. Left front company sent up all spare men, and these were followed by a platoon of the Left support company.

(6). At 6.45 am one Machine Gun was also sent up to the captured position, but soon afterwards messages arrived to say the firing line was too thick, and the STRAND communication trench completely blocked with troops, so orders were sent for all men of the battalion to withdraw from the front and return to their original trenches in ZOUAVE WOOD. This took some time, but by 9.30 am the various platoons had got back. Very good work was done by the bombing parties and the platoons employed in clearing the communication trenches, as the German bombardment was very heavy and increasing in violence as time went on.

(7). The Machine Gun sent up to the CRATER also returned to ZOUAVE WOOD, and was placed in the left support trench on its right flank.

(8). As the day wore on, work of clearing the STRAND trench became impossible owing to the violent bombardment. The trenches of the Left front line also became untenable, so the company there, less the platoon of the extreme left, was ordered to side-slip to the right, which movement was carried out successfully by 3.0 pm.

(9). At 10.30 am the 4 platoons who had been carrying for the Durham L.I., returned to their original positions after having joined in the attack on the CRATER - STABLES ridge.

(10). The shelling in the afternoon increased in intensity, but all the troops held their ground without faltering, and particularly good work was done by the Headquarters and Company messengers, communication being kept up uninterruptedly all day. The Battalion Lineman and Signal/Sergeant were frequently out repairing the telephone lines.

(11). After 6.0 pm the bombardment moderated considerably, but salvoes of heavy shell were fired at intervals till 9.0 pm. Battalion was relieved by West Yorks at 11 pm.

11.8.15.   Sd. J.L.J.Clarke. Lieut. Colonel,
Commanding 1st East Yorkshire Regiment.

Machine Guns.

Headquarters
6th Division.

I attach herewith a report by 2nd Lieut. Wiehe, 2/D.L.I. on the action of our own Machine guns and those of the Germans, in the attack on HOOGE on the 9th.

I asked Lieut. Wiehe to make this report as I thought it might be of interest as I think it is, but there are some other points which he told me personally which he has not brought out in his report.

He was very much struck with the solidity of the German Machine Gun team dug-outs, but apparently they do not keep their guns in them at night — most of their guns therefore suffer in the bombardment. This rather suggests that in positions in the line where one can be heavily bombarded, machine guns or at any rate some of them should be kept under cover by day and night, but in those portions of the line were the enemy are so close that a bombardment is impossible, and one's only fear is a sudden rush, machine guns should be mounted in position ready loaded at night.

I think the principle of very strong dug-outs for Machine Gun teams is of first importance, as from what I understand if the Germans had had their guns under cover in their bomb-proof dug-outs, they might have made it very unpleasant for our men if they had mounted them and come into action when our bombardment lifted.

The floors of these dug-outs must be below the level of the trench to get sufficient covering on top, and will

will have to be provided with a pump and proper arrangements for keeping them from being flooded.

I think a couple of bomb throwers with a small supply of bombs could be usefully attached to each Machine Gun, as a machine gun is very helpless from a bomb attack by the enemy.

The subject of ammunition supply in an attack is a difficult one, and as far as one can see, can only be overcome by having a great number of carriers. There seems to have been no reason why the Lewis Guns should have been worse off than the others, but there supply of magazines is absolutely inadequate for an attack. There should be at least 50 with each gun, which could be carried by 8 or 9 men.

As reported by Staff Captain —

B. Bridgford

17/8/15.
Brigadier Gen'l.
Commanding 18th Infantry Bde.

I think the idea of having bomb throwers with each machine gun is good.

Also very strong dug outs for M.G. detachments might be made.

17-8-15.
B. Bridgford Br Gen
Cmdg 18th Bde

To. The B.M.G.O. 18.I.B. 6. Division.
From. G. I. Wiehe 2Lt. M.G.O. 2. D.L.I.

15 — 8 — 15. Poperinghe.

In the attack on Hooge on August 9th I noticed the following points regarding German machine guns.

During the bombardment of the enemy's trenches by our guns, it seemed that the German machine guns were in no way protected in bomb proof shelters, for when the trenches were captured I saw a gun lying completely in the open, practically unharmed, but not in or near any position. In this case the gunners had been sheltering some distance from the gun, and were all killed. There were no traces of any ammunition lying near the gun.

I saw a broken gun position which had undoubtedly been for a machine gun. It commanded the approach along the bank of the Étang Bellewarde near the Stables. In this position was a recess for ammunition, but this was empty, to the left of the position was a bomb proof shelter. This did not seem to have suffered, except for a severe shaking, as a shell had destroyed the supposed gun emplacement. The shelter was made of very strong supports, upon which were laid iron sheets about ½" thick on these sheets were concrete sandbags, and finally earth to a height of about 3' or 4'. As per diagram.

2.

The shelters were dug down about 2 feet below the bottom of the trench, and the aperture was roughly 2 feet above the bottom of the trench. The parapet and parados was made chiefly of Concrete Sandbags. Chiefly the parados

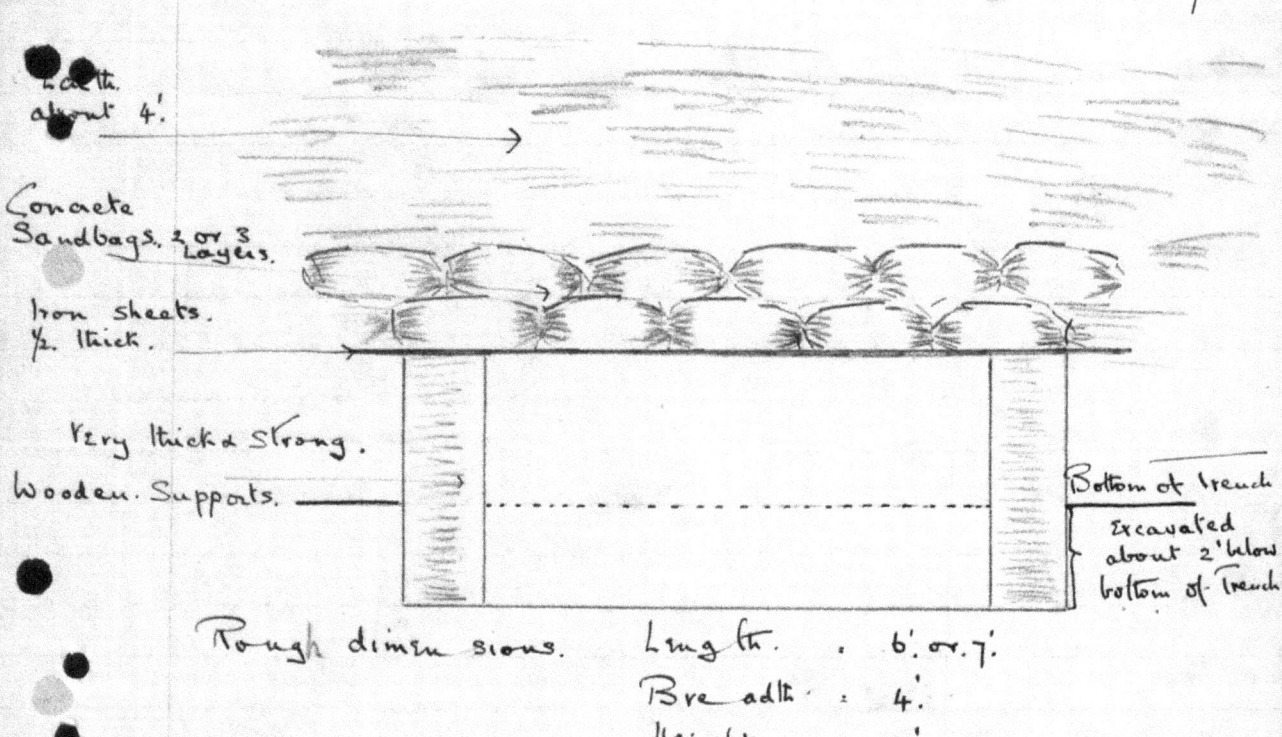

Depth about 4'.

Concrete Sandbags. 2 or 3 Layers.

Iron sheets. ½" thick.

Very thick & Strong. Wooden Supports.

Bottom of Trench Excavated about 2' below bottom of Trench

Rough dimensions. Length . 6'. or 7'.
Breadth : 4'.
Height . = 4'.

There were strong bits of timber supporting the roof. On the 10th this shelter had suffered, but if a few men had been inside, none would have been killed as it did not wholly collapse.
Undoubtedly a well constructed shelter of this description would stop a great deal of hammering with shells of smallish calibre.

In this engagement if the enemy had made a proper counter attack, which would have been delivered by means of bombing parties, our machine guns would have been almost helpless, as the land was a mass of communication trenches. This difficulty I overcame by having a couple of bomb throwers near each gun. It seems as though reserve machine gunners should be trained bomb throwers, for the purpose of protecting the gun. This was one position roughly.

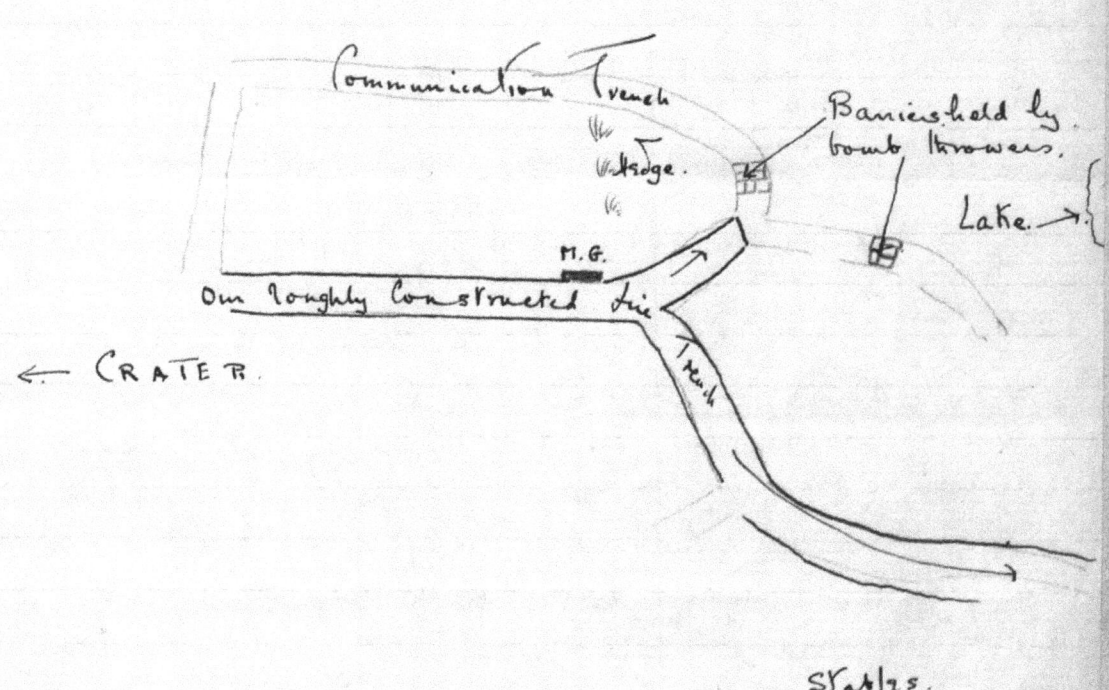

I experienced great difficulty in getting the ammunition to resup, for 4 Maxims I managed to collect about 20 boxes (belts). The 2 Lewis Guns received no ammunition at all. All Ammunition Carriers were hit, except a few who collapsed from sheer fatigue, each man being rather heavily weighted. The Machine Gun teams advanced in this formation:—

Support line 1st line. [M.G. Team.] [Team.] [ ] [Team.]

Front line. 1st line [M.G. Team.] [ ] [Team.] [Team.]
← Platoon →
←————— Company —————→

There were roughly 12 men per gun.

At 8.30 am. 10th Aug. there were 13 men including N.C.O's in the whole section. The majority were hit on the ridge during the assault.

The Guns found practically no targets to fire at. One gun, in front of the stables near the Road, scattered a large group of the enemy in the wood; this gun commanded a path through the wood, marked by red rings on the trees.

G. G. Wicks 2/L.
M.G.O. 2. W.K.I.

6th Div. No.
9/6/22.

6th Corps.

A few points brought out during the late operations at HOOGE may be of interest and are therefore forwarded.

1. I ordered the captured line to be wired as soon as possible. This was done by the R.E. in most gallant manner directly after the position was captured, but with too great a loss in officers and men. I consider it a mistake to wire at all before nightfall. It is costly in men, it marks our position, it advertises the fact that we do not mean a further advance, and it is unnecessary in the present state of German troops, and the efficiency of our Artillery barrage.

2. I gave a definite line to be made good. This appeared to be necessary as a further advance towards the Lake would have led the troops into low ground, and where connection with our former line was long and difficult. At the same time I am convinced that more ground could have been gained. The opportunity for such extension on both flanks could only have been seized by some one in authority on the spot, if the Fort 13, Q.5, Q.3 line, and the BELLEWAARDE position had been previously prepared for assault, the wire cut, and assaulting troops ready. It is of course doubtful whether sufficient Artillery was present to prepare a length of front of such an extent, but it seems clear that at any rate wire should be cut for some distance on both flanks of the actual line to be assaulted, and the Heavy Artillery, less counter-batteries, prepared to turn all their fire on to one, or both flanks as soon as the original objective is seen to be in our possession.

3. The tendency is to have too many men on the captured
position

position, caused (1st) by the need for bringing enough weight to crush any opposition which may be met, and (2nd) by the augmentation of the fighting line by carrying parties. It is essential to thin out the line as quickly as possible directly the position is captured, otherwise every shell tells.

4. It is important to observe the fall of the enemy's shell fire for some days previous to the assault, in order to clear those areas of troops on the day of assault as much as possible. Where this was done little loss was suffered; where it was neglected much was incurred.

5. There was much waste of bombs due to unaimed fire, and to faulty methods of carrying bombs. Better training, and better contrivances will meet the case.

6. A large supply of water should be stored as close as possible to be sent up at once.

7. Some special strong dug-outs near the battle-field for wounded to crawl into would save lives, and these should be close to exits of recognised communication trenches.

8. More Medical Officers should be attached to assaulting battalions.

9. The removal and burial of the dead, and supply of quick lime as early as possible, needs special arrangements.

10. The anti-shrapnel helmets were considered effective, and saved many men from nasty wounds; but they must be made more distinctive than they are at present for their shape and colour, i.e. a slate blue, now lead to their wearers

being

being fired at by our own men. This actually happened on several occasions.

Major General,
Commanding 6th Division.

SECRET.

6th Div. No.
G/6/24.

6th Corps.

With reference to 2nd Army letter No. G.584, dated 19-8-15 (your G.X.270).

(a). Each Infantry Brigade was supported by its own Artillery Brigade.

The positions of the detached officers were as follows:

(i). 1 Subaltern from Right Artillery Brigade with H.Q. 2nd Durham L.I..

(ii). 1 Subaltern from Left Artillery Brigade with H.Q. 2nd York & Lancaster Regt, but in close touch with H.Q. 1st Shropshire L.I.

(iii). 1 Captain from each Artillery Brigade with H.Q. Infantry Brigade.

(iv). 1 Captain per Artillery Brigade at a selected point in rear of firing line acting as General Observing Officer for his Artillery Brigade.

(v). 1 Officer per Battery at the Battery Observation Station.

These officers had no orders as to changing their positions.

The officer attached to Battalion H.Q. had orders not to go in front of Battalion H.Q., unless expressly instructed to do so by the Battalion Commander.

In any case, no wire was run out in front of Battalion H.Q.

As soon as the bombardment starts, it is impossible to observe anything from an Artillery point of view, and Observation Officers as such were no use. Any observation that could be done later was done by (iv) and (v), who

remained

remained in their set positions all day. They could only observe after the attack had taken place.

Officers (i), (ii) and (iii) are purely liaison officers, and did excellent work in letting the Artillery H.Q. know how the Battalions in front line were situated, and in forwarding the requirements of these Battalion Commanders. F.O.O. is, under the circumstances, a misnomer.

Plans of the Divisional and Artillery Communications are attached.

(c). RIGHT ATTACK.

The leading companies of the Durhams were about 230 yards from the German trenches, with Grenadiers 50 yards further forward.

LEFT ATTACK.

Leading platoons were within 30 to 40 yards of enemy's trenches.

(d). Copies of Brigade and Battalion reports are attached.

LEFT ATTACK.

The distance to be crossed varied from 75 to 100 yards. Each Battalion employed 2 companies in front line and 2 companies in support.

When the front line was captured, the Commanding Officers of both battalions went up into the line and thinned it out at once by sending men back to the supporting companies.

This operation, an extremely difficult one under the circumstances, was carried out satisfactorily owing to the good discipline of the men, and the direct personal supervision of the officers. So many men actually got back to the supporting trenches, that the Forward Artillery Officers reported that the captured trenches were being abandoned.

To this and to the depth of the captured trenches may be attributed the small casualties suffered from gun-fire on this flank.

RIGHT ATTACK.

The distance to be crossed varied from 300 to 500 yards, consequently supporting troops had to move forward a considerable distance in the open from their assembly position.

The direct assault was carried out by 2 companies of the Durhams supported by the 2 other companies of the same battalion.

The Sherwood Foresters were ordered to directly support the Durhams, being also responsible for the protection of the Durhams right flank by occupying G.1, G.2 and G.3. The left flank of the Durhams attack was protected by parties of grenadiers.

2 companies of the Sherwoods followed closely in support of the Durhams, occupied G.1, G.2 and G.3, pushed up carrying parties, and moved the remainder of the battalion in close support of the Durhams.

In other words, 2 battalions were employed in the right attack.

About 5 am, on the request of the Durham L.I. for reinforcements, 1 company of the East Yorks was pushed up FLEET STREET in support, towards the CRATER.

On further requests for reinforcements the O.C. East Yorks pushed up more men to the front line, probably about a company.

The rather heavy losses suffered in the right attack may be attributed to the following reasons:-

(1). The very intense bombardment, from all directions, of the captured trenches from the CRATER to the East, and especially of the communication trenches leading from SANCTUARY WOOD.

(ii). This part of the captured position was subjected to machine-gun and rifle fire from the neighbourhood of FORT 13 during the whole day.

(iii). The congestion of the communication trenches, due partly to dead and wounded men, and partly to the necessity which existed for men to move up them, as the whole of the ground from the position to SANCTUARY WOOD was swept by Artillery fire, and rifle fire from the East.

(iv). Too many men were moved up to the front line as reinforcements and carrying parties.

The carrying parties employed were as follows:-

RIGHT ATTACK.

1 company East Yorks.)　　The greater part of this company
　　　　　　　　　　　　　) actually joined with the Durham L.I.
　(for Durham L.I.))　　in the attack on THE STABLES.

½ company Sherwood Foresters for their own battalion.

1 company Queen's Westminsters for Durham L.I.

LEFT ATTACK.

Tools were carried by the two supporting platoons of leading companies. York and Lancasters had 20 men, and Shropshire L.I. had 30 men attached to R.E. to carry R.E. stores. Each Sapper had one man attached to him to assist him. Further stores were sent up by reserve companies.

(e). Each platoon had its own Grenade Squad of 7 men, consisting of:-

　　　1 Bayonet Man.
　　　2 Throwers)
　　　　　　　　　) all equally trained as throwers.
　　　4 Carriers)

The Carriers carried 40 grenades, 10 each man, and both Carriers and Throwers were armed with a leaden headed knobkerrie. Of the smaller kinds of grenades, a Carrier can take a double load of 20, and in future the Squads will carry 80 grenades instead of 40. Practically every man in a platoon is ready and trained to take his place as Bayonet Man in a Platoon Squad. These Platoon Squads are an integral part of the Platoon and work with it.

In the Left Attack, two grenade squads worked up OLD BOND STREET, and the remainder entered the front trenches with their platoons, pushing at once down the communication trenches driving the Germans before them.

In the Right Attack, the grenade squads of the two leading companies were kept for blocking communications after the capture of the position, while the squads of the 2 Reserve Companies were used to work in front of the assaulting battalion and on its left flank.

It was found that one squad was sufficient for each communication trench, supplemented by extra carriers.

The position is shown on a sketch map.

The fresh supply of grenades was in all cases not quick enough. Carriers should be ready to go up at once to a captured position, and a regular supply each hour or half hour after that. If squads have to work up long communication trenches, extra carriers must be attached, and these need not necessarily be trained grenade men.

It is not considered possible to employ larger squads than the Platoon Squad, which have proved very handy.

All Grenadiers should be taught how to use German grenades. Great use was made of German grenades by nearly all our parties.

(f). RIGHT ATTACK.

The Germans commenced to shell our front line trenches on the right almost as soon as our bombardment commenced, also ZOUAVE WOOD which was unoccupied.

At about 6 am, G.1, G.2, G.3 and S.1 and S.2 were

heavily

heavily shelled, losses in the Sherwood Foresters becoming serious.

LEFT ATTACK.

The support trenches occupied by The Buffs were shelled at once, causing little loss.

The assembly trenches of the York & Lancasters and the Shropshire L.I. were undiscovered up to the moment of the assault, and suffered few casualties.

Heavy shelling of the HOOGE position itself commenced about 4.30 am and continued throughout the day.

(g). Little time was available for long reconnaissance for hostile machine-gun positions.

Those which were located about 4.17 were effectually dealt with by our Artillery, as were all other machine guns, most of which were destroyed or buried.

The Germans had not been in occupation of the HOOGE position long enough to make their normal type of emplacements, and this fact added to the difficulty of locating their positions accurately.

Except from the direction of FORT 13 and BELLEWAARDE WOOD, little loss was experienced from machine-gun fire during the attack.

Major General,
Commanding 6th Division.

OPERATION ORDERS IN CONNECTION WITH
OPERATIONS AT HOOGE ON 9TH AUGUST.

SECRET

8th Div.
G.S.175.

:- OBSERVATION PLACES :-

Reference - Sheet 28, N.E., 1/20,000, and attached sketch map.

The following are suggested points for observing the enemy's lines:-

(1). I.17.d.1.7.

From here a good general view of HOOGE trenches may be obtained.

(2). I.12.c.1.1. (S.E. corner of the wood).

This is a point of view on rising ground. From here one can see the ground just East of G.10, and also across to BOND STREET and FLEET STREET.

(3). I.18.c.7.8.

The area enclosed by BOND STREET to its junction with THE STRAND, thence to House E, F.2 and S.E.a., can be seen from here.

(4). J.13.c.1.7.

A good view of the S.E. area of the HOOGE trenches obtained from here.

The positions of Brigade Headquarters are:-
Southern Brigade, 43rd Inf. Bde. at I.19.b.2.0.
Northern Brigade, 42nd Inf. Bde. in RAMPARTS, 200 yards South of MENIN ROAD.

:NOTES FOR CONFERENCE:

Matters to be settled by Brigadiers.

(1). Position of Battle Station.

(2). Position of R.E. store Advanced Depots. Wire piquets. Sandbags. Trench covers. French wire.

(3). Position of Bomb Stores. Tool Depots. Ammunition and Rifle Grenade Depots.

(4). Evacuation trenches for wounded and down traffic. Sentries for the same. Sign boards.

(5). Water. Petrol tins ?

(6). Storing of packs.

(7). Flags. Number to be carried.

(8). Carrying of shovels.

(9). Reconnaissance of position.

(10). Plan of attack.

(11). Means of getting out of trenches. Ladders ?

(12). Communication Trenches. Russian Saps. German barrage. Probably best to pack front trench.

(13). C.O's "postes-de-commandement".

(14). Respirators.

(15). Wire cutters.

(16). What R.E. required.

(17). Iron ration and first field dressing.

(18). What rations to be carried.

(19). Getting up Machine Guns.

(20). Exact arrangements for occupation of captured position.

(21). Lines of runners.

(22). Visual signalling.

(23). Carrying of sandbags by men attacking.

(24). Dressing stations, and evacuation from.

(25). Position of First Line Transport.

(26) Very lights.

(27)

SECRET.   Copy No........

-: 6th DIVISION OPERATION ORDER No. 27 :-

5th August, 1915.

Reference :- ZILLEBEKE map, 1/10,000, and sketch map.

1. The Army Commander has selected the 6th Division to
   retake the ground recently captured by the Germans near
   HOOGE.

2. The Major-General Commanding intends to assault on the
   8th August with the 16th and 18th Infantry Brigades,
   holding the 17th Infantry Brigade in Reserve.

3. The ultimate object of our operations is to
   secure the high ground North of the CRATER and in the
   direction of Q.19, P.7, and to establish ourselves on a
   line through the STABLES and Q.14 towards Q.19.
   The G.O.C. considers that our best chance of success is to
   reduce the men in front line to a minimum, hold important
   points with machine guns, establish communications, and
   relieve men in front line as opportunity offers.

4. With the ultimate object of maintaining ourselves
   North of the CRATER and on the line mentioned in para. 3,
   the attack will be carried out as follows :-

-: R I G H T   A T T A C K :-

Commander :- Br. Genl. H.S.AINSLIE, C.M.G.

18th Infantry Brigade.   ) Will attack from SANCTUARY
) WOOD, with their Right on
26th Trench Howitzer Battery.   ) G.1, G.2, G.3, and their
) Left on THE STRAND.
1st London Field Company R.E.   )

The first objective of this attack is the establishment
of a line continuing G.3 across the MENIN ROAD, North
of the houses, to the CRATER, exclusive.

2.

The Right flank of this attack is to be protected by troops of the 4ath Division, and by the guns, but a counter-attack from the direction of Q.8 must be guarded against by occupying G.2, G.3 and wiring it.

As this attack progresses, troops will be detailed to work down G.7, G.8 and BOND STREET towards OLD BOND STREET, and meet troops of the 16th Infantry Brigade advancing from the West.

:LEFT ATTACK:-

Commander:- Br. Genl. C.L.NICHOLSON.

16th Infantry Brigade. } Will attack from the
38th Trench Howitzer Battery. } direction of G.10 and S.3.a., with their
12th Field Company R.E. } Right on OLD BOND STREET.

The first objective of this attack is the capture of the line CRATER (inclusive) to Q.20 (inclusive), pushing on and consolidating Q.19, P.7.

During the advance, troops will be despatched to work East down BOND STREET, G.8 and G.7 to meet troops of the 18th Infantry Brigade.

RESERVE.   5.   The 17th Infantry Brigade,

see 18th Bde orders   31st Trench Howitzer Battery,

"B" Squadron Northants Yeomanry M.G.Detachment,

will be in Reserve, and will be posted as follows:-

Headquarters 17th Infantry Brigade.)
31st Trench Howitzer Battery.) (about)
Northants Yeomanry M.G.Detachment.) GOLDFISH CHATEAU.

1 Battalion................................YPRES.
1 Battalion................................VLAMERTINGHE.
2 Battalions...............................A.30.
1 Battalion................................POPERINGHE.

5.

ARTILLERY. 6. The Artillery preparation has been continuous for some days.

From 2.45 am to 3.15 am on the morning of the 8th, the Artillery will bombard the enemy's defences.

During the last ten minutes of this bombardment, the Infantry detailed for the assault will deploy under cover of the Artillery fire, and advance as near as possible to the enemy's position and lie down, our own wire being removed during the night. A detailed Artillery programme will be issued.

ASSAULT. 7. At 3.15 am precisely, the guns will lift and the Infantry will assault, and push on as rapidly as possible. The Infantry must advance exactly at the time ordered regardless of what the Artillery are doing. Synchronisation of watches will be arranged for by 8th Division.

DEPOTS. 8. R.E. Depots, Ammunition and Bomb Stores, VERY Light and Rifle Grenade Stores will be established in each Brigade area.

SANDBAGS. 9. Every man will carry two sandbags.

RATIONS. 10. One days preserved rations, and the Iron Ration will be carried.

PACKS. 11. Packs will NOT be carried.

SCREENS. 12. (a). Yellow screens will be used to indicate that our troops have gained a certain position, and cannot advance further without Artillery support.

FLAGS. (b). Blue-and-yellow flags will be waved by selected N.C.O's to indicate that our shells are falling short.

PRISONERS. 13. Prisoners taken will be disposed of as follows:-

16th INFANTRY BRIGADE.

Despatched under small escort to West end of communication trench at I.16.b.2.6., where they will be taken over by Divisional Cyclists and conducted to the SALLYPORT.

18th INFANTRY BRIGADE.

Despatched under small escort to ZILLEBEKE, where they will be taken over by the Northamptonshire Yeomanry and conducted to the SALLYPORT.

The A.P.M. will arrange for further transfer.

MEDICAL. 14. Separate instructions re Medical arrangements will be issued by the A.D.M.S.

MAPS & DOCUMENTS. 15. No maps, diaries, or documents will be carried by anyone taking part in the attack.

REPORTS. 16. Advanced 6th Divisional Headquarters will be established at the RAMPARTS, I.14.b.2.5. at 4 pm on 7th August.

17. Acknowledge.

G. F. Boyd.
Lieut. Colonel,
General Staff, 6th Division.

Issued at 10.30 am.

```
Copy No. 1 to 16th Infantry Brigade.
  ..  .. 2  .. 17th Infantry Brigade.
  ..  .. 3  .. 18th Infantry Brigade.
  ..  .. 4  .. G.O.C. R.A.
  ..  .. 5  .. C.R.E.
  ..  .. 6  .. "Q".
  ..  .. 7  .. Signals.
  ..  .. 8  .. A.D.M.S.
  ..  .. 9  .. 6th Corps.
  ..  .. 10 .. No. 2 Group H.A.R.
  ..  .. 11 .. 14th Division.
  ..  .. 12 .. 46th Division.
  ..  .. 13 .. Office.
  ..  .. 14 .. Office.
```

Note. The operation was carried out on the 9th and the 8th

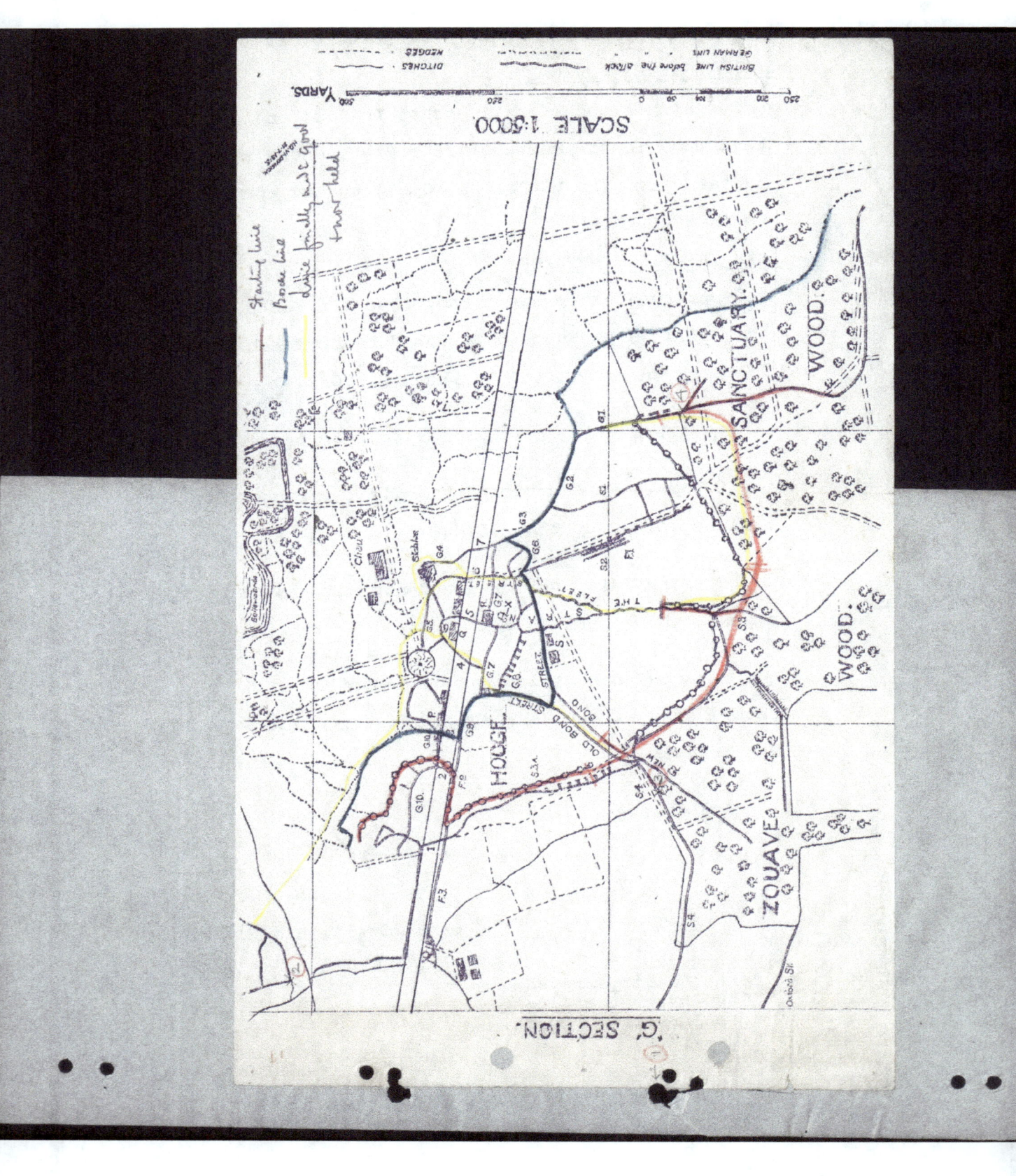

SECRET.   VIth DIVISIONAL ARTILLERY OPERATIONS ORDERS   Copy.....

(on O.O. No.27 of VIth Division)
===

5th August, 1915

Ref. $\frac{1}{10,000}$ ZILLEBEKE Map and Special Map $\frac{1}{5,000}$

1. The VIth Division has been selected to retake the ground recently captured by the Germans near HOOGE.

2. The Major General Commanding intends to assault on the 8th August with the 16th and 18th Infantry Brigades, holding the 17th Infantry Brigade in reserve.

3. The 6th Divnl. Artillery with the assistance of the Army Artillery will support the Infantry.

The Artillery under C.R.A., 6th Division, for this purpose is grouped as follows :-

Group	Commander	Batteries	Brigade
A.Group.	(Major L.C.L.Oldfield)	21st Battery, 42nd Battery, 53rd Battery	2nd Brigade, R.F.A.
		B.Battery 48th Brigade, 14th Divn.	
B.Group.	(Lt.Col.W.Evans)	110th Battery, 111th Battery, 112th Battery	24th Brigade, R.F.A.
		C.Battery 47th Brigade, 14th Divn.	
C.Group.	(Lt.Col.L.M.Phillpotts)	24th Battery, 34th Battery, 72nd Battery	38th Brigade, R.F.A.
D.Group.	(Lt.Col.H.M.Davson)	43rd Battery, 87th Battery	12th Brigade, R.F.A.
E.Group.	(Col. G.C.Dowell)	B.Battery, D.Battery	49th Brigade, 14th Divn.
		No.6 Siege Battery, R.G.A.	

107th Bty.) 23rd Bde. 3rd Division attached 46th Division will
129th Bty.) co-operate and are designated 'F' Group.

4. The ultimate object of our operations is to secure the high ground North of the CRATER, and in the direction of Q.19. P.7., and to establish ourselves on a line through the stables and Q.14 towards Q.19.

5. With this object in view, the attack will be carried out as follows:-

RIGHT ATTACK.

The 18th Infantry Brigade will attack from SANCTUARY WOOD with their right on G.1. G.2. G.3 - and their left on the STRAND.

2.

The first objective of this attack is the establishment of a line continuing G.3 - across the MENIN ROAD, North of the Houses, to the CRATER, exclusive.

The 46th Divisional Artillery is forming a barrage on the flank of this attack from R.2 to the South.

LEFT ATTACK.

The 16th Infantry Brigade will attack from the direction of G.10 and S.3.a. with their right on OLD BOND STREET.

The first objective of this attack is the capture of the line CRATER (inclusive) to Q.20 (inclusive), pushing on and consolidating Q.19. P.7.

From 2.45 a.m. to 3.15 a.m. on the morning of the 8th the Artillery will bombard the enemy's defences.

During the last ten minutes of this bombardment, the Infantry detailed for the assault will deploy under cover of the Artillery fire, and advance as near as possible to the enemy's position and lie down.

7. At 3.15 a.m. precisely, the guns will lift and the Infantry will assault and push on as rapidly as possible.

8. The tasks and timing of the tasks are attached in Appendices 1 to 3.

9. The official time will be wired to an officer of each Group at mid-night 7/8th. This officer will be detailed to attend the telephone a few minutes before that hour: similar arrangements will be made for passing the time from Group Hd.Qrs. to Units.

10. During the advance F.O.Os. will not go forward further than Battalion Hd.Qrs. unless specifically ordered by Battalion Commanders.

11. For the purposes of this operation the Divnl. Artillery is under the orders of C.R.A. - a contact officer of Artillery will be provided at Hd.Qrs. of 18th Infantry Brigade by O.C. A.Group; and one at Hd.Qrs. of 16th Infantry Brigade by O.C. B.Group. These officers will be connected by wire to their Group Hd.Qrs.

3.

12. There is no special allotment of ammunition made for these operations.

O.C. Groups will be guided in the expenditure by the nature and the special circumstances of each task, and all expenditure will be at their discretion.

13. Visual signalling must be arranged in all cases and alternative lines for wires.

14. Yellow screens will be used to indicate that our troops have gained a certain position, and cannot advance further without Artillery support.

Blue and Yellow flags will be waved by selected N.C.Os. to indicate that our shells are falling short.

Advanced 6th Divisional Artillery Headquarters will be established with 6th Divnl.Hd.Qrs. at the Ramparts at I.14.b.2.5. at 4 p.m. on 7th August – All information of any kind is to be immediately forwarded there.

16. Acknowledge.

R.H. Haining
Captain, R.A.
Brigade Major Royal Artillery, 6th Division.

Issued at.....p.m.

Copy No.1 to A.Group.
,, No.2 to B.Group.
,, No.3 to C.Group.
,, No.4 to D.Group.
,, No.5 to E.Group.
,, No.6 to 23rd Brigade (F.Group.)
,, No.7 to M.G.R.A. 2nd Army.
,, No.8 to B.G.R.A. VIth Corps.
,, No.9 to 2nd H.A.R.
,, No.10 to 14th D.A.
,, No.11 to 46th D.A.
,, No.12 to 49th D.A.
,, No.13.14.15. to 6th Divn.

-: 16TH. INFANTRY BRIGADE :-

COMMUNICATIONS.

1. <u>Telephones</u>. Double wires from battle post to O.Cs. Battle Posts Extra reels to be taken on with front line.

2. <u>Orderlies</u>. (a) (i). Battalions to have 6 orderlies at Battalion Headquarters, and 4 with each Company Headquarters.

    One Officer per battalion to be detailed in charge of these orderlies. He is to remain with the C.O. and arrange dispatch of all orderlies both to Companies and Brigade Headquarters.

    (ii) Every message to Brigade Headquarters to be sent in duplicate by different routes in writing if possible.

    Every orderly to be told that he is to put his message on a telephone if he finds one on his way - if there is an officer at the telephone.

    Every message from Battalions is to be numbered and the time of despatch put on it.

    This is very important, otherwise it is impossible for Brigade Headquarters to know if all messages have been received, or the situation at a given time.

    (iii) As soon as possible a communication trench from the most advanced line back to Battalion Headquarters is to be dug for the orderlies to use - A very shallow one is better than nothing.

    (iv) Casualties amongst orderlies must be immediately replaced.

    (b) In addition to the two orderlies per Battalion already detailed for Brigade Headquarters two more per battalion are to report to Brigade Headquarters Battle Post at midnight 7th/8th August.

3. <u>Visual Signalling</u>. Every possible use to be made of Semaphore, Helio, Dietz Discs, lamp and flag, provided that the messages cannot be read by the enemy.

    Battalion Commanders must not expect to get "R.D." or any other acknowledgement from Brigade Headquarters by the same means.
    All their messages will therefore be repeated twice and if possible three times.

5th August, 1915.
                                       sd/H.HEADLAM, Captain,
                           Brigade Major, 16th Infantry Brigade.

Copies to O.C. Units and Signal Section.

Ref. 1/10,000 ZILLEBEKE. 6th DIVISIONAL ARTILLERY OPERATIONS. 8/VIII/15.
Ref. 1/5,000 Special Sheet.

Appendix 1.

BOMBARDMENT.
2.45 a.m. - 3.15 p.m.

UNIT.	TASK.	REMARKS.
'A' Group. (1). 1 Battery.	Engage Wall running from I.18.b.8.4. to I.13.a.5.3. - and trench on South side of wall.	High Explosive to be used to destroy machine gun emplacements, observation posts &c.- and mask the advance - also to damage parapet of trench.
(2). 2 Batteries.	Front and second line hostile trenches from OLD BOND STREET to G.1. - inclusive.	High Explosive (and Shrapnel for second line or communication trenches at discretion)
(3) 1 Battery.	On trench running through R.2 from I.13.c.8.5. to I.13.c.8.5.	High Explosive - to damage machine gun emplacements and to keep the occupants from enfilading our advance.
'B' Group. (1). 3 Batteries.	On trenches along front from P.7. Q.19. Q.18 through Crater to Stables - and communication trenches and trenches in rear in the line Q.19. P.6. Q.14. Q.15.	High Explosive and Shrapnel at discretion.
(2). 1 Battery.	To deal with Q.20 entirely. I.18.a.6.8.	High Explosive.
'C' Group. (1). 2 Batteries.	Barrage selected points in trenches from HOULERS RAILWAY to BELLEWAARDE FARM and P.8 and communication trenches and trenches in rear.	High Explosive and Shrapnel.
(2). 1 Battery.	Barrage along Railway, and any known crossings.	
'D' Group. (1). 3 guns.	On Wall I.18.b.8.4. to I.13.a.5.3. and trench S. of Wall.	Lyddite.
(2). Remainder.	On houses on EERIE ROAD from I.18.b.1.5. to Q.13. - and points in rear Q.18 Q.14. Q.15.	Lyddite.

Appendix 1.cont.

BOMBARDMENT - continued.

UNIT.		TASK.	REMARKS.
'E' Group.	(1) 1 Battery 4.5"	On German line front line trench from OLD BOND STREET to G.3.	Lyddite.
	(2) 1 Battery 4.5"	On Q.18. Q.19. P.6 & P.7 and trenches joining these points.	Lyddite.
	(3) 1 Battery 6" Howr.	On Q.20 - (A.Redoubt). I.18.a.6.8.	
'F' Group.	(1). 1 18-pr. Battery.	On Q.8. Q.11. Q.10. Q.9 and communication trenches.	H.E. or Shrapnel.
	(2). 1 4.5" Howr. Bty.	On German front line trenches from OLD BOND STREET to G.3. Also Q.16 and Q.11.	Lyddite.

Appendix 2.

FIRST LIFT.
3.15 am. - 3.20 a.m.

UNIT.		TASK.	REMARKS.
'A' Group.	(1). 1 Battery.	Remains on wall from I.18.b.8.4. to I.13.a.5.3.	High Explosive.
	(2). 3 Batteries.	Barrage from I.13.c.6.5. through R.2. & Q.5 to Q.8.	Shrapnel.
'B' Group.	(1). 2 Batteries.	Barrage on line P.8. P.7. P.6. Q.14.	Shrapnel.
	(2). 2 Batteries.	On trenches in line Q.18.Crater Q.15.Stables.	H.E. and Shrapnel at discretion.
'C' Group.		No change.	
'D' Group.		No change.	
'E' Group.	(1). 1 Battery. 4.5"	About Q.11. Q.8. Q.5. - and trenches joining these points.	Lyddite.
	(2). 1 Battery. 4.5"	About Q.18. Q.19. P.6. and P.7. and trenches joining these points.	Lyddite.
	(3). 1 Battery 6" Howr.	On B.Redoubt - (area enclosed in triangle between I.13.a.0.4. I.13.c.6.5. I.13.a.6.1.)	
'F' Group.	(1). 18-pr.Bty.	On Q.8. Q.11. Q.10 and communicating trenches.	H.E. or Shrapnel.
	(2). 4.5" Howr. Bty.	On Q.18. Q.15. Q.10 and trenches adjoining.	Lyddite.

Appendix 3.

SECOND LIFT.
3.20 a.m.

UNIT.		TASK.	REMARKS.
'A' Group.		No change.	A steady rate of barrage fire, until orders are received, or reliable information as to the situation (Manning)
'B' Group. (1)	4 Batteries.	Barrage on line P.8. P.5. P.4. P.3. Q.12. Q.9.	
'C' Group.		No change.	
'D' Group.	(3 Guns. (Remainder.	Continue on wall. Barrage along line P.4. P.3. Q.12. and in rear - engaging strong points.	
'E' Group. (1)	1 Battery 4.5"	About points Q.11. Q.8. and Q.5. and trenches joining them.	,,
(2).	1 Battery 4.5"	About points Q.9. Q.10. and in rear engaging strong points.	,,
(3).	1 Battery 6" Siege.	No change.	,,
'F' Group. (1)	18-pr. Bty.	No change.	,,
(2).	4.5" Howr. Bty.	About points Q.4 Q.3. Q.7. Q.2. and in rear.	,,

The times shewn on each Appendix are to be strictly adhered to.

Where "No change" appears in "Task" Column, the task of previous Appendix continues to be performed.

5th August, 1915.

R.H. Manning
Captain, R. A.
Brigade Major Royal Artillery, 6th Division.

SECRET.   Copy No.........

6th DIVISIONAL ARTILLERY OPERATION ORDER
No. 2.
****

6th August 1915.

Reference 1/10,000 ZILLEBEKE map,
    and 1/5,000 Special map.

1.   With reference to para. 3 of VIth Divisional Artillery Operation Order No. 1. dated 5/8/1915, additional artillery as enumerated below will be under the C.R.A., VIth Division, for the purpose of the operations detailed :-

    2 batteries of French 75's m.m guns.

    2 Mountain guns (No.6M.B.,R.G.A.) from 46th Division.   SMB?

    1 18-pr. gun from 46th Division.

2.   The additional artillery will be disposed as follows :-

    1 French Battery will be attached to "A" Group.

    1 French Battery will be attached to "B" Group.

    The single 18-pr gun and 2 Mountain guns will be grouped with "F" Group.

3.   Amended Appendices (1 to 3) of the tasks and timing are attached.

    The appendices attached to VIth Divisional Artillery Operations Order No. 1, of 5th August, are cancelled.

                            sd/R.H.HAINING,   Captain, R.A.
                    Brigade Major, Royal Artillery, 6th Division.

Copy No. 1. to 'A' Group.
  ,, No. 2. to 'B' Group.
  ,, No. 3. to 'C' Group.
  ,, No. 4. to 'D' Group.
  ,, No. 5. to 'E' Group.
  ,, No. 6. to 'F' Group.
  ,, No. 7. to M.G.R.A. 2nd Army.
  ,, No. 8. to B.G.R.A. 6th Corps.
  ,, No. 9. to 2nd H.A.R.
  ,, No.10. to 14th Division.R.A.
  ,, No. 11.to 46th Division.R.A.
  ,, No.12. to 48th Division R.A.
  ,, No.13.)to VIth Division.
      No.14.)
      No.15.)
                                                Issued at 8 a.m.7th.

APPENDIX 1.

Ref. 1/10,000 ZILLEBEKE
& 1/5,000 Special Map.

TH. DIVISIONAL ARTILLERY. OPERATIONS 8/8/15.

BOMBARDMENT.
2.45 a.m. to 3.15 a.m.

UNIT.		TASK.	REMARKS.
"A" Group.	(1). 1 Battery. 18-pr.	Engage Wall running from I.18.b.8.4. to J.13.a.5.3. and trench on South side of Wall.	
	(2). 3 Batteries. 18-prs.	Front and Second line German trenches from G.3. to their Junction with OLD BOND STREET – thence North along G.9. to MENIN ROAD and BARRIER.	
	(3). 1 Battery. 75 m.m.	Barrage on B. redoubt from J.13.a.4.0. to J.13.c.5.5.	
"B" Group.	(1). 1 Battery. 18-pr.	On work Q.20 (I.18.a.6.8.)	Bombardment from 2.45 a.m. to 3.15 a.m.
	(2). 3 Batteries. 18-prs.	Along P.7. Q.19. to CRATER thence to Q.15 and to South side of MENIN ROAD.	
	(3). 1 Battery. 75 m.m.	Barrage along P.8. to P.5.	
"C" Group.	(1). 2 Batteries. 18-prs.	Barrage along trenches from ROULERS RAILWAY to BELLEWARDE FARM and P.8. Also communication trenches and trenches in rear.	
	(2). 1 Battery. 18,pr.	Barrage along Railway and Crossings.	
"D" Group.	(1). 3 (4.5") Hows.	On Wall I.18.b.8.4. to J.13.a.5.3. and trench S. of Wall.	
	(2). 5 (4.5") Hows.	G.9. to Q.18. and work at Q.20. (A. Redoubt).	
	(3). 5 (R.5") Hows.	G.5. to Q.15. and Q.13. and trenches adjoining.	

APPENDIX 1. (continued).

2.

UNIT.		TASK.	REMARKS.
'E' Group.	(1). 1 Battery. (4.5" Hows)	From Junction of OLD BOND STREET and German Front line trench northwards to G.9. and Barrier on MENIN ROAD.	
	(2). 1 Battery. (4.5" Hows).	From G.10.a. and along houses on MENIN ROAD to CRAteR and Q.18.	
	(3). 6 (6") Howrs.	On A. Redoubt (Q.20) I.18.a.6.8.	Bombardment from 2.45 a.m. to 3.15 a.m.
'F' Group.	(1). 1 Battery. 18-pr.	From Q.8. to Q.11 and Q.10.	
	(2). 1 Battery. (4.5" Hows).	Front line German trenches from G.3. to their junction with OLD BOND STREET and Q.16.	
	(3). 1 Gun (18.pr.)	On Wall I.18.b.8.4. to J.13.a.5.3.	
	(4). 2 Mountain Guns.	On houses N. of MENIN ROAD in J.13.a.7.4. and Eastwards.	

APPENDIX 2.

3.

FIRST LIFT.

3.15 a.m. to 3.20 a.m.

UNIT.	TASK.	REMARKS.
'A' Group. (1). 1 Battery. 18-pr.	No change.	
(2). 5 Batteries. 18-prs.	Barrage from Q.5. through Q.8. to Q.11 and to North of MENIN ROAD.	
(3). 1 Battery. 75 m.m.	No change.	
'B' Group. (1). 1 Battery. 18-pr.	⎫ Barrage along P.8, P.7, P.6. to Q.14.	
(2). 5 Batteries. 18-prs.	⎬	
(3). 1 Battery. 75 m.m.	⎭ No change.	
'C' Group. (1). 2 Batteries. 18-pr.	⎫ No change.	
(2). 1 Battery. 18-pr.	⎭	
'D' Group. (1). 5 (4.5") Hows.	No change.	
(2). 5 (4.5") Hows.	P.7. to P.6. and Q.14.	
(3). 4 (4.5") Hows.	Q.14 to Stables.	
'E' Group. (1). 1 Battery. 4.5" Hows.	From Q.5. through Q.8. to Q.11 - and N. of MENIN ROAD.	

This lift only lasts five minutes. Where "No change" is shewn the original targets in Appendix 1 continue to be engaged.

APPENDIX 2. (continued).

4.

UNIT.		TASK.	REMARKS.
'E' Group. (continued).	(2). 1 Battery 4.5" hows.	P.6. to Q.14.	
	(3). 4 (6") Hows.	B. Redoubt from J.13.a.4.0. to J.13.c.6.5.	
	(4). 2 (6") Hows.	P.3. to P.4.	
'F' Group.	(1). 1 Battery 18-pr.	Q.8. and Q.9. to Q.10.	
	(2). 1 Battery 4.5" Hows.	Q.13. though Stables to G.5.	
	(3). 1 Gun 18-pr.	No change.	
	(4). 2 Mountain Guns.	No change.	

APPENDIX 3.

5.

SECOND LIFT:
3.20 am

UNIT.		TASK.	REMARKS.
'A' Group.	(1). 1 Battery. 18-pr.	No change.	
	(2). 3 Batteries. 18-pr.	No change.	
	(3). 1 Battery. 75 m.m.	No change.	
'B' Group.	(1). 1 Battery. 18-pr.	⎫ Barrage along P.5, P.4, P.3. to Q.9.	A Steady rate of Barrage fire until orders are received or reliable[?] information obtained.
	(2). 3 Batteries. 18-prs.	⎬	
	(3). 1 Battery. 75 m.m.	⎭	
'C' Group.	(1). 2 Batteries. 18-prs.	⎫ No change.	
	(2). 1 Battery. 18-pr.	⎭	
'D' Group.	(1). 3 (4.5" Hows).	No change.	
	(2). 5 (4.5" Hows).	From P.4. to P.3.	
	(3). 4 (4.5" Hows).	From P.1. to Bridge over moat in I.12.d.7.8.	
'S' Group.	(1). 1 Battery. 4.5" Hows.	No change.	

APPENDIX 3 (continued).

6.

UNIT.		TASK.	REMARKS.
'E' Group. (continued).	(2). A1 Battery. 4.5" Hows.	Q.12. to Q.9.	
	(3). 4 (6" Hows).	No change.	
	(3a). 2 (6" Hows).		
'F' Group.	(1). 1 Battery. 18-pr.	No change.	
	(2). 1 Battery. 4.5" Hows.	From North of MENIN ROAD to Q.10 and Q.9.	
	(3). 1 Gun 18-pr.	No change.	
	(4). 2 Mountain Guns.		

The times shown in each appendix are to be strictly adhered to.

Where "No change" appears in "Task" column, the task of previous Appendix continued to be performed.

sd/R.H.HAINING. Captain, R.A.
Brigade Major, Royal Artillery, 6th Division.

6th August, 1915.

FIRST PHASE.

S E C R E T.

No. 2 Group Heavy Artillery Reserve.

Amended time table in connection with Operations of 6th Division

9th August, 1915.

Reference ZILLEBEKE Trench Map Scale 1/10,000.

TIME.	BATTERY.	OBJECTIVES.	REMARKS.
	5th Brigade.		
	12th Siege (9.2" Howitzer) (3).	(a) Support trenches S. of MENIN ROAD. (b) Houses & Trenches on N. of MENIN ROAD.	Will fire at (a) till 3.5 a.m. when fire will be lifted to (b) until 3.15 a.m.
	35th Siege (8" Howitzers) (2).	Old German Front Line Trench opposite CRATER.	
2.45 a.m. to 3.15 a.m.	7th Siege (6" Guns) (3).	1 Gun CHATEAU WOOD 1 Gun Woods in J.20.b. 1 Gun Searching down MENIN road.	Remaining Gun available for counter-battery work.
	9th Brigade.		
	108th Battery (60 pounders) (4).	2 Guns HOOGE WALL. 2 Guns Trenches at Q.4.	Remaining Guns of Brigade, four 4.7" standing by for counter battery work.
	71st Battery (4.7" Guns) (4).	Trench Q.5 - Q.8 - Q.11.	
	13th Brigade.		
	31st Battery (60 pounders) (2).	Trenches round BELLEWARDE FARM.	Remainder of Brigade: two 60 pounders and eight 4.7" guns available to support 49th Division if required, and for any necessary counter-battery work in Northern Sector.

FIRST PHASE.

FIRST PHASE (continued).

TIME.	BATTERY.	OBJECTIVES.	REMARKS.
		11th Brigade.	
2.45 a.m. to 3.15 a.m.	24th Battery (60 pounders) (2).	Trench at Q.5.	Remaining Guns of Brigade, two 60 pdrs standing by for counter-battery work.
	122nd Battery (4.7" guns) (4).	Trench Q.11 - Q.10.	
	123rd Battery (4.7" Guns) (4).	Sweeping with Shrapnel Trenches S. of MENIN ROAD from first "O" of HOOGE to Q.11.	

NOTE - Two 8" Howitzers of 20th Siege Battery and one 15" Howitzer of R.M.A.Brigade will be available for use in support of 49th Division if required.

\#oOo\#

No. 2 Group Heavy Artillery Reserve.

SECOND PHASE (1st Lift.)

TIME.	BATTERY.	OBJECTIVES.	REMARKS.
		5th Brigade.	
	12th Siege.	2 Howitzers on Trench running East from Q.14, 1 Howitzer on HOOGE WALL (Q.11 - Q.8.)	
	25th Siege.	P.8. - P.5.	
3.10 a.m.	7th Siege.	1 Gun NONNE BOSCHEN WOODS. 1 GUN WESTHOEK. 1 Gun down MENIN ROAD from CLAPHAM JUNCTION TO GHELUVELT.	
to		**9th Brigade.**	
	108th Battery.	As in First Phase.	
	71st Battery.	Trench Q.10 - Q.7.	
3.20 a.m.		**13th Brigade.**	
	31st Battery.	As in First Phase.	
		11th Brigade.	
	24th Battery.	As in First Phase.	
	122nd Battery.	Trench Q.7 - Q.9.	
	123rd Battery.	Trench Q.12 - Q.9.	

No. 2 Group Heavy Reserve Artillery.

THIRD PHASE (2nd Lift).

TIME.	BATTERY.	OBJECTIVES.	REMARKS.
	5th Brigade.		
	12th Siege.)		
	25th Siege.)	As in Second Phase.	
3.00	7th Siege.)		
a.m.	**9th Brigade.**		
to	All batteries as in Second Phase.		
3.25	**13th Brigade.**		
a.m.	As Before.		
	11th Brigade.		
	24th Battery.	Trench Q.4 – Q.3.	
	122nd Battery.	Trench Q.3 – Q.6.	
	123rd Battery.	Trench Q.6 – P.1.	

No. 2 Group Heavy Artillery Reserve.

FOURTH PHASE (3rd Lift).

TIME.	BATTERY.	OBJECTIVES.	REMARKS.

5th Brigade.

	12th Siege.	One Howitzer blocking Communication Trench at P.7. and working up North as Infantry make ground. * One Howitzer blocking P.3. and Trench running N. One Howitzer along HOOGE WALL (Eastern Half).	* NOTE. As soon as our Infantry have taken the Redoubt the fire of this Howr must be shifted Northward to Trench junction I.12.c.8.3. (just above house shown on map).as we intend pushing on and occupying P.7. (Vide 6th Division Orders).
3.25 am to uch time s our nfantry ave stabli_hed hemselves.	25th Siege.	As Before.	
	7th Siege.	As Before.	

9th Brigade.

	108th Battery.	As Before.	
	71st Battery.	Trench Q.3 - Q.2.	) It is probable that) soon after 3.25 a.m.) these batteries will) be required for counter) battery work.) The time at which they) will have to be taken) off the trenches depends) of course on the action) of the German Artillery.

13th Brigade.

As Before.

11th Brigade.

24th Battery.	As in Third Phase.	
122nd Battery.	As in Third Phase.	
123rd Battery.	As in Third Phase.	

NOTE:- The further action of the Guns depends on the situation which may arise, and cannot be legislated for in detail beforehand.

Copy No. ----------

OPERATION ORDER No. 3.

by

Lt.Colonel, F.W.TOWSEY, Commanding 18th Infantry Brigade.

6th August 1915.

Reference ZILLEBEKE Map 1/10,000, and Sketch Map.

1. The Army Commander has selected the 6th Division to retake the ground recently captured by the Germans near HOOGE.

2. The 16th and 18th Infantry Brigade will attack on the 8th August. The 17th Infantry Brigade will be in reserve.

3. The ultimate object of our operations is to secure the high ground north of the CRATER and in the direction of Q.19. P.7. and to establish ourselves on a line through the STABLES and Q.14 towards Q.19.

The G.O.C. considers that our best chance of success is to reduce the men in the front line to a minimum, hold important points with Machine Guns, establish communications, and relieve men in the front line as opportunity offers.

4. With the ultimate object of maintaining ourselves North of the CRATER and on the line mentioned in para 3., the attack will be carried out as follows :-

RIGHT ATTACK.

Commander:- Lt.Colonel F.W.Towsey.

18th Infantry Brigade.)	Will attack from SANCTUARY WOOD,
81st Trench Howitzer Battery.)	with their Right on G.1. G.2. G.3.
1st London Field Co. R.E.)	and their left on the S BAND.

The first objective of this attack is the establishment of a line continuing G.3. across the MENIN ROAD, North of the houses, to the CRATER, exclusive.

The right flank of this attack is to be protected by troops of the 46th Division, and by the guns, but a counterattack from the direction of G.8. must be guarded against by occupying G.2. G.3. and wiring it.

LEFT ATTACK.

Commander :- Brigadier General C.L.Nicholson.

16th Infantry Brigade.) Will attack from the direction
38th Trench Howitzer Battery.) of Q.10 and S.5.a., with their
12th Field Company R.E.) Right on OLD BOND STREET.

The first objective of this attack is the capture of the line
CRATER (inclusive) to Q.20 (inclusive), pushing on and consolidating
Q.19. P.7.

During the advance troops will be despatched to work East down
BOND STREET, G.8. and G.7. to meet troops of the 16th Infantry Bde.

----

5. Distribution of the Brigade.

The D.L.I. will assemble in the northern portion of SANCTUARY
WOOD with right resting on G.1. and left on their junction with
East Yorks.

The Sherwood Foresters will assemble in SANCTUARY WOOD
immediately in rear of the D.L.I.

The East Yorks will continue to hold ZOUAVE WOOD.

The Q.W.Rifles will be in reserve in MAPLE COPSE.

The West Yorks will be in the ramparts in YPRES.

Units will be in these positions by 2.30 a.m. on the 8th and
will report to Brigade Headquarters when moves are complete.

6. Plan of Attack. The D.L.I. will lead the assault. The Sherwood
Foresters will support the D.L.I. The East Yorks will continue to
hold ZOUAVE WOOD. The Q.W.Rifles will be held in reserve.

7. The Assault. The D.L.I. will advance on the front contained
between G.1., G.2., G.3., on the East, and the STRAND on the West,
and will have for an objective the establishment of a line continuing
G.3., across the MENIN ROAD, North of the Houses, to the CRATER exclusive.

As this attack progresses the D.L.I. will detail men to work
down G.7., G.8., and BOND STREET towards OLD BOND STREET and meet
troops of the 16th Infantry Brigade advancing from the West.

The Sherwood Foresters will closely support the D.L.I. and will
specially provide for the protection of their right front by occupying G.1. and advancing men up G.1. G.2. & G.3. simultaneously with
the advance of the D.L.I.

The Sherwood Foresters will detail men to turn G.1., G.2. G.3., as far as its junction with the MENIN ROAD into a fire trench and will hold it. The Sherwood Foresters will also be responsible for opening up and improving S.1. and S.2. for purposes of communication as the attack progresses.

The East Yorks are responsible for opening up and improving the STRAND and FLEET STREET as far as its junction with S. as means of communication.

8. **Co-operation of Artillery and time of Assault.**

From 2.45 a.m to 3.15 a.m. on the 8th, the Artillery will bombard the enemy's defences.

During the last ten minutes of this bombardment (i.e. beginning at 3.5 a.m.) the infantry detailed for the assault will deploy under cover of the artillery fire and advance as near as possible to the enemy's position and lie down.

At 3.15 a.m. precisely, the guns will lift and the infantry will assault and push on as rapidly as possible. The Infantry will advance exactly at the time ordered, regardless of what the artillery are doing. The setting of watches will be arranged for by the Bde.

9. **Sandbags.** Every man will carry 2 sandbags at least.

10. **Depôts.** A depot for all R.E.Stores, Brigade Reserve of Hand Bombs and Brigade ammunitions Reserve will be established on the edge of SANCTUARY WOOD at I.24.b.1.5.

Three Depots of Battalion Bombs will be formed at :-

The South end of G.1. by Sherwood Foresters.
" " " S.2. by Durham L.I.
" " " STRAND by East Yorks.

11. The D.L.I. and Sherwood Foresters will detail carrying parties to take up R.E.Stores. These parties will move up close behind the assaulting troops. The 1st London Field Coy. will allot parties of R.E. to those two battalions.

12. **Communication.** The two main communication trenches allotted to the Brigade are OXFORD STREET, and the ZILLEBEKE communication Trench

13. **Battle Police.** The East Yorks will provide two police posts, one at western edge of MAPLE COPSE and the other at the R.E. Depot in SANCTUARY WOOD.

14. **Rations.** One days preserved rations, and the iron ration will be carried. Water bottles will be full.

15. **Packs.** Packs will not be carried.

16. **Maps and Documents.** No maps or documents or diaries will be carried by anyone taking part in the attack.

17. **Prisoners.** Prisoners will be despatched under small escort to ZILLEBEKE where they will be taken over by the NORTHAMPTONSHIRE Yeomanry who will conduct them to the SALLYPORT.

18. **Medical.** Separate instructions re Medical arrangements will be issued.

19. **Screens.** Yellow screens will be used to indicate that our troops have gained a certain position, and cannot advance further without Artillery support.

20. **Reports.** Advanced Brigade Headquarters will be in Eastern part of MAPLE COPSE.

21. ACKNOWLEDGE.

sd/F.G.MAUGHAN. Captain,
Brigade Major, 18th Infantry Bde.

Copy No. 1. West Yorks.
2. East Yorks.
3. S.Foresters.
4. D.L.I.
5. Q.W.Rifles.
6. 1st London Fd.Coy.R.E.
7. 16th Infantry Brigade.
8. 31st Trench Howitzer Battery.
9. 6th Division.
10. Retained.

16TH. INFANTRY BRIGADE.

The attached plan of operations is based upon the following appreciation of the situation:-

Given that the artillery bombardment has been effective the assaulting Battalions will have little or no difficulty in establishing themselves on the line assigned to them without employing more than half their force. Each Battalion will then still have half a battalion in hand to fill up casualties in the assaulting companies and enable the line reached to be consolidated.

If Battalions use up their whole reserves and are still repulsed it is considered unlikely that the enemy will push home his advantage as such a course would only bring him into the low ground S. of the MENIN ROAD where he would be at the mercy of a strong counter-attack.

For these reasons, only two companies of the 1/Buffs will be moved up (vide paras. 2 and 6 of Plan of Operations) in support of the assaulting battalions, as it is thought that these will be quite sufficient to deal with any enemy who might break through the line, or to replace casualties in the assaulting battalions and enable them to maintain at least their original line, and probably the line G.10 - MENIN ROAD - to South of the CRATER, until a fresh attack could be organised.

The Commanders of these two companies of the 1/Buffs must get into position to watch closely the course of events. Should the enemy drive back the assaulting battalions and follow them up they will at once act on their own initiative and counter-attack without hesitation.

Captain,

8th August, 1915.　　　Brigade Major, 16th Infantry Brigade.

16TH. INFANTRY BRIGADE

Plan of Attack for morning of 8th August 1915.

"A". PRELIMINARY MOVEMENTS.

1. The 1/K.S.L.I. and 2nd York. & Lancaster Regiment will be in position in their fire and assembly trenches by 1.30 a.m. The movement must be carried out absolutely quietly, and once in position the troops must keep perfectly still.

2. By 1 a.m. the 1/The Buffs will be in position as follows :-
   - 1 Company in F.2.
   - 1 Company in Southern branch of OXFORD STREET.
   - 2 Companies in G.H.Q. line - between junction of OXFORD STREET with G.H.Q. line and the MENIN ROAD.

3. The 1/Leicestershire Regiment will be employed digging up to midnight 7th/8th, and will then retire to the ramparts where they will remain ready to move at once if called upon.

"B" ASSAULT.

4. The Artillery bombardment begins at 2.45 a.m. and continues till 3.15 a.m. precisely.

5. During the last 10 minutes of this bombardment the 1/K.S.L.I. and 2nd York & Lancs Regiment having previously quietly cut all wire in front of our line, will start creeping forward to their objectives.

At 3.15 a.m. they will advance to the attack in the formation and strength arranged by Battalion Commanders.

They will establish themselves on approximate line F.7. - Q.19 - Q.14. by digging a new trench in a suitable line.

The R.E. Sections attached to Battalions will assist and help to wire in the new line.

When established this line is to be held with as few men and as many machine guns as possible.

Any troops not required to hold the new line will be withdrawn by Battalion Commanders - 2nd York & Lancs Regt. to the line G.10. - H.12. 1/K.S.L.I. to the line of the MENIN ROAD.

6. The O.C. 2nd York & Lancaster Regiment can call on the company of 1/The Buffs in F.2. for support if necessary.

Similarly, O.C. 1/K.S.L.I. can call upon the company of the 1/Buffs at South

South-East end of OXFORD STREET.

Battalions will inform Brigade Headquarters if they call upon these Companies.

7. If the two companies of 1/The Buffs are called upon by 1/K.S.L.I. and 2nd York & Lancs Regt, the Brigadier will decide whether to replace them by remaining companies 1/The Buffs in G.H.Q. line.

If these companies are moved forward they will be replaced by two companies 1/Leicestershire Regiment from the Ramparts.

                     Captain,

6th August, 1915.   Brigade Major, 16th Infantry Brigade.

Copy No......

16TH. INFANTRY BRIGADE OPERATION ORDER NO :-

Ref:- ZILLEBEKE Sheet, 1/10,000.
& Sketch Map "G" Sector.
(issued with notes on HOOGE). 6th August, 1915.

1. The Army Commander has selected the 6th Division to retake the ground recently captured by the Germans near HOOGE.

2. The ultimate object of the operations is to secure the high ground N. of the CRATER and in the direction of Q.19. P.7., and to establish ourselves on a line through the STABLES and Q.14 to Q.19.

3. The attack on the left of the line is allotted to the 16th Infantry Brigade and attached troops (12th Field Co.R.E. and 38th Trench Howitzer Battery). The right attack is allotted to the 18th Infantry Brigade and attached troops. The 17th Infantry Brigade is in Reserve West of YPRES.

4. The first objective of the 16th Infantry Brigade attack is the capture of the line - CRATER (inclusive) to Q.20 (inclusive) pushing on and consolidating Q.14. Q.19. and just South of P.7.

5. The Brigade will attack as follows:-

(a) 1/K.S.L.I. - CRATER (inclusive) to junction of dotted trench (just North of Q.18) with Q.20.

(b) 2nd York & Lancs Regt. from above named trench junction exclusive to left end of Q.20.

(c) 1/The Buffs - 2 companies in G.H.Q. line between MENIN ROAD and Junction of G.H.Q. line and OXFORD STREET.

1 Company in the southern branch at East end of OXFORD STREET, 1 company in F.2.

(d) 1/Leicestershire Regt. - in the Ramparts.

(e) 12th (Field) Company R.E. - less 2 sections - in the Ramparts.

The 1/K.S.L.I. is responsible for maintaining contact with the 18th Infantry Brigade, and the 2nd York & Lancaster Regiment for maintaining communication with the 1/K.S.L.I.

Special instructions have been issued to Officers Commanding Units.

6. The Artillery preparation has been continuous for some days.

From 2.45 am. to 3.15 am. on morning of the 8th the Artillery will bombard the enemy's defences.

During the last ten minutes of this bombardment the leading companies of the 1/K.S.L.I. and 2nd York & Lancs Regt. will advance (creep forward) as near as possible to the enemy's position and lie down.

Any wire in front of our line is to be removed during the night. At 3.15 a.m. precisely the guns will lift and the Infantry will assault and push on a quickly as possible.

The advance must be made exactly at time ordered regardless of what the Artillery are doing.

Synchronisation of watches will be arranged.

During the attack the 1/K.S.L.I. will despatch parties headed by bombers to work down BOND STREET and G.S. and to get in touch with 18th Infantry Brigade.

8. Immediately the line CRATER- Q.20 is occupied, battalion bombers, accompanied by R.E. working parties, will work up all communication trenches towards German lines.

9. O.C. 2nd York & Lancs Regt. will arrange to dig back a communication trench to Q.10. as soon as Q.20 is occupied. All use is to be made of the sapheads already running out from Q.10. towards German line. He will also detail a party to dig out the existing trench from Q.10. to H.13. Parties of the 42nd Brigade will also work on this trench from H.13. towards Q.20.

Similarly the 1/K.S.L.I. will open up communication trenches running back from Q.18 to the MENIN ROAD.

10. Machine Guns and Trench Howitzers are to be brought up to captured line at once.

11. R.E. Stores of 30,000 sandbags, wire, 400 shovels, pickets, are dumped at southern end of H.12.

12. S.A.A. Reserves of 200 boxes S.A.A. have been put at places sel selected by Commanding Officers, 1/K.S.L.I. and 2nd York & Lancs.

13. Sandbags. Every man will carry four sandbags.

14. <u>Packs</u>. will be stored under Battalion arrangements.
15. <u>Rations</u>. One day's rations and the Iron ration will be carried.
16. <u>Screens</u>. (a) German screens must not be pulled down.

(b) Yellow screens will be issued and put up to show that troops have gained a certain position and cannot advance further without artillery support.

(c) Blue and Yellow flags will be waved by selected N.C.Os. to indicate ~~that~~ to our Artillery that our shells are falling short.

(d) Bombers will mark their progress up trench by yellow and green flags.

17. <u>Prisoners</u>. Prisoners are to be collected under Battalion arrangements and sent back under small escrot by communication Trench "Z" to point where it reaches G.H.Q. line, where Divisional Cyclists will take over. A receipt must be obtained.

18. <u>Battle Police</u>. 1/Leicestershire Regiment will put battle police
(1) at point where OXFORD STREET joins S.6. - S.8.
(2) at East end of Communication Trenches Y. and Z. and of the Communication Trench on North of MENIN ROAD.

Duties of the police are to collect stragglers and send them back to their units in parties. They are to send back any unwounded men who are helping back wounded men. Police to be in position by 2.30 a.m.

19. <u>Medical</u>. Separate instructions are being issued.

The Brigadier expects that lightly wounded men will stick at their posts.

All walking cases must bring back their arms and equipment if they possibly can do so.

20. <u>Maps and Documents</u>. No maps or documents are to be carried by anyone taking part in the attack.

21. <u>Reports</u>. Brigade Headquarters will be established at 12 midnight 7th/8th at a point in OXFORD STREET in I.17.d.5.8.

ACKNOWLEDGE.

sd/H.HENDLAM, Captain,
Brigade Major, 16th Infantry Brigade.

Issued at 5 p.m. by Signals.

VI.Divn.
G.S.6/6/.

NOTES REGARDING COUNTRY AND TRENCHES ABOUT H O O G E.

The position at HOOGE, which has been taken by the Germans, is on the end of a spur running East and West which is followed by the MENIN ROAD. This position overlooks a wide extent of country to the West.

South of the MENIN road the ground slopes fairly uniformly from HOOGE to the west, and towards ZOUAVE and SANCTUARY WOODS to the South.

The MENIN road runs on an embankment as far East as a point due South of the crater.

The South-western part of ZOUAVE WOOD is thick and affords good cover, and it gets gradually thinner towards the N.E. edge where it is so thin as to afford practically no concealment.

There is a slight hollow in the N.E. corner of I.18.c.

TRENCHES etc.,
across the
MENIN ROAD.

Nos. 1 & 2. are tunnels under the road.

No. 3. is a cut about 5' deep.

No. 4. is a barricade in a dilapidated state.

No. 5. is a trench and barricade.

No. 6. is a trench.

No. 7. is a trench with barricade.

POINTS mentioned
as likely to
harbour MACHINE
GUNS.

(1) Junction of FLEET STREET and STRAND.

(2) Trench F.1.

(3) MARSH FARM (marked "S" on map).

(4) Old French dug-out at point marked "X" on map.

(5) Mound at West end of TUNNEL HOUSE (marked "R" on map).

(6) BULL FARM (marked "Q" on map).

GENERAL DESCRIPTION
of TRENCHES as they were
when handed over by
the 3rd Division.

F.3. Four lines of assembly trenches, much knocked about. These were dug and occupied in one night and have since been a good deal shelled.

F.2. Very poor communication trench, almost non-existent.

G.10. A strong narrow trench, fairly well wired on North side and running out into saps towards West and N.W.

G.9. A fire trench facing N., badly traversed and poor.

G.10.a. A trench along the road, badly enfiladed from ISLAND POST (the group of houses marked "P" on map.)

From Eastern end of G.10.a. a communication trench runs North into the fire trench West of the crater. This C.T. was shallow, unrevetted and unfinished.

Trench West of crater. A former German trench, very strong, well traversed and provided with good dug-outs. It has a hedge along the South side of it, a layed hedge formerly thickly wired.

Crater. North edge prepared for defence by us, with a parados.

Communication Trench from Crater to BULL FARM (house marked "Q" on map). Very shallow, ground here dead to Chateau.

G.5. (from BULL FARM TO STABLES). A strong parapet but poor parados.

There is a C.T. across from G.5. to G.4., south of STABLES.

G.4. A moderate trench.

G.7. West of TUNNEL HOUSE (house marked "R" on map). This trench is stated to be nearer to the road than the map shows it.

It is described as a good fire trench with shelter trench 5 yards south of it. At its East end it goes into a tunnel as do the last few yards of THE STRAND. East of the house G.7. is bad.

G.8. A fire trench with T-headed firing bays facing South. Trench much knocked about.

G.6. A goodish trench, also facing South.

G.3. A fairly good fire trench.

G.2. A fairly good fire-trench (since reported to have been knocked to pieces.

G.1. A good fire trench with good parados.

S.1. A very bad trench.

S.2. A good trench prepared for fire to east and wired.

There is a Communication Trench connecting S.2. with G.1., not shown between S.1 and G.1.. It is described as bad.

OLD BOND STREET. Described as bad in every way.

NEW BOND STREET. Part in wood very shallow. From edge of wood onwards good.

THE STRAND. Was a good communication trench.

FLEET STREET. Was not a good trench.

Communication Trench immediately North & South of No. 4 Barricade is practically non-existent. The ground at this point is very wet.

Communication Trench North of and parallel with G.6. bad.

---------------------*******---------------------

SECRET

G. 6/9

-: ADDITIONAL NOTES ON HOOGE :-

MACHINE GUN POSITIONS.   Against an advance from the south on to the MENIN ROAD it is stated that very little fire could be brought from works North of the road. Besides any fire from the trenches occupied by the Germans south of the road, that part of the force attacking between G.1. and S.2. would be exposed to fire from the work Q.4. - Q.5. - R.2. - R.1. (Fort 13), and from the wall along the south side of the road, immediately North of Q.8. - Q.11. This wall is believed to screen several machine guns and enfilades G.1. and S.1.

The ground West of S.2. is stated to be dead to fire from the east.

North of the line Q.20 - Q.18. - CRATER - STABLES, the ground is exposed to fire from the trench P.5. - P.8.. P.5. is a very likely machine gun position which would require to be dealt with before an attack could hope to reach the S.W. corner of the lake.

The island P.2. used to have a machine gun on it, exact position not certain, which commanded the ground between the CHATEAU and the south shore of the lake.

There is a slight mound near the south end of the bridge to the southern island, which used also to harbour a machine gun, and commanded part of the same ground.

GENERAL DETAILS.   From the line CHATEAU - CRATER the ground slopes very slightly to the north down to the shore of the lake. The southern part of this area contains a fair number of trees, part being an orchard. The northern half is open.

The two roads leading north from the CRATER had formerly a stout hedge along each of them, and the belt between them is described as difficult to move through on account of fallen trees and ruined out-houses.

(2)

The woods south of the lake, east of the CHATEAU, are described as completely shattered by shell fire, forming a regular abbatis.

Along the western edge of the lake is a very big "bund" - about 10' high and 12' thick.

----------------*****----------------

DIVISIONAL OPERATION ORDERS NOS. 28, 29, 30 & 31.

War Diary

Copy No. 13

-:6th DIVISION OPERATION ORDER No. 28:-

18th August, 1915.

Reference:- Map, sheet 28, 1/40,000.

1. On night 19th/20th August, the 16th Infantry Brigade will take over that part of the line held by the 7th Infantry Brigade (H.Q. CANAL BANK).
The line now held by the 7th Infantry Brigade is the LEFT SECTOR of our old line, i.e. from the WIELTJE Salient (inclusive) to the Sap running towards the MORTELDJE ESTAMINET (inclusive).

2. All arrangements for relief to be made direct between Brigadiers concerned. No movement of 16th Infantry Brigade to take place before dusk.

3. Artillery reliefs will be arranged later.

4. The 16th Infantry Brigade after taking over the line will temporarily come under the command of the G.O.C. 49th Division for tactical purposes. (H.Q. 49th Division are at H.7.c.8.6.).

5. No. 38 Trench Howitzer Battery is at the disposal of the G.O.C. 16th Infantry Brigade. The O.C. to report at H.Q. 16th Infantry Brigade POPERINGHE at 10 am tomorrow for orders.

6. Trench stores and trench bombs to be taken over.

7. Completion of relief to be reported by 16th Infantry Brigade to 49th Division, and repeated to 6th Division.

8. Acknowledge.

Lt. Colonel,
General Staff, 6th Division.

Issued at 8.30pm.

Distribution overleaf.

Distribution:-

    Copy No. 1 to 16th Infantry Brigade.
     ..   .. 2 .. 17th Infantry Brigade.
     ..   .. 3 .. 18th Infantry Brigade.
     ..   .. 4 .. G.O.C. R.A.
     ..   .. 5 .. C.R.E.
     ..   .. 6 .. "Q".
     ..   .. 7 .. Signals.
     ..   .. 8 .. A.D.M.S.
     ..   .. 9 .. 6th Corps.
     ..   .. 10 .. 14th Division.
     ..   .. 11 .. 49th Division.
     ..   .. 12 .. Office.
     ..   .. 13 .. Office.

SECRET

War Diary

Copy No. 19

6th DIVISION OPERATION ORDER No. 29:-

Reference:- 1/10,000 map, 28 N.W., Sheet 2.
           "   " LA BRIQUE.

20th August, 1915.

1. On the night 23rd/24th August the 18th Infantry Brigade will take over from the 41st Infantry Brigade, 14th Division, and from the 16th Infantry Brigade, the line from a point just North of CRUMP FARM (I.5.a.) to a point just North of LIVERPOOL STREET (C.22.c.2.2.).
   On the night 24th/25th, the 16th Infantry Brigade will extend its left about 500 yards, and take over the line from the 146th Infantry Brigade, 49th Division, up to a point about C.14.d.9.9.

2. Arrangements for the above reliefs to be made direct between the Brigadiers concerned.
   H.Q. 41st Brigade is at old 18th I.B. H.Q., CANAL BANK.
   H.Q. 146th Brigade is on CANAL BANK, Western side, 200 yards N. of No. 4 bridge.

3. Trench stores, trench bombs, also ammunition and rations at defended posts, will be taken over.

4. From the 25th instant the defences of POTIJZE and ST JEAN are allotted to the 18th Infantry Brigade, and a permanent garrison of 2 platoons will be kept there at present.
   WILSON FARM is allotted to the 16th Infantry Brigade, a permanent garrison of one platoon being kept there by night only, (at FRASCATI by day).

5. Boundaries between Divisions for Defence are as follows:-
   <u>On the North.</u> From C.14.d.8.9 through letter D in centre of C.14.d., thence just West of KNARESBOROUGH CASTLE, C.14.d.6.1. to C.21.c.4.9., thence along CONEY STREET (exclusive) to Bridge No.4 (common to both 6th and 49th Divisions).

2.

    <u>On the South.</u>   Point just North of CRUMP FARM - BOND STREET (inclusive to 6th Division) - POTIJZE defences - LOWER POTIJZE - ~~PRESTON HOUSE~~ Sqr I 2 (central) - Bridge No. 1.a. (to 14th Division).

6. The G.O.C. R.A. 6th Division will communicate direct with the G.O.C. R.A. 3rd Division as to details of relief of Artillery, which must be completed by the night of 26th/27th August.

7. Communication trenches are allotted as follows:-

    <u>16th Inf. Bde.</u> THREADNEEDLE STREET and all communication trenches North.

    <u>18th Inf. Bde.</u> All communication trenches South of THREADNEEDLE STREET to BOND STREET (inclusive).

8. Dividing line between Brigades for defence of the X line is where THREADNEEDLE STREET cuts the X line.
Dividing line between Brigades on the CANAL BANK is a point just opposite the RED HART ESTAMINET.

9. Completion of relief to be reported to 6th Division H.Q.

10. Acknowledge.

                                      G. F. Boyd
                                            Lt. Colonel,
                              General Staff, 6th Division.

Issued at 8.15 pm.

```
Copy No.  1  to  16th Infantry Brigade.
  ..  ..  2  ..  17th Infantry Brigade.
  ..  ..  3  ..  18th Infantry Brigade.
  ..  ..  4  ..  G.O.C. R.A.
  ..  ..  5  ..  C.R.E.
  ..  ..  6  ..  "Q".
  ..  ..  7  ..  Signals.
  ..  ..  8  ..  A.D.M.S.
  ..  ..  9  ..  6th Corps.
  ..  .. 10  ..  14th Division.
  ..  .. 11  ..  49th Division.
  ..  .. 12  ..  3rd Division.
  ..  .. 13  ..  Office.
  ..  .. 14  ..  Office.
```

Copy No. 14

War Diary

6th DIVISION OPERATION ORDER No. 30:-

21st August, 1915.

Reference:- Map sheet 28, 1/40,000.

1. On the night 24th/25th August, the 17th Infantry Brigade will be relieved in the HOOGE position by the 7th Infantry Brigade, 3rd Division.
All arrangements for relief to be made direct between the Brigadiers concerned.

2. On relief, the 17th Infantry Brigade will go into billets in Huts in A.30 and POPERINGHE, and be in Corps Reserve.

3. The two Field Companies R.E., and 26th Trench Howitzer Battery will go into rest billets under arrangements to be made by "Q" 6th Division.

4. The Machine Guns, Northamptonshire Yeomanry, will be withdrawn and return to the Squadron, as also the working parties Northamptonshire Yeomanry now in YPRES.

5. Ammunition, tools and trench stores to be handed over, and a list submitted to 6th Division Headquarters.
1,000 first-class and 2,000 second-class grenades will be handed over.

6. Completion of relief to be reported to 6th Division H.Q.

7. Acknowledge.

Lt. Colonel,
General Staff. 6th Division.

Issued at 3 pm.

Copy No. 1 to 16th Inf. Bde.	Copy No. 8 to 6th Corps.
" " 2 " 17th Inf. Bde.	" " 9 " Mounted Troops.
" " 3 " 18th Inf. Bde.	" " 10 " 3rd Division.
" " 4 " G.O.C. R.A.	" " 11 " 14th Division.
" " 5 " C.R.E.	" " 12 " 46th Division.
" " 6 " "Q".	" " 13 " A.D.M.S.
" " 7 " Signals.	" " 14 " Office.
	" " 15 " Office.

SECRET.   Copy No. 12

War Diary

-: 6th DIVISION OPERATION ORDER No. 31 :-

1st September, 1915.

Reference:- Map, sheet 28, 1/40,000, and map scale 1/10,000.

1. On the night 3rd/4th September, the 17th Infantry Brigade will relieve the 16th Infantry Brigade in the Left Sector of our line. Rations and ammunition at WILSON FARM will be handed over.

   All arrangements for relief to be made direct between the Brigadiers concerned, and completion of relief reported to 6th Division Headquarters.

2. BRIELEN and the Farm H.5. central will be placed at the disposal of G.O.C. 17th Infantry Brigade; the 18th Infantry Brigade will withdraw one battalion to the Wood A.30.

3. The 38th Trench Howitzer Battery will relieve the 26th, and be attached to the 17th Infantry Brigade.

4. On relief, the 16th Infantry Brigade will go into billets and huts under arrangements to be made by "Q" Staff 6th Division.

5. As little movement as possible must take place before dusk, unless the weather is particularly unfavourable for aerial observation. In any case special precaution must be taken, and it is advisable under present conditions to avoid the POPERINGHE Road East of VLAMERTINGHE.

6. Acknowledge.

                                              Lieut. Colonel,
                                         General Staff. 6th Division.

Issued at 12 noon.

   Copy No. 1 to 16th Inf. Bde.   Copy No. 6 to "Q".
    "   " 2 .. 17th Inf. Bde.   "   " 7 .. Signals.
    "   " 3 .. 18th Inf. Bde.   "   " 8 .. 6th Corps.
    "   " 4 .. G.O.C. R.A.   "   " 9 .. A.D.M.S.
    "   " 5 .. C.R.E.   "   " 10 .. 14th Division.
                                    "   " 11 .. 49th Division.
                                    "   " 12 & 13 to Office.

SUMMARY OF INFORMATION.

SUMMARY OF INFORMATION NO 70.

22nd August, 1915.

1. OPERATIONS - AUGUST 21st/22nd.

   After his heavy bombardment of some of our battery positions on the 20th., the enemy has been quiet, and there is nothing to record in the past 24 hours. In the bombardment on the 20th over 800 shell were fired by the enemy, inflicting total casualties of 1 killed, 7 wounded and 21 horses hit; no material damage was done.

2. MARCONI WIRELESS PRESS - LONDON, AUGUST 21st.

   RUSSIA - A great battle still rages in the Gulf of RIGA, firing being heard hundreds of miles away. Germany maintains silence about the battle, but PETROGRAD stated last night that large forces of the enemy's fleet had penetrated into the Gulf and fighting continued. This is the second occasion on which the German fleet has attempted to force a way into the Gulf. The German offensive against RIGA from the sea coincides with the capture of KOVNO, which removed the greatest obstacle to a more rigorous prosecution of the German campaign in the Baltic provinces. It is suggested by a French expert that RIGA may be abandoned. A Berlin message says the Germans are now attacking the South-West front, BREST - LITOVSK. Vienna reports that the effect of this advance has been to crowd together within the precincts of the Fortress, large Russian forces whose retreat is restricted to a few crossings of the BUG.
   A Zeppelin approaching VILNA has been brought down by Russian fire. On board were an engineer officer, eight soldiers, photographic apparatus, a small machine gun, ten explosive and a quantity of incendiary bombs. The airship was damaged in four places.
   PETROGRAD newspapers announce that an order will shortly be issued abolishing, during the war, Jewish residential restrictions regarding towns except PETROGRAD and MOSCOW.

   BALKANS. - ITALY is reported to have sent an ultimatum to TURKEY, and war is regarded in Germany as inevitable. An Allies' message suggests a rupture in negotiations between TURKEY and BULGARIA. The former has 40,000 men at KIRK KILLISSE on the BULGARIAN frontier. The Turks are erecting new and strong fortifications on a line from NILIVRI on the Sea of MARMORA, 36 miles West of Constantinople, and have concentrated 40,000 troops there. The line is to replace that in GALLIPOLI should the latter be abandoned.

   GERMANY - In the Reichstag to-day the question by Herr LIEBKNECHT, Socialist Deputy, as to whether the Government was disposed to abandon the idea of any annexation whatever and enter into immediate peace pourparlers if other belligerents were similarly inclined, was answered by Herr Von JAGOW, who said, "I think I have the consent of the majority of the House if I decline to reply, as at present it would be unsuitable. LIEBKNECHT made an attempt to speak, but was prevented by continual applause and shouts. Subsequent attempts by LIEBKNECHT were prevented by loud laughter and applause.

   S/S ARABIC. - It is still not definitely known how many persons were lost in the sinking of the ARABIC, the number of missing passengers being now given as 16 including 2 Americans. 38 of the crew were drowned. The total deathroll, if no more survivors are found, will be 54. Any action America may take appears to depend on whether the ARABIC tried to ram the submarine, Washington being already satisfied that no warning was given the liner before the attack. The American press comments in bitter terms on the outrage, one journal saying, "A break is certain".

3. GERMAN WIRELESS NEWS.

The communique is a short one. It is stated that E. of KOVNO Von HINDENBURG took 450 prisoners and 6 guns, and on fighting West of TYKOCIN the Russians lost 610 prisoners and on fighting West of GALLWITZ'S Army has taken BIELSK and 4 machine guns. Von to have broken the enemy's resistance yesterday and to have taken 1,000 prisoners. Von MACKENSEN'S left wing is pressing forward over the BUG, and further progress was made in front of BREST - LITOVSK.

4. EXTRACT FROM VII CORPS SUMMARY.

FROM THIS WEEK'S ISSUE OF THE "BERLIN LOKAL ANZEIGER".

How Tommy Dungbeetle captured a German gun.

The realisation that he was a real member of Kitchener's Millions only dawned on Tommy Dungbeetle when he found himself in Flanders.

Up till this moment the whole thing had struck him as a sort of "Monkey Theatre", and he had neverhhad such a feeling of regret at having come as when the Germans started to shoot. It seemed to Tommy Dungbeetle that they were all shooting at him.

In reality Tommy was no fighter. He had quite a good time the whole in the slums until one day he committed the following apalling blunder.

One fine day Tommy stood in front of his favourite "Pub" in the East End when a band came along making fearful noises, accompanied by soldiers who said that the country was in danger and would "go under" unless people like Tommy Dungbeetle sprang to the rescue.

Tommy's feelings of honour were however not disturbed and he would probably have remained standing in his place, had not a long-legged Scot in kilt suddenly shaken him by the hand and reminded him with a wink of a former "blind" they had had together.

Tommy certainly could not remember having had a "bust" with this particular individual, but as the Scot beckoned him with friendly hand towards the "Pub" he did not trouble about such niceties and went in.

Soon a couple of sisters of his host came along and some other "merry souls". Tommy was happier than he had ever been in his life and finally blind drunk. He awoke with a few pounds in his pockets in barracks !!

He did not like "drill" but as the officers told yarns every day of the glorious life he would lead in Germany where he would be absolutely free to do as he liked and where the Jewellers' shops were full of good things, he could already see himself rich beyond the dreams of avarice, and meeting the Duke of Argyle as a friend at his place in the country.

Then came the second critical period. One evening he was happy and drunk in "Old England" and the following morning sober and sorry in France.

He did not like the sight of the wounded, but they were soon put into reserve billets which were quite safe and comfortable.

"The French will do the work" he was told with a confidential grin. So Tommy rather enjoyed the war. There was plenty of jam and cake and meat, so things were quite pleasant.

One day, however, something terrible must have happened, for the officers had long faces though they said nothing.

What he did hear caused Tommy to shiver. A brigade had encountered the Bavarians and hardly a man had come back.

Then it was said that it was not so bad after all - in fact that nothing had happened except that the Bavarians had been beaten and they were going to finish them off. Tommy was to help.

The two divisions with the band at the head marched off along

3.

the broad country road. It was a lovely day and Tommy felt in the best of spirits and sang "It's a long way to Tipperary" with the others.

This was lovely - this was not war at all...........

Suddenly a loud report, the singing stopped, and the earth all round Tommy seemed to rise up. Shrieks and screams filled the air and Tommy rushed about like a mad animal as the German guns got to work.

All round the dead were strewn. Suddenly Tommy's head encountered a gun. All his fear left him. Had he not been promised £50 if he captured a gun. In the distance he saw thick gray columns of men. He waved his arms and shouted. Some men advanced and he cried out, "Gentlemen, I have captured a gun and you are my witnesses."

A fearful box on the ears was the only reply and a voice neither Scottish nor English said "You ———— this is not a ———— Theatre".

Only when he found himself deep in Germany did Tommy realise that he had captured an English gun.

———————

signature
Lieut.
for Major ES.

22/8/15.

1st London Rif.

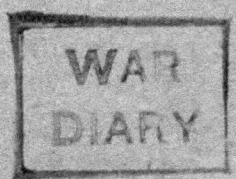

GENERAL STAFF

6th DIVISION

SEPTEMBER

1915

Attached:

   Div. Operation Orders.
   Paper G/6/4.
   Summaries of
      Information.

Poinst brought
out on the
operations at
   HOOGE.

6th Division

— Confidential —

121/0991

War Diary
of
General Staff 6th Division

From 1.9.15 To 30.9.15

Vol XIII

Army Form C. 2118.

WAR DIARY
or
INTELLIGENCE SUMMARY.
(Erase heading not required.)

Instructions regarding War Diaries and Intelligence Summaries are contained in F. S. Regs., Part II. and the Staff Manual respectively. Title pages will be prepared in manuscript.

Hour, Date, Place	Summary of Events and Information	Remarks and references to Appendices
Sept 1st	Hostile aeroplane dropped 2 bombs near 18th Bde trenches, no damage. Quiet day. 16th & 18th Bdes holding line.	
Sept 2nd	A good deal of shelling on 16th Bde lines and also YPRES otherwise nothing of interest.	
Sept 3rd	Raining hard. Trenches very wet + we are as bad as we are. 17th Bde relieved 16th Bde. Enemy's artillery active. 17th & 18th Bdes holding line	
Sept 4th	Hostile aeroplane driven off by m.g. rifle fire by 18th Bde.	
Sept 5th	Very wet.	
Sept 6th	Hostile aeroplanes active. One of their drones by one of our planes an hour after it was reported. St Jean shelled by heavy howr at 2.30pm	O.O. no 32 attached

Army Form C. 2118.

WAR DIARY
or
INTELLIGENCE SUMMARY.
(Erase heading not required.)

Instructions regarding War Diaries and Intelligence Summaries are contained in F. S. Regs., Part II. and the Staff Manual respectively. Title pages will be prepared in manuscript.

Hour, Date, Place	Summary of Events and Information	Remarks and references to Appendices
Sept 8th	2 Germans brought down by 17th Bde. Otherwise almost uneventful front.	
Sept 9th	Considerable shelling round TURCO FM. Enemy firing a few incendiary shell. St Jean Church much reduced in height by shelling. YPRES had a real good dosing. 16th Bde relieves 18th Bde	
Sept 10th	Enemy carried out a fine demonstration against our line, chiefly into little Willie, doing some damage, about 4–5 am. 17th and 16th Bdes holding line. A rifle now captured belonging to 234 Regt. Retaliation failed through error.	
Sept 11th	Nothing doing	
Sept 12th	Munition workers reached YPRES to be suitably impressed. 1 officer + 3 men suffocated by an official A.8.	

WAR DIARY
or
INTELLIGENCE SUMMARY.

(Erase heading not required.)

Army Form C. 2118.

Hour, Date, Place	Summary of Events and Information	Remarks and references to Appendices
Sept 13th	Steady shelling along the line. 2 Huns sniped by 16th Bde. Boche firing a glot of red and green lights.	O.O. 33. Uncred.
Sept 14th	1 Hun sniped by 16th. IRSH Fsn shelled intermittently with HE. from 11 am till 3·35pm.	O.O. 34 in real
Sept 15th	Special RE. reconnitered Lt POLLITT. Quiet day 18th Bde relieves 17th Bde	
Sept 16th	16th and 18th Bde holding the line. Nothing doing	
Sept 17th	Nothing doing	
Sept 18th	Nothing doing	
Sept 19th	A good deal of shelling.	O.O. 35 in rear

WAR DIARY
or
INTELLIGENCE SUMMARY.

(Erase heading not required.)

Army Form C. 2118.

Hour, Date, Place	Summary of Events and Information	Remarks and references to Appendices
Sept 20th	Hostile aeroplanes active. Nothing else doing.	
Sept 21st	Very quiet day.	
Sept 22nd	Sudden bursts of hostile rifle fire during night. YPRES heavily shelled. 17th Bde relieves 16th Bde 17th and 18th Bde relieving the line	
Sept 23rd	Very quiet	
Sept 24th	Very gentle wind, slightly East. Very quiet day.	
Sept 25th	The wind was very slight in the early morning, but W of SW. During the night the hour for the gas demonstration was brought in an hour till 5.50 a.m. The gas bombs moved very effective, and created a great deal of alarm and despondency along the whole front. The Germans lit fires, threw over pellet bombs and directed a heavy fire along his lines	see O.O. 36.

Army Form C. 2118.

WAR DIARY
or
INTELLIGENCE SUMMARY
(Erase heading not required.)

Instructions regarding War Diaries and Intelligence Summaries are contained in F. S. Regs., Part II. and the Staff Manual respectively. Title pages will be prepared in manuscript.

Hour, Date, Place	Summary of Events and Information	Remarks and References to Appendices
Sept 26th	Trenches all along the Front, Cornellie, Caines were about 80 but little demonstration was a distinct success. No germans left their trenches. A Belgian aeroplane over YPRES early in morning without marks of identification. Quiet day	
Sept 27th	Line now divided into three Bde sections viz one Brigadier and Staff at a rest commanding six battalions belonging to different Bdes. Quiet day.	
Sept 28th	Quiet day.	
Sept 29th	After heavy shells into POTIJZE and FORTUIN COTTAGE & PRESO STREET shelled.	
Sept 30th	Quiet day.	

E.L.comine Maj SS

DIVISIONAL OPERATION ORDERS NOS. 32, 33, 34, 35 & 36.

SECRET. *War Diary* Copy No. 12

:6th DIVISION OPERATION ORDER No. 32:-

7th September, 1915.

Reference:- Map sheet 28, 1/40,000.

1. On the night 9th/10th September, the 16th Infantry Brigade will relieve the 18th Infantry Brigade in the right sector of the 6th Division line.

    All arrangements for relief to be made direct between the Brigadiers concerned.

2. On relief, the 18th Infantry Brigade will go into billets in POPERINGHE and huts in A.30, under arrangements to be made by "Q" Staff 6th Division.

3. The 18th Infantry Brigade on relief will be in 6th Corps Reserve. Hd. Qrs. 18 Rue des Pots, POPERINGHE.

4. All trench stores etc. to be handed over, and work now in hand to be completed before any new work is commenced.

5. As little movement as possible must take place before dusk, unless the weather is particularly unfavourable for aerial observation. It is advisable under present conditions to avoid the POPERINGHE - YPRES Road East of VLAMERTINGHE.

6. Command of the sector to pass to G.O.C. 16th Infantry Brigade at 10 pm, 9th, and completion of relief reported to 6th Division Headquarters.

7. Acknowledge.

Lt. Colonel,
General Staff, 6th Division.

Issued at noon.

Copy No. 1 to 16th Inf. Bde.   Copy No. 7 to Signals.
"   "   2 .. 17th Inf. Bde.   "   "   8 .. 6th Corps.
"   "   3 .. 18th Inf. Bde.   "   "   9 .. A.D.M.S.
"   "   4 .. G.O.C. R.A.   "   " 10 .. 14th Division.
"   "   5 .. C.R.E.   "   " 11 .. 49th Division.
"   "   6 .. "Q".   "   " 12 & 13 to Office.

SECRET.   *War Diary*   Copy No. 13

:6th DIVISION OPERATION ORDER No. 33:-

13th September, 1915.

Reference:- Map sheet 28, 1/40,000.

1. On the night 15th/16th September, the 18th Infantry Brigade will relieve the 17th Infantry Brigade in the left sector of our line.
Arrangements to be made direct between the Brigadiers concerned. Machine Gunners to be relieved either before, or after, as is most suitable.

2. The 38th Trench Howitzer Battery will relieve the 26th Trench Howitzer Battery, and be attached to the 18th Infantry Brigade at present.

3. On relief, the 17th Infantry Brigade will go into billets and huts in POPERINGHE and A.30, respectively, under arrangements to be made by "Q" Staff 6th Division, and will be in 6th Corps Reserve. Hd. Qrs. 18 Rue des Pots, POPERINGHE.

4. The G.O.C. 18th Infantry Brigade will take over command of the sector at 10 pm on the 15th, and report completion of relief to 6th Division Headquarters.

5. As little movement as possible must take *place* before dusk, unless the weather is particularly unfavourable for aerial observation. It is advisable under present conditions to avoid the POPERINGHE - YPRES road East of VLAMERTINGHE.

6. Acknowledge.

Lieut. Colonel,
General Staff. 6th Division.

Issued at 11.30 am.

Copy No. 1 to 16th Inf. Bde.   Copy No. 7 to Signals.
"   "   2 .. 17th Inf. Bde.   "   "   8 .. 6th Corps.
"   "   3 .. 18th Inf. Bde.   "   "   9 .. A.D.M.S.
"   "   4 .. G.O.C. R.A.   "   " 10 .. 14th Division.
"   "   5 .. C.R.E.   "   " 11 .. 49th Division.
"   "   6 .. "Q".   "   " 12 & 13 to Office.

SECRET.   Copy No. 13

-: 6th DIVISION OPERATION ORDER No. 34 :-

14th September, 1915.

Reference :-   Map, sheet 28, scale 1/40,000.

1. 6th Division Operation Order No. 33 is cancelled.

2. With a view to carrying out the re-adjustment of the line as outlined in my G/1/33/21, the following moves will take place under arrangements to be made by Brigadiers concerned :-

3. On the night 15th/16th September :-
   (a). The 18th Infantry Brigade will relieve the 16th Infantry Brigade in the right sector of our line. Command will pass to G.O.C. 18th Infantry Brigade at 10 pm, and completion of relief reported by him to 6th Division Headquarters.

   (b). The battalions of the 17th Infantry Brigade on the CANAL BANK and in BRIELEN will be withdrawn to billets in POPERINGHE, and their places occupied by two battalions of the 16th Infantry Brigade. These two battalions will be at the disposal of the G.O.C. 17th Infantry Brigade for defensive purposes.

   (c). One battalion of the 16th Infantry Brigade will bivouac in the grounds of VLAMERTINGHE CHATEAU, and one will occupy the French dugouts in H.11.

4. On the night 16th/17th September :-
   (a). The 16th Infantry Brigade will relieve the 17th Infantry Brigade in the left sector of our line, and the 17th Infantry Brigade (less two battalions in POPERINGHE) will go into huts in A.30. Command of the sector to pass to G.O.C. 16th Infantry Brigade at 10 pm, and completion of relief reported by him to 6th Division Headquarters. The 17th Infantry Brigade on relief will be in Corps Reserve. Headquarters at Rue des Pots, POPERINGHE.

   (b). The 38th Trench Howitzer Battery will relieve the 26th Trench Howitzer Battery, and be attached to the 16th Infantry Brigade.

2.

5. On the night 22nd/23rd September, the 17th Infantry Brigade will relieve the 16th Infantry Brigade in the left sector of our line. Command of the sector to pass to G.O.C. 17th Infantry Brigade at 10 pm, and completion of relief reported by him to 6th Division Headquarters. On relief, the 16th Infantry Brigade will be in Corps Reserve. Hd. Qrs. Rue des Pots, POPERINGHE.

6. On the night 26th/27th September, the 16th Infantry Brigade will take over its own section of the line as detailed in my G/1/33/21, except that the 16th Infantry Brigade will include B.16. Further details will be issued later.
By this date the adjustment of the line between the 17th and 18th Infantry Brigades will have been completed, under arrangements to be made between the G.O.C's 17th and 18th Infantry Brigades.

7. As little movement as possible must take place before dusk, unless the weather is particularly unfavourable for aerial observation. It is advisable under present conditions to avoid the POPERINGHE - YPRES Road East of VLAMERTINGHE.

8. Acknowledge.

G. F. Boyd
Lieut. Colonel,
General Staff. 6th Division.

Issued at 9.15 am.

```
Copy No. 1 to 16th Inf. Bde.    Copy No. 7 to Signals.
  ..  .. 2 .. 17th Inf. Bde.      ..  .. 8 .. 6th Corps.
  ..  .. 3 .. 18th Inf. Bde.      ..  .. 9 .. A.D.M.S.
  ..  .. 4 .. G.O.C. R.A.         ..  .. 10 .. 14th Division.
  ..  .. 5 .. C.R.E.              ..  .. 11 .. 49th Division.
  ..  .. 6 .. "Q".                ..  .. 12 & 13 to office.
```

War Diary

SECRET.   Copy No. 11

6th DIVISION OPERATION ORDER No. 35:-

Reference:- Map, Sheet 28, 1/40,000.   19th September, 1915.

1. On the night 21st/22nd September, the 18th Infantry Brigade will take over that part of the line held by the 41st Infantry Brigade, 14th Division, as far as I.5.d.5.1.

   Details of relief to be arranged between Brigadiers concerned, and completion of relief reported.

2. 41st Infantry Brigade has arranged to hand over all trench stores and bombs. A list of these will be forwarded to 6th Division Headquarters.

3. Machine Gun Detachments will be relieved on the night 20th/21st, under arrangements to be made between Brigadiers concerned.

4. The G.O.C. 17th Infantry Brigade will place one battalion at the disposal of G.O.C. 18th Infantry Brigade as a Reserve. This battalion will move into position on night 21st/22nd. An officer from this battalion will report at 18th Infantry Brigade Headquarters at 2 pm tomorrow, 20th instant, when the position assigned to it by the G.O.C. 18th Infantry Brigade will be pointed out. One company and 2 machine guns must occupy the KAAIE Salient.

5. Acknowledge.

                                          G. F. Boyd.
                                          Lieut. Colonel,
Issued at 8.30 pm.   General Staff, 6th Division.

```
Copy No. 1 to 16th Inf. Bde.    Copy No. 6 to Signals.
  ..  ..  2 .. 17th Inf. Bde.     ..  ..  7 .. "Q".
  ..  ..  3 .. 18th Inf. Bde.     ..  ..  8 .. A.D.M.S.
  ..  ..  4 .. G.O.C. R.A.        ..  ..  9 .. 14th Division.
  ..  ..  5 .. C.R.E.             ..  .. 10 .. 6th Corps.
                                  ..  .. 11 & 12 to Office.
```

SECRET.   War Diary   Copy No....8....

-: 6th DIVISION OPERATION ORDER No. 36 :-

23rd September, 1915.

Reference:- Trench map, and special map issued herewith.

1. (a). The French and British Armies in the West are about to assume the offensive.

   (b). The 5th Corps, with the 14th Division attached, is to attack the position about BELLEWAARDE and to the South on the 25th instant.

   (c). The 3rd Division will capture the line J.19.a.7.9 – 9.9 – J.13.c.9.2 – 7.9 – 6.9 – J.13.a.6.1 – 5.0 – 4.3 – 2.5 – 0.7 – I.18.b.7.7 – 6.8 – 6.9 – I.12.d.4.1 – I.12.d.2.4. The 14th Division will capture the line I.12.d.2.4 – 1.6 – 2.9 – 0.9 , I.12.a.7.1 – 7.2 – 6.4 – 2.4 – 0.4, and join up with their front line South of the ROULERS Railway. The final bombardment will take place from 3.50 am to 4.20 am on the morning of the 25th instant, and the assault at 4.20 am precisely. At 4.19 am a mine will be exploded under the enemy redoubt at I.12.a.0.4.

   (d). The 6th Corps (less 14th Division) is to carry out a demonstration along its whole front, assisted by the Artillery of the 36th French Corps on the left.

2. The demonstration mentioned in para. 1(d) is to take the form of:-

   (a). Bombardment of selected points.
   (b). Wire-cutting.
   (c). Simulation of a gas attack.

3. The 6th Division will carry out a demonstration as follows:-
   (a). On the 24th instant, the Divisional Artillery will bombard points in the enemy's lines and cut wire, under orders to be issued by the C.R.A., and at a time to be notified later.

The

6th DIVISION OPERATION ORDER No. 36 (continued). 2.

The points selected, and the fronts on which the wire is to be cut will be notified by Artillery Brigade Commanders to the Infantry Brigadiers concerned. The fronts on which the wire has been cut will be kept under Infantry and Artillery fire during the night 24th/25th.

(b). The 17th and 18th Infantry Brigades will be provided with material for producing smoke. On the morning of the 25th instant, if the wind is suitable, and at a time to be notified, a smoke/cloud will be maintained for 30 minutes along the front. Special instructions are issued with regard to this.

(c). To assist the attack of the 14th Division, at 4.20 am on the 25th September the 18th Infantry Brigade will bring as heavy fire as possible to bear on the area North of a line drawn through points 0.8, 2.7, 4.7 in I.12.a., the German communications along the Railway, and the trenches between the Railway and OSCAR FARM.

4. Acknowledge.

G. F. Boyd
Lieut. Colonel,
General Staff. 6th Division.

Issued at 11.20 pm.

Copy No. 1 to 16th Inf. Bde.
" " 2 " 17th Inf. Bde.
" " 3 " 18th Inf. Bde.
" " 4 " G.O.C. R.A.
" " 5 " C.R.E.
" " 6 " 6th Corps.
" " 7 and 8 to Office.
" " 9
" " 10

PAPER G/6/4.

SECRET

6th Div. No.
G/6/4.

~~16th Infantry Brigade.~~
17th Infantry Brigade.
18th Infantry Brigade.

---

1.   Certain appliances are being issued to Brigades for the purpose of simulating a gas attack:-

  (a). Paynes smoke candles   (lasts 3 minutes).

  (b). 18-pdr. grenades......(lasts 6 minutes).

  (c). Threlfallite No. 1....(lasts 3 minutes).

  (d). Red Mixture grenades..(lasts 1 minute).

2.   The object to be attained is to make a dense smoke for 30 minutes along our front.

   The whole operation naturally depends upon the wind; and those portions of the front unfavourable will not be dealt with.

   For instance, with a wind in the N.W., trenches B.12 and B.11 will not be used.

   Similarly, with a S.W. wind, B.12, B.13 will not be used.

   If wind is entirely unfavourable, grenades will not be used at all.

   Battalion Commanders must so arrange that supplies are used at the most favourable points.

  (a). Grenade or candle should be thrown over the parapet at 10 yards interval, under no circumstances closer, a fresh grenade being thrown as the old one expires.

  (b). None of the gas generated is poisonous.

  (c). None of the grenades are dangerous to handle. All are lighted with the common lighter with fuze set at $3\frac{1}{2}$ seconds.

  (d). The fumes of the Threlfallite and red mixture make the eyes smart, and they should be thrown well clear of the parapet.

(e)

(e). A certain amount of flame is generated, and the grenade should be thrown into a hole where possible.

(f). All grenades should be kept 'lighters up' before throwing.

3. Issue will be made as follows:-

It is advisable to give each front a proportion of each kind of grenade.

	Paynes Candles.	18-pdr.	Threlfallite.	Red Mixture.
17th Infantry Bde.	150	380	750	A proportion.
18th Infantry Bde.	220	620	1250	

E. Ironside
Major,
General Staff.

Points on the Operations
at HOOGE.

EXTRACT FROM REPORT BY G.O.C. 8th DIVISION, IN REPLY

TO QUESTIONS ASKED BY 2nd ARMY.
==

1. <u>Close co-operation of Artillery F.O.Os with the Infantry.</u>
   <u>Where were the F.O.Os placed during the various phases of</u>
   <u>the attack. ?</u>

   (a). Each Infantry Brigade was supported by its own Artillery Brigade.
   The positions of the detached officers were as follows :-

   (i). 1 Subaltern from Right Artillery Brigade with H.Q.2nd Durham L.I.

   (ii). 1 Subaltern from Left Artillery Brigade with H.Q. 2nd York & Lanc Regt., but in close touch with H.Q. 1st Shropshire L.I.

   (iii). 1 Captain from each Artillery Brigade with H.Q. Infantry Brigade.

   (iv). 1 Captain per Artillery Brigade at a selected point in rear of firing line acting as General Observing Officer for his Artillery Brigade.

   (v). 1 officer per battery at the Battery Observation Station.

   These officers had no orders as to changing their positions.
   The officer attached to Battalion H.Q. had orders not to go in front of Battalion H.Q. unless expressly instructed to do so by the Battalion Commander.
   In any case, no wire was run out in front of Battalion H.Q.
   As soon as the bombardment starts, it is impossible to observe anything from an Artillery point of view, and Observation Officers as such were no use. Any observation that could be done later was done by (iv) and (v), who remained in their set positions all day. They could only observe after the attack had taken place.

   Officers (i), (ii) and (iii), are purely liaison officers, and did excellent work in letting the Artillery H.Q. know how the Battalions in front line were situated, and in forwarding the requirements of these Battalion Commanders. F.O.O. is, under the circumstances, a misnomer.

2. <u>What were the arrangements made for the bombing parties. ?</u>

   (a). Each platoon had its own Grenade Squad of 7 men, consisting of :-

   1 Bayonet Men.
   2 Throwers.)
   4 Carriers.) All equally trained as throwers.

The

The Carriers carried 40 grenades, 10 each man, and both Carriers and Throwers were armed with a leaden headed knobkerrie. Of the smaller kinds of grenades, a Carrier can take a double load of 20, and in future the Squads will carry 80 grenades instead of 40.

Practically every man in a platoon is ready and trained to take his place as Bayonet Man in a Platoon Squad. These Platoon Squads are an integral part of the Platoon and work with it.

It was found that one squad was sufficient for each communication trench, supplemented by extra carriers.

The fresh supply of grenades was in all cases not quick enough. Carriers should be ready to go up at once to a captured position, and a regular supply each hour or half hour after that. If squads have to work up long communication trenches, extra carriers must be attached, and these need not necessarily be trained grenade men.

It is not considered possible to employ larger squads than the Platoon Squad, which have proved very handy.

All Grenadiers should be taught how to use German grenades. Great use was made of German Grenades by nearly all our parties.

8th Corps.

A few points brought out during the late operations at HOOGE may be of interest and are therefore forwarded.

1. I ordered the captured line to be wired as soon as possible. This was done by the R.E. in most gallant manner directly after the position was captured, but with too great a loss in officers and men. I consider it a mistake to wire at all before nightfall. It is costly in men, it marks our position, it advertises the fact that we do not mean a further advance, and it is unnecessary in the present state of German troops, and the efficiency of our Artillery barrage.

2. I gave a definite line to be made good. This appeared to me necessary as a further advance towards the Lake would have led the troops into low ground, and where connection with our former line was long and difficult. At the same time I am convinced that more ground could have been gained. The opportunity for such extension on both flanks could only have been seized by some one in authority on the spot, if the Fort 13, Q.5, Q.6 line, and the BELLEWAARDE position had been previously prepared for assault, the wire cut, and assaulting troops ready. It is of course doubtful whether sufficient Artillery was present to prepare a length of front of such an extent, but it seems clear that at any rate wire should be cut for some distance on both flanks of the actual line to be assaulted, and the Heavy Artillery, less counter-batteries, prepared to turn all their fire on to one, or both flanks as soon as the original objective is seen to be in our possession.

3. The tendency is to have too many men on the captured position, caused (1st) by the need for bringing enough weight to crush any opposition which may be met, and (2nd) by the augmentation of the fighting line by carrying parties. It is essential to thin out the line as quickly as possible directly the position is captured, otherwise every shell tells.

4. It is important to observe the fall of the enemy's shell fire for some days previous to the assault, in order to clear those areas of troops on the day of assault as much as possible. Where this was done little loss was suffered; where it was neglected much was incurred.

5. There was much waste of bombs due to unaimed fire, and to faulty methods of carrying bombs. Better training, and better contrivances will meet the case.

6. A large supply of water should be stored as close as possible to be sent up at once.

7. Some special, strong dug-outs near the battle field for wounded to crawl into would save lives, and these should be close to exits of recognised communication trenches.

8. More Medical Officers should be attached to assaulting battns.

9. The removal and burial of the dead, and supply of quick lime as early as possible, needs special arrangements.

10. The anti-shrapnel helmets were considered effective, and saved many men from nasty wounds; but they must be made more distinctive than they are at present for their shape and colour, i.e. a slate blue, now lead to their wearers being fired at by our own men. This actually happened on several occasions.

No.S/8/22
14th Aug.1915.

Major General,
Commanding 8th Division.

16th INFANTRY BRIGADE.

EXTRACT FROM REPORT ON THE OPERATIONS AT HOOGE 9th AUG. 1915.

4. Our own bombs were most effective, and both battalions also picked up and used the German bombs freely.

Our men appear to have used a great many bombs without seeing a good target for them; consequently both battalions ran short at times.

A great many bombs were dropped or fell out of the boxes, which are cumbersome.

It is suggested that bombers should carry nothing but bombs and a slung rifle or a revolver.

The supplying of bombs to the firing line was difficult, and the positions of reserve depots required thinking out. The system of supply of bombs to the firing line required to be more organised.

Very large reserves of bombs are suggested.

Probably what is most required is a better carrying apparatus in order to avoid bombs falling out all over the place; and also more definite superintendence of the throwing of bombs. Undoubtedly large numbers were wasted by being thrown at nothing, and by being used at times when rifle fire would have been more effective.

5. The wires between battalions and the Brigade Headquarters were broken at once.   *   *   *

6. Both battalions agree as to the efficacy of the shrapnel helmets, which saved several men from nasty wounds.

7. The 1st Shropshire L.I. report that several Germans pretended to be dead, and then got up and shot our men in the back after they had passed. These men were dealt with. One man of the 2nd York and Lancs Regt was set on fire by an explosive bullet. Clips of reversed bullets were found. The morale of German troops was distinctly bad. They were apparently greatly demoralised by the bombardment.

8. Each battalion employed two companies in front line and two in reserve.

The advance was made in lines of platoons at about 40 yards intervals.

Morale of our men was all that could be desired. They behaved splendidly under very heavy shell fire.

Officers were able to keep good control.

Men got a little out of hand in their desire to get on further, and some who advanced too far were probably killed by our own barrage.

9. SOME SUGGESTIONS.

(a). A larger supply of water must be stored ready to be sent up at once.

(b). Some special strong dug-outs should be made ready for wounded to crawl back to.

(c). Stretcher parties were very late in arriving. They should be on the spot immediately it is dark.

(d). More Medical Officers are required to each battalion going into action. The 1st Shropshire L.I. had an extra one on this occasion.

It is suggested that one Medical Officer should be up in the firing line, and a second in the Regimental Aid Post.

(e). More runners required - to be posted on relay system. Well buried wires would be a help, but in this case there is no time to do this thoroughly.

(f). Sanitary measures to be taken immediately position is held require to be arranged for.

10. In conclusion, I submit the following points with regard to which I think valuable experience has been gained :-

(a). The necessity for disposing supporting troops away from the probable areas of enemy shell fire.
As far as this Brigade is concerned, it was recognised beforehand that this area was bounded by the MENIN ROAD - the South edge of ZOUAVE WOOD - OXFORD STREET - and G.H.Q. line back to the MENIN ROAD. This area was entirely cleared, and the supporting troops disposed in the trench running South from the South arm of OXFORD STREET, in the West end of OXFORD STREET, and in HALFWAY HOUSE, suffered practically no loss.

(b). The absolute necessity for good communication trenches. The existing ones were, in my opinion, badly sited and not nearly deep enough or sufficiently protected.

* * * *

(c). Where no natural cover exists for Collecting and Dressing Stations, strong deep dug-outs should be constructed some little way off but connected with recognised communication trenches.

* * * *

(d). Bombing parties should be supplied with bombs by some system of sending them up from reserves at regular intervals to certain points, thus obviating the necessity of sending back for them.
The whole system of bomb carrying equipment requires organisation. The boxes at present in use for certain types of bombs are most unsatisfactory.

(e). The question of disposal of the dead in a captured trench which it is intended to hold is one which requires careful previous arrangement. Burial parties previously detailed should start work as soon as possible by day if the situation permits, but in any case as soon as it is dark. Parties should not be too big, each under a selected N.C.O. with an officer to superintend the area. Quicklime should be provided beforehand. Each party should, if possible, be accompanied by a trained R.A.M.C. orderly to minimise the risk of badly wounded men being buried.

* * * * *

EXTRACT FROM 16th INFANTRY BRIGADE OPERATION ORDER
of 8th AUGUST 1915.
==================

* * * * * * *

10.   Machine guns and trench howitzers are to be brought up to captured line at once.

11.   R.E.Stores of 20,000 sandbags, wire, 400 shovels, pickets, are dumped at southern end of H.12.

12.   S.A.A. reserves of 200 boxes S.A.A. have been put at places selected by Comdg.Officers, 1/K.S.L.I. and 2nd York & Lancs.

13. Sandbags.   Every man will carry four sandbags.

14. Packs.   Will be stored under battalion arrangements.

15. Rations.   One day's rations and the iron ration will be carried.

16. Screens.   (a).   German screens must not be pulled down.

              (b).   Yellow screens will be issued and put up to show that troops have gained a certain position and cannot advance further without artillery support.

              (c).   Blue and Yellow Flags will be waved by selected N.C.O's to indicate to our artillery that our shells are falling short.

              (d).   Bombers will mark their progress up trench by yellow and green flags.

* * * * * * *

18. Battle Police.   1/Leicester Regt. will put battle police :-

    (1). At point where OXFORD STREET joins S.6 - S.8.

    (2). At east end of communication trenches Y and Z and of the communication trench on N of MENIN road.

        Duties of the police are to collect stragglers and send them back to their units in parties.   They are to send back any unwounded men who are helping back wounded men.   Police to be in position by 2-30 a.m.

* * * * * * *

20. Maps and documents.   No maps or documents are to be carried by anyone taking part in the attack.

                                        (sd) H.Headlam, Captain,
                                             Brigade Major,
                                             16th Infantry Brigade.

Issued at 5 p.m. by Signals.

Page 2. Last paragraph. As far as I am aware, no bombers in this B⁻ᵈᵉ have had an opportunity of seeing a German Bomb. Instruction in the means of lighting the fuzes &c, of a German bomb could be easily given, & might be useful. As enormous quantities of these bombs are usually captured.

Page 3. Para 3.
Para 4.
Para 6.
Para 7.
Para 8.
Para 9 — Would it be possible to get a supply of these helmets. Especially for the sentries who will have to be more or less exposed during German retaliation to our bombardment

Page 4. Para 7.

SECRET.

~~140th Inf Bde~~
~~141st Inf Bde~~
142nd Inf Bde
~~47th Div Arty~~
~~47th Div Engrs~~
~~"Q"~~

The following notes from the experience gained by 6th Division at HOOGE are forwarded in continuation of this Office G/435.

1. **Time when the heavy shelling by the enemy commenced.**

    The Germans commenced to shell our front line trenches on the right almost as soon as our bombardment started. The assembly trenches, some of which were dug in a hollow two days before the attack and others on the night immediately preceding it, were undiscovered up to the moment of assault.

    About three hours after the attack the trenches previously occupied by the enemy on our right were heavily shelled, occasioning serious losses among our troops. The heavy shelling of the HOOGE position itself commenced about an hour and a quarter after the assault and continued throughout the day.

2. **Action of enemy's machine guns.**

    Very few of the German machine guns fit to fire were left in the front line.
    Except from the direction of a portion of the enemy's line on the right not attacked, little loss was experienced from machine gun fire during the assault. Later machine guns opened from places in BELLEWAARDE WOOD and from a house at the West end of HOOGE, - this was knocked out by a trench mortar.

3. **Losses from shell fire.**

    After the capture of the position there was a tendency to have too many men in certain parts of it. This resulted in unnecessarily heavy losses from shell fire as soon as the enemy's artillery was turned on to the captured trenches.
    In other portions this was avoided by the Battalion Commanders going up to the line and thinning it out by sending men back to the supporting companies.

                                        General Staff,
                                    47th (London) Division.

2nd Sept. 1915.

G/435/1.

SUMMARIES OF INFORMATION.

SUMMARY OF INFORMATION NO. 89.

2nd September 1915.

1. OPERATIONS - September 1st/2nd.

Near the CANAL one of our catapult bombs landed amongst a German working party near the salient West of 5 CHEMINS EST. The enemy retaliated for our shelling but did no damage.

On the rest of the front there is nothing to report.

Our heavy artillery were active during the day. They retaliated on ZONNEBEKE, POELCAPELLE, and WESTHOEK for the shelling of YPRES. When firing on BELLEWAARDE FARM apparently a bomb store was hit, as an explosion occurred. The firing on FORTIN 13, South East of HOOGE, is reported to have been very effective. Many trees were blown down and earth and planks were blown into the air.

2. EXTRACT FROM FRENCH OFFICIAL COMMUNIQUE.

From 6.0 to 7.50 the English Fleet bombarded the Belgian coast. The enemy replied feebly by firing at NIEUPORT and the TRIANGLE WOOD. We countered their batteries up to 11 o'clock.

3. MARCONI WIRELESS NEWS - London, 1st September.

Russia.

The German admission yesterday of a partial check in their advance against the Russian left wing, rather understated the case. A series of vigorous attacks along the entire front in GALICIA preceded as usual by massed artillery fire, has been repulsed and the enemy losses have been extremely heavy. In some districts the Grand Duke reports the enemy was obliged to retire precipitately and in Russian counter-attacks about 3,000 prisoners, half of whom were Germans, and a large number of guns were captured. Flanking movements in the North have made no further progress. The enemy has been checked in an attempt to cross the DWINA. Near FRIEDRICHSTADT and on the VILID the Russians have developed an offensive movement.

Italy.

General CADORNA announces further progress on the CARNIC PLATEAU, and the capture of more trenches in the TRENTINO.

In the ISONZO, a picked body of Trailleurs has made an attack on the Austrian machine guns and mortars that have been annoying the Italian approach, and have silenced them.

The strong enemy position on MONTE MARONIA, North of MONTE MAGGIO has been captured in face of a furious artillery fire.

4. EXTRACTS FROM GERMAN WIRELESS.

Western Theatre of War.

No change. North East of BAPAUME, an English aeroplane was brought down by one of our aviators.

South-eastern Theatre of War.

The troops of V. BOTHMER stormed the heights of STRYTA against great opposition,

The number of prisoners taken by the German troops on the East and South Eastern fronts has reached the number of 2,000 officers and 269,839 men, 2,370 guns, and considerably more than 560 machine guns. At KOVNO we captured in round figures 20,000 men and 227 guns, and at NOVO GEORGIEVSK 90,000 men (among them 15 Generals and over 1,500 other officers), 1,200 guns and 150 machine guns.

The number of prisoners taken by the German and the Austro-Hungarian troops since the 2nd May has now passed well over one million.

NOTE: The discrepancy in the proportion of officers to men between the figures given for the whole front and those given for NOVO GEORGIEVSK is noticeable. The losses of the Field Army in men and guns is not as great as might have been supposed from reading the daily German Communiques.

5. NEWS FROM GERMAN SOURCES.

Berlin.

"LA NORDDEUTSCHE ALLEGEMEINE ZEITUNG", expresses the admiration of Germany for the heroic defence of the DARDANELLES by the Turkish Army which has struggled for several months against several hundred thousands of the enemy, abundantly supplied with every kind of engine of war, supported by strong squadrons and a very heavy artillery, and who have attacked them without respite. Germany is proud of her Turkish Ally.

6. EXTRACT FROM VII CORPS SUMMARY - 1st Sept.

A telegram from ROME states that the position in Turkey has become worse during the last week. The difficulties of the defence in the GALLIPOLI peninsular increase from day to day, owing to inability to solve satisfactorily the problem of supply. Supplies cannot come by sea, and the roads to the mainland are constantly under the fire of the Allied artillery. Shortness of food is creating great discontent amongst the Turks, who no longer are allowed periods of repose, since their replacement by fresh troops has become impossible.

Major, G.S.

2/9/15.

SUMMARY OF INFORMATION NO. 90.

3rd September 1915.

1. OPERATIONS - September 2nd/3rd.

    The last twenty-four hours have been quiet and there is little to report. YPRES was heavily shelled at 4 p.m. and again at 6 p.m. Near BELLEWAARDE FARM our "TOBIES" did some effectual retaliation. Towards the CANAL the enemy's artillery were more active, probably in response to the French artillery, which has been administering strong and intermittent doses. Our snipers on this flank claim four Germans.

2. NEWS FROM FRENCH SOURCES.

    BREMEN has placed with all the export houses of the United States, a firm order for the purchase of 1,000,000 bales of cotton for delivery at direct or indirect destination, at the wish of the vendor. An order of such importance under the circumstances indicates urgent need and contradicts all the German official declarations, which pretend not to be inconvenienced by the Allied decision making cotton a contraband of war.

3. MARCONI WIRELESS NEWS - London, September 2nd.

    Dardanelles.

    A fine exploit by British submarines has been accomplished in the DARDANELLES. It is officially announced in PARIS that in addition to the transport sunk on August 20th by an aeroplane, there must now be added four torpedoed by British submarines; two at ACBASHILIMAN, and two between GALLIPOLI and NAGARA. The guns of the warships have sunk several vessels anchored in the STRAITS.

    French Front.

    The big artillery actions on the Western front continue. This is the eighth day of the attack of the big guns. In ARTOIS, ARGONNE, and the VOSGES, the French Official report says that tonight's fire was very efficacious and our batteries silenced the enemy.

    The French communique, reporting on the death of PEGOUD, says :-

    "In the course of a plucky fight on Tuesday morning over PETITE-CROIX, 2nd Lieutenant PEGOUD met with a glorious death. The aviator, who was alone in an aeroplane, made a daring attack on a German machine upon which he fired, emptying several belts of ammunition in his machine gun. He was himself hit by a bullet which killed him instantly, his machine falling to the ground within our lines."

    Russia.

    The latest news from PETROGRAD shews that 7,000 prisoners were captured by the Russians in their success on the GALICIAN front. Very little change is reported on the remainder of the front up to the BALTIC. The Germans are now attacking GRODNO.

    Germany's Submarine Policy.

    At the moment of the announcement that Germany intends to modify her submarine policy in accordance with the American demand, comes the news that Admiral Von TIRPITZ, the inspirer of the piracy

2.

policy is to take a long holiday owing to illness. It is known that for some time the German Chancellor has opposed the Chief Pirate's plan. It would appear that the Kaiser has come over to Von BETHMANN HOLLWEG'S view, hence Von TIRPITZ'S holiday.

South Africa.

General SMUTS, Minister of Defence, interviewed at JOHANNESBURG yesterday, said recruiting for the South African contingent would continue until the war was successfully ended.

3/9/15.

R.J. Ingham
Major, G.S.

1st Ln Coy R.E.

SUMMARY OF INFORMATION NO. 81.

4th September 1915.

1. OPERATIONS - September 3rd/4th.

   There has been no activity along the front during the last 24 hours; the weather has been too bad. The enemy opposite the centre portion of our line is reported to have at least as much water to compete with as we have. Near the CANAL the enemy appears only to have fired two trench mortar bombs. The French artillery added to the enemy's enjoyment by intermittent heavy shelling.

   The prisoner captured near the VERLORENHOEK ROAD on the night 2nd/3rd gave the following account of his experiences.

   He said he had started out with a patrol of three men under a N.C.O. It was very dark and raining. After they had gone a short way they lost the N.C.O., and soon after they found they were lost. After discussion, he disagreed with his two comrades as to the way back, and they separated, he going his way and they theirs. In a short time he suddenly came on the English trenches and was challenged but got away. Soon after he stumbled on our trenches again and was heavily fired on. This time he got two bullets through his coat, one through the trouser leg, just above the knee, and a fourth which just grazed his left arm, but he managed to get away, only to come on our trenches for a third time, when he gave himself up.

   On being questioned he stated that though his regiment had suffered heavy losses in April and May, they still had a good number of experienced officers left in whom they had confidence. Things were going well in Russia and everyone was certain of ultimate victory. The daily losses in the regiment are small, one or two men per company from shrapnel fire or snipers and that was all. By trade he was a commercial traveller, and apparently an admirer of the fair sex. He was not at all pleased to have been captured.

2. MARCONI WIRELESS NEWS - London, 3rd September.

   French Front.

   The PARIS Official wireless communique, received in the afternoon of the 3rd September, reports violent fighting in the VOSGES, as a result of which the enemy has recaptured some of his lost trenches on a front of 250 metres. The Germans pretended, says the bulletin, to have recaptured the line LINGEKPF - BAVENKOPF but as a matter of fact the French retain the bulk of their positions. The usual afternoon communique issued in PARIS today reports a continuance of artillery activity during which no notable incident occurred.

   Russia.

   GRODNO, having served its purpose in checking the enemy's advance as long as possible, has been abandoned by the Russians. The enemy have occupied both GRODNO and LIDA.

   In the North the Russian advance between the SVENTA and the VILIA continues and two villages have been carried at the point of the bayonet by Russian Cavalry, who drove the Germans back in disorder. Here, and on the right bank of the VILIA, captures of men and munitions have been made.

   In GALICIA the Russians have assumed a partial offensive at the mouth of the STRYPA, in which they have captured prisoners, maxims and a quantity of stores, and between the STRYIA and the BUG the enemy has again suffered heavily in rearguard actions.

Italy.

In the VAL SUGANA the enemy in their efforts to check the Italian advance on the FRENT are shelling DONCEGNE. ROVENETO is said, in an unofficial message, to have been evacuated.

On the CARSIC PLATEAU, further trenches containing arms and ammunition have been taken from the enemy.

ARRIVALS AND SAILINGS OF OVERSEA STEAMERS.

In the week ending Wednesday, it is officially announced the total arrivals and sailings of oversea steamers of over 300 tons of all nationalities to and from the United Kingdom Ports, was 1,353 and the number of merchant vessels sunk or captured was three with a gross tonnage of 6,757. No fishing vessels were sunk or captured.

The German "concessions" with regard to America are regarded here as arising from impotence and not humanity.

"Order Pour Le Merite".

According to the "KOELNISCHE ZEITUNG", the Kaiser has conferred the "Order Pour Le Merite" on ENVER PASHA, the Turkish Minister of War.

Balkans.

A SOFIA telegram states the Duke of MECKLENBERG, who has arrived there as a guest of the Royal Family, is accompanied by Doctor Von ROSENBERG, Reporter on Balkan Affairs to the German Ministry of Foreign Affairs. The Duke has had an interview with Monsieur RADOSLAVOFF, the Bulgarian Premier.

3. ASPHYXIATING GAS (From the "MATIN").

At SOKAL, Russian aviators dropped some bombs on the gas depot of the enemy. The gas spread round the depot and took the enemy by surprise. 26 Officers and 700 men were poisoned.

4. GERMAN LOSSES IN OFFICERS TO THE MIDDLE OF JULY 1915. (From French sources.)

Calculations based on the German Official Casualty Lists give the minimum number of losses. The figures given below include for each arm, Senior Officers, Lieutenants, and N.C.Os. acting as Officers.

	Killed.	Wounded.	Missing.	Prisoners.	Grand Total
Generals	53	77	2		132
Infantry	13,406	26,615	2,175		42,196
Cavalry	557	1,036	231		1,824
Artillery and Pioneers	1,484	3,401	131		5,016
Services	521	815	293		1,629
Prisoners				1,244	1,244
TOTALS	16,021	31,944	2,832	1,244	52,041
Totals to June 1st	13,805	26,827	2,349	993	43,972

4.9.15

SUMMARY OF INFORMATION NO 92.

5th September, 1915.

1. ### OPERATIONS - SEPTEMBER 4th/5th.

   If anything the enemy's artillery was rather more active than usual against our trenches, but a number of shells were apparently blind. Of 20 shells fired at BURNT FARM 12 never exploded.

   The enemy's infantry is as busily engaged as ours in repairing and draining their trenches. A patrol sent out North of WIELTJE Road last night encountered none of the enemy.

   The ARRAS Front. - It is reported that early on the morning of September 3rd several parties of the enemy were stopped by our machine gun fire when moving along the road. In the case of one party of 8 men only 2 got up and ran into a wood; the remainder were apparently wounded. On this portion of the front it is reported that early one morning one of our sentry posts was startled to find that he overlooked a considerable extent of the enemy's trench which was apparently being much used at that time. After the occurrence had been reported to an officer, and when all the available accommodation had been taken up, a machine gun was turned on with considerable effect. The enemy were caught with their trousers down.

2. ### MARCONI WIRELESS PRESS.

   LONDON - SEPTEMBER 4th - Particularly violent fighting is again announced in to-night's French communique. The explosion of several mines has further seriously damaged enemy works. The Communique deals with Germany's difficulties regarding new effectives. It is shown that the enemy is in a serious position. In one period of six weeks the officer casualties amounted to the huge total of somewhat over 8,000.

   RUSSIA - A more hopeful feeling now prevails in Russia, there being no noticeable relaxation of the tension on the front. The morale of the Russians is unimpaired while the enemy is apparently much exhausted. Russia's latest report on the evacuation of GRODNO says that a furious conflict raged in the Northern and Western suburbs. The fact that Berlin claims only 40% prisoners shows how skilfully the Russian withdrawal was conducted. There is further activity on the flanks. On the DWINA in the North the Germans claim to have captured a fortified bridgehead about 30 miles from RIGA, while in the South Russia admits a further retreat in Galicia. The latter, however, was evidently carried out to conform with the retirement further North in the direction of HUTZK. Here VIENNA states the Russians are now making a stand along the whole front.

   BALKANS - A Rome telegram states that SERBIA and ROUMANIA are concentrating considerable forces along the route which would have to be taken by German armies in order to join hands with the Turks. 150,000 Roumanians are said to be concentrated at SEVERIN, near the junction of the AUSTRIAN, SERBIAN and ROUMANIAN frontiers.

   GENERAL - The Central Powers are again manoeuvring for favourable peace terms having let it be known what their terms are, and have sought to bring both the United States and the Vatican into the new move. It was with object partly that the "Concession" was made to Washington over the submarine piracy. Doctor Wilson, however, refuses to be made a catspaw, and has made it known there can be no question of intervening with the object of closing hostilities as the Allies are determined to go on. Commenting hereon the New York Sun says, "We take it no one who reads the signs of the times can any longer doubt the Kaiser and his ministers are pulling all wires within reach

P.T.O.

2.

to end the conflict which, however brilliant in some exterior manifestations has already brought desolation and disaster upon Germany, and threatens total ruin if continued". The New York World says, "When Germany is ready to talk peace seriously and talks that kind of peace which will not only render justice to the wronged but will guarantee civilisation against the moloch of Militarism, the Government and people of the United States will immediately respond".

A raiding party has been landed for the first time from a submarine. The incident occurred in the ISMIA GULF in the Sea of MARMORA, British seamen being sent ashore to blow up a bridge. The undertaking did not quite succeed, however, the bridge being only partially destroyed.

3. FROM FRENCH OFFICIAL COMMUNIQUE.

German losses on the Eastern Front. (G.H.Q. 4th Sept.)

We learn from the official lists that the Guard Corps has suffered the following losses between May 15th and August 31st:-

Regiment	Officers	Men
1st Foot Guard Regt.	53 officers	3,005 men.
2nd -do-	33	1,209
3rd -do-	17	2,116
4th -do-	30	1,609
5th -do-	29	1,254
1st Grenadier Guards Regt.	96	2,823
2nd -do-	55	2,588
3rd -do-	63	2,732
4th -do-	75	2,414
5th -do-	24	950
1st Reserve Guards Regt.	40	1,681
2nd -do-	24	1,108
TOTALS.	539 officers	23,690 men.

Extract from a letter written by the chaplain of a German ambulance in Russia (B.R. of VI Army).

14th Aug., 1915.

It is true that our victorious war in Russia is costing us frightful sacrifices. This is much brought home to us at our ambulance as well as among the member of our faith. But it cannot be otherwise, and a great success requires a great sacrifice. May God will it that the war does not last too long.

B.J. Ingham.
Major, G.S.

5/9/15.

SUMMARY OF INFORMATION NO 93.

6th September, 1915.

1. OPERATIONS.

    Yesterday evening a hostile aeroplane was persuaded by means of rifle and machine gun fire to abandon his usual tactics of patrolling up and down the line. The enemy were seen baling and rebuilding their parapet; one of their number was shot in the performance of his duties.

2. FRENCH BULLETIN.

    In the North we carried out a bombardment to demolish the Fortin of HET SAS. The enemy replied on our first line.
    On the night of the 3rd/4th there was an intermittent bombardment to the S.E. of the Bois CARRÉ, which became rather violent in the ROCLINCOURT - CHANTECLER sector. There was great artillery activity in the region of BRETENCOURT.
    During the 4th there was an intermittent bombardment of the FOSSE CALONNE BULLY - GRENAY near SOUCHEZ, and shells of all calibres and aerial torpedoes in the NEUVILLE and ROCLINCOURT sectors.

3. MARCONI WIRELESS PRESS.

    RUSSIA. - The latest communique from PETROGRAD plainly confirms the view that the situation in the East has markedly improved. The mass of the German army probably lies between GRODNO and KOBRIN sector which roughly forms the centre of the front. In this region the German advance continues slowly, and its immediate objective is not very clear. On the extreme North we find the Russians were able to cross to the left bank of the DWINA near the village of LINDEN, and drove the enemy from the river bank. On the DWINA and at FRIEDRICHSTADT the Germans gained ground and the railway to JACOBSTADT is threatened.

    FRENCH FRONT. - The great artillery bombardment which the Allies have been pouring upon the enemy for 11 days has not yet given place to fighting at close quarters.

    TURKEY. - A despatch from SALONICA to the Echo de Paris states; "Lack of munitions is being felt in Turkey. Old stocks are beginning to be depleted. Coal and metals are also lacking, and very often munitions factory chimneys give out no smoke for several days".

    GENERAL. - According to a telegram from Queenstown the Allan liner Hesperian was attacked last night by a German submarine. She was carrying between six and seven hundred passengers, and happily the enemy's missile failed. The Hesperian remained afloat and presumably in response to signals of distress, assistance was sent and reached her in good time.

4. EXTRACTS FROM A LETTER FROM ONE OF THE OFFICERS OF THE E 13.

                                    C/o The British Legation,
                                         Copenhagen.

    What a disastrous ending to our trip, but I am glad to say we are all well.
    We went ashore on Wednesday night with only about 6 miles more of

P.T.O.

2.

the tricky channel to go through, and nothing on earth could get her off. In the morning a Danish torpedo-boat came to us and took me back to their guardship. At the same time a German destroyer arrived on the scene, but as we were in neutral water he could not touch us, so he lay quite close and jeered, and told them (I had gone to the guardship by this time) to look pretty as he was going to take their photographs, and then he said: "There are plenty of Germans where you are going to". Then he steamed away and came back later with another destroyer. When she was some way away she hoisted a signal which we could not read and then suddenly fired a torpedo, which missed, and hit the bottom and blew up. Then she opened fire with every gun she had, and L --- gave the order to get into the water as the boat was on fire from the 1st shell. Then these beasts started firing at our men in the water with machine guns (Maxims) and also with shrapnel, but thank God their shooting was bad, and only 6 men were hit one of them being our cook, but they managed to get him ashore. Besides the five shot ten more were drowned as they were all in their clothes and the water is nearly fresh water so they could not float when they were tired. The Danes were very good and did everything they could for us, besides picking up the remainder of the crew in their boats.

I had to watch all this coming back from the guard ship, and it -- well, I can't describe it, but seeing all my own men in the water absolutely defenceless, and the hail of shot all round them - perhaps you can imagine what I felt like. My one prayer now is that we are not interned and that I may go straight to another boat, and I shan't be satisfied till I have sunk a German.

We have spent the last two days in a Danish battleship, and their kindness to us all has been too wonderful for words. They have reclothed us in all their best and have been so nice to us

The only thing that makes me feel most happy is, that after the Germans had finished battering our boat the White Ensign was still flying at the masthead, and in the afternoon I went over to the dear old boat and hauled it down with my own hands, and now it is in my possession hanging along the wall beside my bed; it is riddled with small shrapnel and maxim holes, but quite intact.

Hobbes.
Lieut.

6/9/15.   Major, G.S.

7th September 1915.

1. OPERATIONS.

Yesterday evening the enemy were very busy baling their trenches after the recent rains, and repairing the parapet. Enemy working parties were much worried by our fire.

At 10.35 this morning it was reported that three German aeroplanes were continually patrolling up and down over the enemy's lines.

At 12 o'clock it was reported that a German aeroplane had been brought down by a British aeroplane. The German machine fell within the enemy's lines about C.7.d.

2. FRENCH OFFICIAL COMMUNIQUE.

Northern region. Our artillery caused a magazine explosion in the German lines.

An Albatross in good condition has come down at PARIS, the aviators being made prisoners.

3. MARCONI WIRELESS NEWS: London, September 6th.

The torpedoing of the "HESPERIAN".

It is officially announced that the Allan liner "HESPERIAN", torpedoed off the South of Ireland on Saturday night, sank this morning while returning to QUEENSTOWN. It is feared that some lives were lost. Three thousand sacks of mails went down. Official America is waiting for a full report.

German Submarine Losses.

A letter from the Rt. Hon. A.J. BALFOUR, First Lord of the Admiralty, to the Press, states : "Whilst the losses inflicted on German submarines have been formidable, the British mercantile tonnage is at this moment greater than when the war started."

Russia.

In the Eastern theatre of war the Russians admit German success on the river DWINA in the region of FRIEDRICHSTADT, South East of RIGA. The Russians were compelled to recross the river near LINDEN owing to the bridges being set on fire by the German artillery. This exposes the Russian communications with RIGA, which is in danger of being cut off.

In the retreat from GRODNO the Russians have eluded the attempt of the enemy to encircle their forces.

On the rest of the front the Russians are delivering strong counter-attacks, particularly against the Austrians in GALICIA.

Details have been received today of a successful naval action in the BLACK SEA, when Russian destroyers attacked cruiser "HAMIDIEH" and two torpedo boats and put them to flight, after damaging the cruiser.

Balkans.

The moment for final decision on the part of BULGARIA is rapidly approaching. This is supported by a statement from GENEVA that ROUMANIA has called men from SWITZERLAND, ordering them to join their regiments.

French Front.

The latest French communique announces continued bombardment with artillery of all calibres in the war zones North and South of ARRAS.

Four German aeroplanes bombed the open town of LUNEVILLE causing unfortunately many casualties amongst the civilians, many being women and children. In retaliation for this forty of our aeroplanes bombarded the military depot of SARREBRUCK, doing much damage.

4. **THE GERMAN 16½" GUNS.** (From the "TIMES", September 6th.)

The "TELEGRAAF" learns the following details concerning the 42 cm. guns of the German artillery :-

200 men are necessary for each gun and the mounting takes 25 to 26 hours, as every gun is composed of 172 parts. The complete gun weighs about 87 tons and the foundation plate nearly 37 tons. 12 railway wagons are necessary for the transport of one single gun. The gun is electrically fired from a distance of 300 yards. The projectile weighs about 880 lbs., and is 1.63 metres long. Each shot costs 11,000 Marks (£550).

The range of the guns may be estimated from the fact that the Forts of LIEGE were destroyed from a distance of 22.8 kilometres (about 14 miles).

5. **EXTRACT FROM A LETTER OF AN OFFICER FIGHTING IN EAST AFRICA.**

28th May 1915.

..............Our difficulties out here are enormous. Never before has civilised war been attempted in the tropics of Africa, and it has yet to be proved feasible. Desert, water, health and transport are our main difficulties, the latter being of every conceivable form, including donkeys, mules, camels, cattle, ponies, motors, railway, tramway, road push-carts, ox-wagons, porters, and sometimes none at all.

Wild beasts are a great nuisance to us. Several of the men have already been caught bending by lions and rhinos. One of our patrols was held up by a splendid elephant which was eventually shot. On the Victoria Nyanza it is no uncommon occurrence to have all the mules stampeded by some hungry hippopotamus roaming the lines by moonlight in search of grain and hay. The mules wake up and clear out, the hippo throws a fit and goes off squealing and carrying all before him, plunging into the water festooned with tents, barbed wire, and all the latrine accommodation of the camp.

The Germans are behaving none too well out here in Africa and we are getting our slice of frightfulness. The behaviour to natives is cruel in the extreme. They got a native guide near the railway the other day and tied a rope round his waist so tight that his entrails came out of his anus; he died. There is also a white woman with the Germans, the wife of one of their officers who accompanies their patrols and commits every atrocity unchecked. Her latest effort was to shoot one of our officers who fell wounded into her hands, and whilst he was held down by niggers she mutilated him. We hope to catch her one of these days when God help her!

7/9/15.

Major, G.S.

-:6th DIVISION:-

NEWS SHEET.

LONDON. September 8th.

The full official statement regarding last night's air raid issued this afternoon and published in full shows that three Zeppelins were concerned. Fifty-six casualties are reported, ten deaths, twenty seriously hurt, twenty-three slightly hurt, and three missing, the latter are believed to have been buried beneath the debris. Of the killed no fewer than eight were women and children, while thirty women and children were amongst the injured and two women included in the missing. The toll of the feebler sex and the little ones should surely satisfy the Huns. Though 15 small dwelling-houses were demolished and some fires were caused, the material damage did not extend beyond this, and obviously has no military significance whatever.

This afternoon's communique from FRANCE reports, that last night was marked by a general artillery action on the Western front with particularly lively engagements in the region of YPRES and in the ARGONNE. Another big raid also has been carried out by the FRENCH, a squadron of aeroplanes attacking the railway station at ST. MEDARD on which 60 shells were dropped. In addition to providing further details of the fighting on the Western front, the FRENCH communique, as received by Reuter, says, that the railway station attacked by FRENCH airmen was that of DIEUZE and that the objective at ST. MEDARD was an aviation camp.

Acting in co-operation with BRITISH Naval airmen, FRENCH machines also bombarded aviation camp at OSTEND.

Official reports from the Eastern front suggest that the temporary lull has been succeeded by some stiff fighting in which, generally speaking, the GERMAN attack was repulsed by the RUSSIANS.

At COPENHAGEN a telegram says that a message from BERLIN reports that the Autumn floods have already started along the Eastern front and that the German advance has received a check, which is impossible for them to overcome.

The CZAR having assumed supreme command of all the forces, has issued an order which says that, "With unshakable assurance in final victory, we shall fulfil our sacred duty to defend our country to the last"

Yesterday's official communique from ROME states that the ITALIAN troops repulsed with heavy losses to the enemy an attack on the slopes of MONTENERO. In the LEDRO valley on Sunday one of the ITALIAN detachments made a surprise attack on a sawmill and on the electric power station at LENZUMO destroying both.

According to a report from ATHENS, a BRITISH submarine operating in the Sea of MARMORA has sunk a TURKISH Transport carrying 11 inch guns to GALLIPOLI. Another message indicates that the TURKS are short of guns in the PENINSULA, so that a loss of this kind may have some serious consequences for them than the sinking of an ordinary supply ship.

Monsieur CRUPPI, Minister of Finance, recently arrived at BUCHAREST from PETROGRAD and spoke enthusiastically of the way in which RUSSIA is developing her prodigious resources for dealing with teutonic invaders who will be utterly unable to maintain themselves during the coming winter. CZAR in course of personal interview assured him of RUSSIAS determination to continue fighting till victory is more fixed than ever.

The recent TURKISH boasts concerning successes constitute as usual an inevitable prelude to the news of the ALLIES successes, concerning which reports are arriving from ROME.

The ITALIAN newspapers unanimously hail enthusiastically the visit of General JOFFRE in his mission for increasing co-ordination of operations. General JOFFRE returned to PARIS yesterday and thence addresses a congratulatory telegram to General CADORNA.

9-8-15. A.B.LAWSON. Major, G.S. 6th Division.

1st London Coy R E

981

SUMMARY OF INFORMATION, NO. 95.

8TH September 1915.

1. OPERATIONS.

Two enemy snipers were bagged yesterday evening. One was in some bushes in front of the German trenches and was silenced by a burst of rapid fire, and the other was up a tree and was shot at and seen to fall.

2. FRENCH OFFICIAL COMMUNIQUE.

Some of the English Fleet bombarded the coast between WESTENDE and OSTEND in the night and early hours of the morning. The Germans bombarded our lines at POLDER in reply but were silenced. They also bombarded the YSER to the South of DIXMUDE, the YPERLEE and YPRES.
Heavy bombardment by the Germans in the sector ROCLINCOURT - CHANTECLER and NEUVILLE.

3. RUSSIAN OFFICIAL COMMUNIQUE.

On the NIEMEN the Germans attempted an offensive. The fighting continues.
South of PELEKSIE the enemy continues to concentrate his main effort for the roads from LOUTZK towards DOUBNO ROVNO, where the general situation remains unchanged.
Near MARBINE we made prisoners 8 officers and 300 men and on the SERETH we took four machine guns and 400 men.

4. MARCONI WIRELESS NEWS - London, September 7th.

Balkans.

A message from ATHENS states that the Turkish torpedo boat destroyer "CARHISSAR", an eight year old boat of considerable value as a scout having regard to her speed of twenty-eight knots, has been sunk in the SEA OF MARMORA by one of the Allies submarines.

Sinking of the "HESPERIAN".

It is now known that 25 persons are missing from the "HESPERIAN", while the body of a lady cabin passenger has been recovered.

New Type of German Aeroplane.

News, via COPENHAGEN, states that the Germans are now experimenting with giant aeroplanes intended to supersede Zeppelins. The machines are biplanes measuring 140 feet across the wing and propelled by a 300 horse power motor with a capacity for carrying eight hours supply of petrol, and expected to suffice for a journey to LONDON and back of five hours.

Persia.

German agencies have lavished money and arms upon every disaffected region of WESTERN PERSIA and there is serious danger of anarchy.

German Submarine.

The German Admiralty admits that U.27 has not returned and must be regarded as lost.

5. ACCOUNT RECEIVED OF OPERATIONS AT BUKOBA ON THE VICTORIA NYANZA -

JUNE 23RD.

It was decided some time back to despatch a combined naval and military expedition to destroy the enemy's base at BUKOBA on the VICTORIA NYANZA. The bulk of our forces, including our mountain guns, were landed about three miles north of BUKOBA at dawn on the 22nd. The landing party then proceeded to clear KARWAZI HILL, assisted by our ships' guns. Meanwhile the enemy's gun had opened fire on H.M.S. "NYANZA" but failed to score a hit. Ships' guns forced the enemy to remove it to another prepared position. At 9 a.m. the enemy's gun again opened fire on H.M.S. "WINIFRED", making very accurate shooting at about 5,000 yards, but again we were fortunate in not actually being hit, though one shell fell but a few yards from the ship. Our landing party had now worked round to a hill about two miles from the town and was faced by the enemy's main position and by noon the whole of our force was heavily engaged with the enemy whose well-concealed machine-guns and sharp-shooters held us up for some considerable time. The enemy's gun again opened on our mountain guns from the northern exit of BUKOBA, but was soon driven to take up a new position at the Protestant Mission to the south of the town, where its great distance made it comparatively harmless. At 3 p.m. the fight was at its hottest, but we gradually gained superiority of fire. The enemy behaved with the utmost gallantry under the heaviest fire and endeavoured to remove one of their machine-guns, which was prevented by the splendid practice of our guns, who sent shell after shell among the gun detachment, finally smashing it up completely. The enemy's artillery made one last effort, but in vain, for darkness finally put a stop to all resistance.

At daylight BUKOBA was at our feet, some two miles distant. The fight was opened by the enemy making an attack on our right centre, closely supported by machine-gun fire, which gave us considerable trouble till our guns silenced it. About 11 a.m. the enemy attempted to withdraw their gun, but this was soon checked by our artillery and a direct hit from one of our mountain guns forced the enemy to abandon the attempt. We recovered it later and brought it aboard our convoy but in the rough weather experienced on the lake it slipped overboard. By 12.30 p.m. the enemy commenced to retire and the Royal North Lancs. entered the town from the West. The German flag over the fort was hauled down by an officer of the Royal Fusiliers at about 1.20 p.m. and the hoisting of the Union Jack announced to all that BUKOBA had fallen. The enemy's verified casualties were 16 killed and 29 wounded, but they are in all probability considerably higher. Our losses were much less than the enemy's and our loss in material was nil.

6. GERMAN AEROPLANE AT CALAIS.

The two German aviators who came down yesterday at CALAIS as was thought from lack of petrol, on examination proved to have come down at CALAIS thinking it was OSTEND, inasmuch as nobody fired at them.

Major, G.S.

8/9/15.

SUMMARY OF INFORMATION NO. 96.

9th September 1915.

1. **OPERATIONS.**

    Yesterday morning when the mist lifted a party of Germans were seen walking in front of their parapet and at least two of them were picked off.
    A Toby shell was put into HAMPSHIRE FARM on the night of the 7th/8th September, which is thought to have destroyed a bomb store, as a dense cloud of smoke was seen.
    Last night, rather more hostile shelling than usual in some sectors, but no damage.

2. **FRENCH OFFICIAL COMMUNIQUE.**

    Constant heavy bombardment in ARRAS sector, near ROYE, between the OISE and the AISNE and in the CHAMPAGNE. In the Western ARGONNE, after an intense bombardment, the Germans delivered an attack with two Divisions which gained a footing at some points in our trenches. Their new attempt at breaking our line was brought to a standstill by violent counter-attacks. As a reply to the bombardment of NANCY, a French squadron bombed the military depot at FRESCATY and the station DES SABLONS at METZ.

3. **RUSSIAN OFFICIAL COMMUNIQUE.**

    No change at RIGA. Attacks were repulsed South of FRIEDRICHSTADT and between the NIEMEN and WILIA. There have been some heavy rear guard fighting near WOLKOWYSK. Our Cavalry charged near WOLOCKKI and captured three officers and 150 men. Near TARNOPOL we held up the enemy's attempted advance.

4. **MARCONI WIRELESS NEWS - London, September 8th.**

    German Air Raid on England.

    The Official Statement regarding last night's air raid, shows that three Zeppelins were concerned. Fifty-six casualties are reported, ten deaths, thirty seriously hurt, twenty-three slightly hurt, and three missing. The latter are believed to have been buried beneath the debris. Of the killed no fewer than eight were women and children, while thirty women and children were included in the missing.

    French Air Raids.

    Another big raid has been carried out by a French squadron of aeroplanes, attacking the Railway Station of ST. MEDARD, on which sixty shells were dropped.
    Acting in co-operation with British Naval airmen, French machines also bombarded the Aviation Camp at OSTEND.

    Russia.

    A COPENHAGEN telegram says that a message from BERLIN reports that the autumn floods have already started along the Eastern front and that the German advance has received a check which it is impossible for them to overcome.

Italy.

Yesterday's Official Communique from ROME states that the Italian troops repulsed an attack, with heavy losses, on the slopes of MONTE MERO. In the LEFRO VALLEY on Sunday one of the Italian detachments made a surprise attack on a sawmill and on the electric power station at LENZURNO, destroying both.

Turkish Transport Sunk.

According to a report from ATHENS, a British submarine operating in the SEA OF MARMORA, has sunk a Turkish Transport carrying 11-inch guns to GALLIPOLI. Another message indicates that the Turks are short of guns in the Peninsula, so that a loss of this kind may have more serious consequences for them than the sinking of an ordinary supply ship.

Balkans.

The recent Turkish boasts concerning successes at ANAFARTA constitute as usual the prelude to the news of Allies successes, of which reports are arriving from ROME.

5. **GERMAN CASUALTIES.**

The German Official Casualty lists show the following losses :-

Western Front.	XIV Corps	...	47,515 men
	VIII "	...	42,172 "
	XVI "	...	41,209 "
Eastern Front.	I Corps..	...	43,466 "
	I Reserve Corps		41,684 "
Corps which have fought on both fronts.	II Corps	...	43,466 "
	Guard Corps	...	42,022 "
	XXI Corps	...	40,804 "

A German Corps at full strength, all ranks, has a total of 44,000 men.

Major, G.S.

9/9/15.

6th DIVISION.

NEWS SHEET.

LONDON. September 9th. Midnight.

The air raid on Tuesday night on the Eastern Counties in which 10 people were killed and 46 injured (23 slightly) was followed by another air raid last night. In last night's air raid the total casualties reported from all sources is 106, of whom 20 are killed, 14 seriously injured and 72 slightly injured. There were 8 women and children killed, and 40 women and children injured. One soldier was killed and three injured. There have now been 19 air raids in England since the war began, and over 300 women and children have been murdered as the result of these raids, which have never had the slightest military significance.

Following upon the sustained attack yesterday morning, an attack which was prepared for by an intense bombardment of asphyxiating shells, delivered by the Germans last night in fresh assault in ARGONNE, says this afternoon's wireless communique. The attack, which was made with great violence, was repulsed, Germans suffering considerable losses.

French airmen continue to show much activity. Their latest achievement being an attack made on CHALLERANG Railway station, fifty bombs being dropped.

In GALICIA near TARNOPOL the Russians have achieved great success capturing about 8000 men, 30 guns and other booty.
Only the impossibility of replying with the same weight of metal prevented them from developing further the success. From GRODNO stubborn German attacks continue in the region of railway station of DRONSKENIKI and towards SKIDEL. In the latter direction Russians have inflicted great losses on the enemy, and have taken scores of prisoners.

A vigorous offensive by Italian troops from the MONT CROCE Pass to CONELICO resulted, says the latest official communique from Rome, in several hostile positions being occupied and trenches seized. Unhappily, defensive organisation of the enemy in naturally formidable position necessitated suspension of offensive movement. Enemy made determined attack on Italian position on MONT MARONIA, but the position still remains in the possession of our Allies.

Report from GALLIPOLI Peninsula - via MITYLENE, speaks of progress on SUVLA front, the sector in KINCH new landing was made.

The perjurer STAHL (?) has confessed that he wilfully endeavoured to mislead United States officials by declaring, in affidavit, that he saw four guns on Lusitania. Sentence will be passed upon him today.

TRADES UNION CONGRESS at Bristol, representing the whole of British Organised Labour, debated yesterday and in practically unanimous agreement (600 in favour, 7 against) passed resolution in following terms:- "That this Congress from first to last opposed systems of Militarism as dangerous to human progress. Considers present action of Great Britain and Allies, Expresses horror at atrocities committed by German and Austrian Military Authorities, and hereby pledges itself to assist the Government, as far as possible, in the successful prosecution of the war.

completely justified.

SUMMARY OF INFORMATION NO 97.

10th September, 1915.

1. OPERATIONS.

Yesterday evening considerable hostile bombing and shelling of our trenches took place. Three attempts by a large hostile aeroplane to fly over our trenches were stopped by rifle fire.
YPRES was constantly shelled in the afternoon.

This morning some sectors of our trenches were heavily shelled and there was much rifle fire.

2. FRENCH OFFICIAL COMMUNIQUE.

The artillery combat around ARRAS continues, in the ROYE district and on the CHAMPAGNE front. In the ARGONNE the enemy attacks were not renewed. The day was marked by a violent artillery duel.
The bombardment was also very heavy in the WOEVRE at BOIS HAUT, in the FORET d'APREMONT, and in the BOIS de MORTMERE.

3. RUSSIAN OFFICIAL COMMUNIQUE.

In the region of NOVZ-TROKI the Germans violently bombarded with asphyxiating gas shells the exits from the lakes occupied by our troops. There were obstinate German attacks towards SKUDEL which we repulsed with heavy losses to the enemy, taking scores of prisoners.
In GALICIA, near TARNOPOL, we gained a great success over the Germans. We learned from prisoners that two German Divisions, assisted by an Austrian Brigade and numerous heavy and light artillery, were preparing to deliver a decisive attack on the night of the 8th September. Forestalling this blow our troops took the offensive and after a fierce attack on the DOLJOUKA on the 7th, the Germans were completely routed. At the end of the fight the enemy commenced an extraordinarily intense bombardment. Not being able to reply with the same energy, we had to content ourselves with the successes gained without attempting to enlarge them.
Besides numerous losses in killed and wounded, the Germans left in our hands more than 200 officers and 8,000 men. We took 30 guns (14 of which were heavies) many machine guns and limbers, and spoils of war. After a short pursuit our troops returned to their original positions on the SERETH. Further to the South in the region of TREMBOUL we made prisoners, more than 40 officers and 2,500 men, with three guns and ten machine guns. Between the DNIESTER and the right bank of the lower SERETH the Austrians took the offensive. Thanks to an attack on the flank, however, by one of our battalions, the enemy were held up and we made prisoners eleven officers and more than 100 men, with machine guns.

4. MARCONI WIRELESS PRESS. - LONDON, 9th September.

Zeppelin Air-raid. - The air raid on Tuesday night in which 10 people were killed and 46 injured was followed by another raid last night. In last night's air-raid, the total casualties reported from all sources were 106, of whom 20 were killed, 14 seriously injured, and 72 slightly injured. There were 8 women and children killed and 40 women and children injured. One soldier was killed and three injured.
There have now been 19 air raids on England since the war began, and over 300 women and children have been murdered as a result. These raids have never had the slightest military significance.

P.T.O.

2.

FRANCE - The Germans last night delivered a fresh assault in the ARGONNE. The attack, which was made with great violence, was repulsed, the Germans suffering considerable losses.

French airmen continue to show much activity, and their latest achievment is an attack on the railway station of CHALLERANGE, 50 bombs being dropped.

ITALY - A vigorous Italian offensive from the MONTE ROSA pass to CONELIC resulted in several hostile positions being occupied and trenches seized, says the latest Official Communique from ROME.

DARDANELLES - A report from the Gallipoli Peninsula speaks of progress on the SUVLA front, the sector in which the new landing was made.

GUNS ON THE LUSITANIA - The perjurer STAHL has confessed that he wilfully endeavoured to mislead United States officials by declaring in affidavit that he saw four guns on the Lusitania, and sentence upon him will be passed to-day.

AIRSHIPS OVER HOLLAND - News from ROTTERDAM states that three airships yesterday performed inexplicable evolutions over Dutch territory, one flying low over the forts on the outskirts of AMSTERDAM.

5. GERMAN PRESS.

The HAMBURGER NEUESTE NACHRICHTEN expresses sincere satisfaction over the sinking of the HESPERIAN. "The entire German people" it says "partake in this satisfaction".

The paper abstains from giving reasons for the sinking of the boat, but it expresses its regrets over the loss of the submarine 27 which was, it says, "the victim of an English crime".

"England", cries this journal, "is silent about the submarine 27! Where is the 27 ? There stands an example of criminal English conduct, a crime of the English fleet, mistress of the seas: or is it perhaps that the 27 was sunk by the ARABIC ?

W. Lyples.
Lieut.
for Major, G.S.

10/9/15.

6th DIVISION.

NEWS SHEET.

LONDON. September 10th, midnight.(by wireless).

It is officially announced today that President WILSON has asked the Austrian Government to recall the Austrian Ambassador at WASHINGTON, as he has admitted that he proposed to his Government to instigate strikes in American factories engaged in making war munitions. It is possible that the German Military Attache may also be recalled.

The Russian victory in the Southern end of the Eastern front assumed greater importance today, and the success at TARNOPOL has been followed by another at TREMBOVLI. Over 17.000 prisoners have been taken, which must mean that two Army Corps have been routed.

It is officially announced today by the British Government that an enemy spy has been tried by court-martial in LONDON, and shot.

Private reports from BERLIN indicate that both Admiral TIRPITZ and Admiral BEHNKE, Chief of the Headquarter Staff, have left their posts.

A Zeppelin has met with an accident near BRUSSELS, and been destroyed. The crew have been killed.

News from the BALKANS indicates the possibility of a conference of all the BALKAN STATES.

Mr. Lloyd George's speech today, at the Trades Union Congress, has created a great impression in ENGLAND and FRANCE, and the help given by the Labour Party to the Government in recruiting has been endorsed by the Congress by a large majority.

Official Press Bureau message this afternoon, says, that since the casualities caused by Zeppelins on the night of Tuesday, the 7th, were published, the bodies of three persons who were missing have been recovered, and four of the persons who were seriously injured have died.
The total number of deaths due to the attack on the 7th are therefore 17, - 5 men, 6 women, and 6 children.

Speech of Lloyd George at National Congress of Trades Unions couched in terms of candid friendship, and delivered with all the fire of his best style. The most important points were:- Firstly, that in this war the role of workers is of paramount importance. Secondly, that Government has set up 16 national arsenals and are constructing 11 more. In order to run the latter they require 80.000 additional skilled men and 200.000 unskilled men and women. Thirdly, he called upon Trades Unions to relax ordinary regulations, and allow mixing of skilled and unskilled labour. Fourthly, that Government have established direct control over 716 establishments, and restricted war profits in all as promised at the previous Treasury Conference. Fifthly, restriction of output must be removed.

2.

Regarding last point Lloyd George definite incidences, and created deep impression. He answered many questions and completely carried Conference with him.

Attention is still directed towards BALKAN STATES and a message from SALONIKA comes through GENEVA, announcing that VENEZELOS has been successful in getting the GREEK, ROUMANIAN, SERVIAN, and BULGARIAN Governments to agree to a conference, to take place shortly at SALONIKA. Conference will be attended by the 4 Premiers and a number of Military Attachés.

News via COPENHAGEN announces that German political circles discuss with lively interest the BULGARIAN Minister's visit to NISH.

Conflicting statements issued from PARIS and BERLIN yesterday concerning fighting in the ARGONNE. German claims of 1.999 prisoners palpably absurd from meticulous exactitude of statistics.
In such instances the advice of the WOLFF BUREAU should probably be followed and figures divided by ten.

A.B.LAWSON, Major,

General Staff.

SUMMARY OF INFORMATION NO. 98.

11th September 1915.

1. OPERATIONS, September 10th/11th.

During the day five of the enemy's steel loopholes were destroyed with a heavy rifle near BELLEWAARDE FARM. Our trenches near CROSS ROADS FARM were very heavily shelled for a quarter of an hour on the morning of the 10th, principally by field guns. The bombardment was followed by heavy rifle fire for five minutes and then by an even more intense bombardment by field guns, which lasted twenty minutes. Our trenches and parapets were damaged but considering the violence of the bombardment the number of casualties was small. Our trenches near WIELTJE were also heavily shelled by field guns and trench mortars and some damage was done to the parapets of the trenches.

The night was quiet on the whole front. An enemy working party was dispersed near the CANAL by machine gun fire at about 9 o'clock.

2. FRENCH OFFICIAL COMMUNIQUE.

In the VOSGES the Germans yesterday attacked the French positions from the LINGEKOPF to the BARRENKOPF, using asphyxiating shells. At the SCHRATZMAENNELE one of the French front line trenches was evacuated on account of the use of flame jets by the enemy. A counter-attack enabled the larger part of the lost ground to be regained.

On the HARTMANNSWEILLERKOPF the French, during a night attack, recaptured the trenches which had been lost.

In the ARGONNE the army of the Crown Prince, which made two attacks with the assistance of asphyxiating shells, have been unable to continue the action. The German despatches announcing the capture of a certain number of prisoners and material, contained fantastic figures. Moreover, there is no mention of the German losses which have been considerable and which are not compensated for by any appreciable gain. For a year the Crown Prince's army has made attack after attack in the ARGONNE and has lost more than 100,000 men without securing a single point of importance.

3. MARCONI WIRELESS NEWS - London, 10th September.

United States.

It is officially announced today that President WILSON has asked the Austrian Government to recall their Ambassador at WASHINGTON, as he had admitted that he proposed to his Government to instigate strikes in American factories engaged in making war munitions. It is possible that the German Military Attache may also be recalled.

Russia.

The Russian victory in the Southern end of the Eastern front assumes greater importance today and the success at TARNOPOL has been followed by another at TREMBOVALA. Over 17,000 prisoners have been taken which must mean that two Army Corps have been routed.

England.

It is officially announced today that an enemy spy has been tried by Court Martial in London and shot.

Mr. LLOYD GEORGE'S speech at the Trades Union Congress has

2.

created a great impression in England and France and the help given by the Labour Party to the Government has been endorsed by the Congress by a huge majority.

Germany.

Private reports from BERLIN indicates that both Admiral TIRPITZ and Admiral BEHNKE, Chief of the Naval Headquarters Staff, have left their posts.
A Zeppelin has met with an accident near BRUSSELS and been destroyed. The crew have been killed.

Balkans.

Attention is still directed towards the BALKAN STATES and a message from SALONIKA, through GENEVA, announces that VENEZELOS has been successful in getting the GREEK, ROUMANIAN, SERVIAN, and BULGARIAN Governments to agree to a Conference to take place shortly at SALONIKA. The Conference will be attended by the four Premiers and a number of Military Attaches.
News via COPENHAGEN announces that German political circles discuss with lively interest the BULGARIAN Minister's surprise visit to NISH.

B/ Bingham.
Major, G.S.

11/9/15.

6th Division.

NEWS SHEET (BY WIRELESS).

LONDON. September 12th.

Once again GENERAL IVANHOFF, the brilliant General who throughout the past terrible month has contested so admirably the German advance in Southern GALICIA, has scored substantial success. In the communique issued at PETROGRAD last night, we are told that the earlier Russian victory at TARNOPOL has been repeated. The CZAR's troops broke down the German resistance, capturing more than two thousand prisoners and a number of quick-firing guns. The Germans have now lost to General IVANHOFF, within the last couple of weeks, something like the strength of an Army Corps. The enemy is in a position in which he certainly cannot afford to lose troops on such a scale. He is committed to an enterprise of stupendous magnitude. Even if his resources in men are far greater than we know them to be, still every soldier would be needed for the task that lies ahead. Tremendous as are the achievements of the German arms in the East, the obvious fact is that nothing decisive has been accomplished, and that steps by which decision can be sought, involve sacrifice, hardships and risks, such as have never before been attempted in warfare. These steps entail an advance into the heart of RUSSIA, though hundreds of miles of hostile and most difficult country. One thing that GERMANY cannot afford to do is to sit still, for that means certain destruction for her. That IVANHOFF's victories seem to indicate serious progress towards KIEFF is out of the question; the North will probably witness the next great enemy effort. Here he will perhaps make a prodigious sacrifice in the hope of reaching PETROGRAD.
His operations on the DWINA proceed, however, very slowly, and there is not the least reason to suppose that the German armies possess the momentum necessary to carry through this gigantic effort. Meanwhile there is no sign whatever, that the plan of forcing upon the retreating RUSSIANS pitched battles in the centre, with their forces divided by vast pripet marshes, will succeed. Taking the line from RIGA to the DNISTER, the impression one receives is that the Germans have shot their bolt, and that the driving power which remains to them is inadequate to carry out any of the alternative plans by which, alone, decisive victory couldn'e secured in RUSSIA before the winter makes campaigning impossible.

The Press Bureau issued this evening the following statement :- A raid was attempted by Zeppelins last night on the East Coast. Bombs were dropped, but there were no casualties and no damage was done.

The afternoon French Official communique states :- North of ARRAS, in the sector of NEUVILLE, there was incessant bomb and grenade fighting accompanied by reciprocal cannonade. A fresh attempt by the enemy against our advanced post at SAPIGNEUL was, like the preceding ones, completely repulsed. To the South of LEINTREY our artillery did effective work on positions around works and concentrations of the enemy.

A German attempt to attack was immediately stopped by our curtain of fire and the fire of our Infantry. There is nothing to report on the rest of the front. Enemy aeroplanes threw some bombs on COMPIEGNE during the day. Our aeroplanes successfully bombarded with heavy shells the German aviation hangars at BRAYVILLE

The New York Evening Star prints quotations which, it says, COUNT BERNSTORFF has made to a friend. One is that,"if diplomatic relations are broken off, German submarines will be instructed to sink anything they see, and this of course means war within two or three days". BERNSTORFF is reported to have said that his Government are very peculiarly placed.

A.B. LAWSON,   Major,
General Staff. 6th. Division.

1st Lu Coy R.E.

1st Ln Coy R.E.   341

SUMMARY OF INFORMATION NO. 99.

12th September 1915.

1. OPERATIONS.

September 10th.

The operations undertaken against the enemy's observation balloons near POELCAPELLE and BECELAERE appear to have been successful. First the fire of the enemy's anti-aircraft guns was drawn and the guns then shelled by our heavy artillery. The aeroplanes carrying out the attack then crossed the German lines and attacked the balloons, which were also fired at while on the ground by some of our heavy guns, the shooting being observed by machines fitted with wireless. The result of the operations was that very few hostile anti-aircraft guns fired at our machines between 11.30 a.m. and 12 noon, all being forced to change their positions. The balloon near POELCAPELLE was damaged either by shell fire or by bombs. The balloon near BECELAERE was deflated, after being moved two or three times.

September 11th/12th.

There is little to report during these twenty-four hours. Some of our heavy guns did some damage on the enemy's trenches about BELLEWAARDE FARM. The enemy retaliated by firing on RAILWAY WOOD.
Two working parties were dispersed during the day near 5 CHEMINS EST. and during the night the enemy commenced to bomb and to fire trench mortarsshells from FARM 14, until our guns retaliated.

2. ZEPPELIN RAIDS.

Zeppelins were again over the Eastern Counties last night.

3. PRESS NEWS FROM GERMAN SOURCES.

"We learn from well informed sources that in the attack by our dirigibles on LONDON during the night of the 8th/9th September, bombs fell in the neighbourhood of HOLBORN VIADUCT. Numerous fires caused by the bombs were observed from the dirigibles, the clear night permitting perfect observation. Near NORWICH numerous bombs were dropped on important industrial works South West of the town and several explosions and fires were observed. At MIDDLES-BROUGH the Docks and big furnaces close to the SOUTH BANK - REDCAR line were particularly damaged. The English Official reports,for reasons which it is easy to understand, are silent regarding the material successes obtained by the German dirigibles and merely announce a certain number of losses in human lives."

4. MARCONI WIRELESS NEWS - London, September 11th.

Russia.

The Russian communique issued on the night of September 10th is again of a cheering character. Enemy counter-attacks in GALICIA have been repulsed and the Russians, again taking the offensive, drove the Austrians in precipitate retreat, capturing about 16 officers and 5,000 rank and file. The Germans, however, appear to be progressing in the direction of DVINSK, though East of GRODNO their heavy attacks were repulsed. A satisfactory feature of the

Russian communique is the repeated reference to the success of their concentrated fire in checking the enemy.

United States.

The German Note to America regarding the "ARABIC" has created a storm which, if it does not eclipse, at least excels the DUMBA crisis. The German pretext that the liner was torpedoed because the submarine commander feared he was going to be attacked is ridiculed.

It is stated that Captain Von PAPEN, German Military Attache, and Herr Von GERHED, the Austrian Consul General, are involved in a dubious affair and will probably be recalled. Count BERNSTORFF is also involved but not so seriously. It is thought that over these two issues the friendly relations of the United States with Germany are strained more towards breaking point than ever.

Mr. J.P. MORGAN personally met the members of the ANGLO-FRENCH COMMISSION who have arrived in NEW YORK to help solve exchange difficulties. The Exchange advanced on the news of the arrival of the Commission and on the issue of the following Statement by the members:-

"The object of our visit is to consult with American Bankers and others as to the best means to be adopted for ensuring regularity of exchange between NEW YORK, LONDON, and PARIS in order that the commerce and industry of those countries may suffer as little as possible during the course of the war."

A message from WASHINGTON states that the FEDERAL RESERVE BOARD has revised its regulations governing the re-discount of Bankers Acceptances by the Federal Reserve. Its action may pave the way towards the establishment of a credit loan which is said to be sought by the Anglo-French Commission.

Germany.

BERLIN claims that on Thursday night a German airship successfully dropped bombs on a Russian naval point d'appui, a Baltic port and its railway works.

Balkans.

According to the BUCHAREST Correspondent of "CORRIERE DELLA SERA" Germany and Austria will not accept the refusal of ROUMANIA to allow munitions for Turkey to pass through her territory and pressure on ROUMANIA is being redoubled by the Central Empires.

England.

The British Steamer "CORNUBIA" has been sunk but the crew were saved. The Lowestoft smack "BOY ERNIE" has been sunk, one man being wounded.

It is officially announced that the Army Council has gladly accepted the offer of the Union Government to raise an Infantry Battalion of Cape coloured men, and also two bearer companies of Indians resident in South Africa.

5. **FRENCH OFFICIAL COMMUNIQUE.**

Great and continued artillery activity is reported on the ARTROIS front to the South of the SOMME, and in the neighbourhood of ROYE. On the AISNE - MARNE CANAL the enemy twice attempted a sudden attack on one of our advance posts near SEPIGNEUL but completely failed. In the ARGONNE the fight with bombs and grenades continued.

B.J. Ingham
Major, G.S.

12/9/15.

-:6th DIVISION:-

NEWS SHEET. (By wireless).

LONDON, September 13th, 1915.

Another attempt was made to raid the East Coast by German aircraft last night. Bombs were dropped but there were no casualties, and the only damage reported was to telegraph wires and windows. This is the second raid in which no damage has been effected.

In France the artillery battle continues. On Russian front Germans are reported from PETROGRAD to be driving to strike decisive blow from one end of the line to the other, the Russian Command, however, has the situation well in control, and in the southern part of their line has followed up its success of last week by a further advance. A writer in the Paris "FIGARO", who had an opportunity of visiting the British Grand Fleet mentions some of ways in which submarine danger is met. At first, he says, submarines thought they could act with impunity, but they now know that when they leave port they have far less chance of returning than of being put to sleep in the eternal depths of the sea.

Parliament opens for the Autumn Session tomorrow. The revised War Budget will be introduced, also a bill for prolonging duration of Parliament.

M.MAHRICE STRAUSS, who has been conducting a tour of enquiry for the "EXCELSIOR" gives an account in that journal of his visit to AMSTERDAM, and afterwards to BERLIN. In BERLIN, he says, what is most desired after victory in RUSSIA, is a big defeat of the French, but then, it is admitted that "these cursed Frenchmen fight like devils".

Germans declare that in the spring, HINDENBURG will take PETROGRAD and MOSCOW, and that at present the German troops are to take possession of ODESSA and the fertile lands surrounding. According to the "FIGARO", Germans are laying down new submarines having wider radius of action. They can be built in 3 or 4 months.

A PARIS telegram states that a cargo steamer VILLE DE MONTAGANEM, belonging to the Compagnie Transatlantique, was sunk on the 9th instant by a submarine flying the German flag. It is believed that the submarine sunk another vessel two hours previously. Two boats of the VILLE DE MONTAGANEM have been picked up by an English steamer and sixteen men rescued. Three men had been slightly injured by shell fragments. Lloyd's telegram states that 21 of the crew are missing.

From well-informed Balkan source it is learnt that the situation in the BALKANS is as follows:-
SERBIAN question with the BULGARIAN Government is regarded with greatest confidence and sympathy. Serbian Government has given its decision to the ENGLISH, FRENCH, RUSSIAN and ITALIAN Governments and these four powers are considering the final opinion which will be submitted to SERBIAN Government. SERBIA is convinced that MACEDONIA is, by history, language, and race SERBIAN, but as offering to ensure further federation of BALKANS, is willing to give up MACEDONIA as a fraternal present to BULGARIA; Cession of MACEDONIA TO BULGARIA, will, however, only be arranged after BULGARIA has joined the ALLIES, and SERBIA has received all lands which are Southern Slav, namely:- BOSNIA, DALMATIA, CROATIA and SLAVONIA. In event of European Powers agreeing to these terms, a new BALKAN FEDERATION will be formed.

A.B.LAWSON, Major,
General Staff.

1st Lon Coy RE

SUMMARY OF INFORMATION NO. 100.

13th September 1915.

1. OPERATIONS - September 12th/13th.

On the morning of the 12th there was considerable shrapnel fire on WIELTJE AND WARWICK FARM. Our snipers on this portion of the front claim one German officer and three men. Near the CANAL our snipers scored three hits.

The enemy's trench mortars were active from near FARM 14. Our reply with heavy trench mortar bombs and sharpnel had good effect.

2. PRESS EXTRACTS.

(i) The Germans are reported to be hurriedly restoring the defences of KOVNO and guns of the heaviest calibre are being mounted.

(ii) According to information from ADRIANOPLE the greater number of the heavy guns belonging to that place which had been transported to BVLAIR have been brought back and hastily replaced in position.

(iii) It is reported that at the re-opening of the French Chamber this week a law will be introduced enabling a new army of at least 700,000 black troops to be placed in the field next spring.

3. MARCONI WIRELESS NEWS - London, September 12th.

Russia.

Again General IVANOFF has scored a substantial success in GALICIA. In the communique issued in PETROGRAD last night we are told that the earlier Russian victory at TARNOPOL has been repeated and more than 2,000 prisoners and a number of quick firing guns have been taken. The enemy is in a position in which he certainly cannot afford to lose troops on such a scale. He is committed to an enterprise of great magnitude and were his resources in men far greater than we know them to be, still every soldier would be needed for the task that lies ahead. Tremendous as are the achievements of German Arms in the East, the obvious fact remains that nothing decisive has been accomplished and that the steps by which a decision can be sought involves great sacrifices, hardships, and risks. These steps entail an advance into the heart of Russia through miles of hostile and difficult country. One thing Germany cannot afford to do is to sit still. IVANOFF'S victories seem to indicate that a serious progress towards KIEFF is out of the question, and the North will probably witness the next great effort of the enemy. Here he will perhaps make great sacrifices in the hope of reaching PETROGRAD. His operations on the DWINA proceed however slowly and there is no reason to suppose the German Armies possess the momentum necessary to carry through this effort. Meanwhile there is no sign whatever that the plan of forcing upon the retreating Russians pitched battles in the centre with their Armies divided by the vast PRIPET MARSHES will succeed. Taking a line from RIGA to the DNEISTER, the impression one receives is that the Germans have shot their bolt and that the driving power which remains is inadequate to carry out any of the alternative plans by which alone decisive victory could be secured in Russia before winter makes campaigning impossible.

Zeppelin Raid on England.

The Press Bureau issues this evening a statement that a raid was attempted by Zeppelins last night on the EAST COAST. Bombs were dropped but there were no casualties and no damage was done.

French Front.

The afternoon French Official Communique states that a fresh attempt by the enemy against the advanced post at SAPIGNEUL was, like the preceding ones, completely repulsed. Near LEINTNEY a German attempt at an attack was stopped by artillery and infantry fire. Enemy aeroplanes threw some bombs during the day in COMPEIGNE. Our aeroplanes successfully bombarded with heavy shells German aviation hangers at BRAYVILLE.

America.

The NEW YORK "EVENING SUN" prints quotations which it says COUNT BERNSTORFF has made to a friend. One is that: "If diplomatic relations are broken off German submarines will be instructed to sink anything they see and this, of course, means war within two or three days." BERNSTORFF is reported also to have said that his Government are very peculiarly placed.

4. FRENCH OFFICIAL COMMUNIQUE - Midnight, 12th/13th September.

In the DARDANELLES the last five days have been very quiet. In the Northern zone the Turks on several occasions have opened a violent infantry and artillery fire but have not left their trenches. In the Southern zone there is nothing particular to report, except effective work by our trench mortars which have destroyed two small strong points and have caused the enemy sensible losses.

13/9/15.

Major, G.S.

GERMAN AEROPLANE BROUGHT DOWN.

It is reported that a German aeroplane was attacked by one of our machines and brought down near STEENWERCKE. The machine came down, as the pilot apparently lost control. Just as it looked as if the machine was going to drop to the ground the engine picked up and it seemed as if the machine would escape. A Company of Infantry which happened to be route-marching in the vicinity and who had watched the incident, seeing the machine apparently escaping, opened fire with volleys at 100 yards range. Both the pilot and the observer were killed and the machine was captured undamaged.

6th DIVISION.

NEWS SHEET. (By wireless).

LONDON, 14th September.

The British Government has appointed Admiral Sir Percy Scott to direct the gun defences of LONDON against enemy aircraft. Sir Percy Scott has been the founder of modern gunnery, and his inventions for gun sighting and directing fire are in use on all ships of the British Navy, and have been widely imitated in other countries. He invented the system of mounting naval guns on land carriages, which was used for the first time in the SOUTH AFRICAN War, and has been been used in the present campaign by both sides.

The ENGLISH coast was visited by a Zeppelin again last night. Bombs were dropped and anti-aircraft guns, both fixed and mobile, were in action. So far as is at present known, there were no casualties and no damage was done.

As a result of an air raid by a German aeroplane on the coast of KENT yesterday, 7 people have been injured, 6 of them being women.

The House of Commons met today after 7 weeks recess. A vote of credit for the financing of the war will be moved tomorrow, and a short discussion took place on the subject of National Services.

Reports from ITALY state, that General JOFFRE during his three days visit to the ITALIAN Army visited all points of front and was greeted with great enthusiasm by the ITALIAN troops. He had interviews with the King, the Commander-in-Chief, the President of the War Council, and with members of the Government.

It is reported from the DARDANELLES that the Turks are preparing for the forcing of the Straits. The fire from the batteries on ASIATIC side has slackened enormously, and enemy forces are beginning to retire into the interior.

The ROUMANIAN Government is reported to have ordered partial mobilization.

Hindenburg's new great effort in NORTH has resulted in the cutting of the PETROGRAD railway between VILNA and DVINSK. His more northerly offensive to West and South West of DVINSK is being vigorously proceeded with. On other parts of the front, the RUSSIANS are fighting successful rearguard actions. They have made further progress in GALICIA and have captured more prisoners and guns. The RUSSIAN communique contains significant statements that in centre of front "our artillery succeeded in developing a powerful fire".

A telegram from ATHENS states, that a squadron of FRENCH torpedo boats while on patrol work have torpedoed and sunk a German submarine between TENEDOS and MYTILENE.

Monsieur GOREYSKIN, Premier, has returned from visit to Imperial Headquarters.

According to the best available information, DUMA will be prorogued until the end of October.

P.T.O

A CHRISTIANIA telegram states, that the Captain of the steamer BESSNEIM reports that his ship was hailed by a German submarine and a BRITISH subject was taken off as prisoner. NORWEGIAN Legation in BERLIN has been ordered to protest to the German Government which has been done.

Mr. Alfred Gwynne Vanderbilt who was drowned in the LUSITANIA disaster on May 7th, has left property in the UNITED KINGDOM of value of £32,606, while pecuniary legacies exceed £2,200,000.

It is reported from NEW YORK that the present plan of ANGLO-FRENCH financial commission is to borrow a billion dollars there on straight BRITISH and FRENCH Government Bonds without collateral security. If the money is obtainable, it is stated all of it will be spent in the UNITED STATES.

In the House of Lords this afternoon, Lord CREWE announced that Lord KITCHENER would make a statement tomorrow with regard to the Military situation.

A.B.LAWSON, Major,

General Staff.

SUMMARY OF INFORMATION NO. 101.

14th September 1915.

1. **OPERATIONS - 13th/14th September.**

    For the last three or four days the reports from the front between the VERLORENHOEK ROAD down to BELLEWAARDE FARM have been that all is quiet. During the morning a battery fired 55 rounds at the German work at I.12.a 7.8. One round apparently blew up some sort of ammunition store.

    At 6.40 p.m. a working party near the salient C.29 Central was dispersed with a Toby shell.

    Towards the CANAL the German second line was shelled and a large amount of debris was thrown up. This drew retaliation on IRISH FARM and FUSILIER FARM. Three Germans were bagged in this section with the aid of "snyposcopes". During the night there was some shelling and trench mortaring of the CANAL bank and the trenches immediately near. Prompt retaliation in kind caused the enemy to stop.

    September 12th.

    A big explosion is reported to have occurred near HOLLEBEKE CHATEAU as a result of our heavy artillery fire.

    On this day the enemy fired 18 heavy shell at the CLOTH HALL in YPRES and the remaining tower was knocked down.

2. **A RUSE DE L'AIR.** (From 2nd Corps Summary.).

    Last week one of our slower pattern biplanes, returning from a reconnaissance over COMINES, was suddenly overhauled by a German fighting plane of much greater power and speed. Our aeroplane was so constructed that the machine-gun could only be fired straight to the front, and there was little use in turning to fight the faster machine. As the hostile machine drew alongside to give the coup de grace, our observer with commendable presence of mind suddenly presented his telescope and levelled it point-blank at the German, while at the same time the pilot blazed off with the forward gun. The German was so taken aback by this manoeuvre from what he took to be an unarmed machine, that he dived suddenly and was seen no more.

3. **MARCONI WIRELESS NEWS - London, September 13th.**

    Air Raid on East Coast.

    Another attempt was made to raid the East Coast by German aircraft on the night of September 12th/13th. Bombs were dropped but there were no casualties and the only damage reported was to telegraph wires and windows. This is the second raid in which no damage has been affected.

    Submarine Warfare.

    A writer to the PARIS "FIGARO" who had an opportunity of visiting the British Grand Fleets, mentions some of the ways in which the submarine danger is met. At first, he says, submarines thought they could act with impunity but they now know that when they leave port they have far less chance of returning than of being sunk.

    According to the "FIGARO", Germans are laying down new

submarines having wider radius of action which can be built in three or four months.

A PARIS telegram states the cargo steamer "VILLE DE MOSTAGANUN", belonging to the COMPAGNIE TRANSATLANTIQUE, was sunk on the night of the 12th/13th September by a German submarine. It is believed the same submarine sank another vessel two hours previously. Two boats of the "VILLE DE MOSTAGANUN" were picked up by an English steamer and sixteen men rescued. Three men had been slightly injured by shell fragments. Twenty-one of the crew are still missing.

Russia.

On the Russian front the Germans are reported from PETROGRAD to be striving to strike a decisive blow from one end of line to other. The Russian Command, however, has the situation well in control and in the Southern part of the line has followed up its successes of the last week by a further advance.

Berlin.

Monsieur MAURICE STRAUSS, who has been conducting a tour of inquiry for the "EXCELSIOR" gives an account in that journal of his visit to AMSTERDAM and afterwards to BERLIN. In BERLIN, he says, what is most desired after victories in Russia, is a big defeat of the French but then it is admitted "these cursed Frenchmen fight like devils". The Germans declare that in the spring HINDENBURG will take PETROGRAD and MOSCOW but that at present the aim of the German troops is to take possession of ODESSA and the fertile lands in the surrounding district.

The Balkan States.

From a well-informed Balkan source it is learnt that the situation in the Balkans is that SERBIA is considering the Bulgarian representations with sympathy. The Serbian Government has communicated its decision to the ENTENTE POWERS, who are considering their final opinion which will be submitted to the Serbian Government. SERBIA is convinced that MACEDONIA is, by history, language, and race, Serbian but as an offering to ensure the future federation of the Balkans, she is willing to give up MACEDONIA as a fraternal present to BULGARIA. The cession of MACEDONIA to BULGARIA will, however, only be arranged after BULGARIA has joined the Allies and Serbia has received all the lands which are Southern Slav namely, BOSNIA, DALMATIA, CROATIA, and SLAVONIA. In the event of the European Powers agreeing to these terms a new Balkan Federation will be formed.

4. FRENCH OFFICIAL COMMUNIQUE - Midnight, 13th/14th September.

The artillery action continues to the North and South of ARRAS, in the sectors of NEUVILLE, ROCLINCOURT, and DAILLY. Our artillery has destroyed the enemy's defences and works. Before ANDECHY several parties of the enemy have been dispersed. In retaliation for the recent bombardments of LUNEVILLE and COMPIEGNE by the enemy's aeroplanes, a squadron of nineteen of our machines visited the town of TREVES on the morning of the 13th September and dropped about 100 shells. The Railway Station and the bank were hit. Other aeroplanes bombarded from a low altitude the Railway Stations of DONAUSCHINGEN on the DANUBE, and of MARBACH in a district where movements of troops had been reported.

14/9/15.

Major, G.S.

FLAMMENWERFER IN ACTION.

The German Flammenwerfer consists of a strong cylinder, 2'6" high by 10" in diameter, which can be carried on a man's back. It is connected by means of stout hose to a projector which contains a jet of about 3/16" diameter, which is surrounded by a circular wick saturated in paraffin wax. This burns during the projection of the liquid and ignites it actually at the jet.

The Flammenwerfer is about half filled with four gallons of a mixture of a light inflammable oil and a heavy tarry oil similar to oil gas residues. It is then charged up to a pressure of 23 atmospheres from a nitrogen cylinder and is ready for action. The wick round the jet is then lighted by means of a small detonator and a charge of slow burning powder and the tap turned on. The pressure of the nitrogen forces out the oil; this inflames at the jet and spreads out in a broad cone of flame and smoke which covers about six yards of front when stationary, has an extreme range of twenty yards and a duration of less than a minute. The jet can, of course, be directed to any angle, and can be sent in short bursts if required.

The chief power of the Flammenwerfer lies in its moral effect, but this need not be feared, provided that troops know what to expect and can protect themselves. The smoke is very dense and black, and the flames are a yellowish red; and during the whole time there is a loud roaring noise. The heat developed in the flame is very great, but practically all the burning takes place in the air, and although some of the heavy oil falls to the ground, it does not burn there as none of the lighter oil is left. This being so, none of the flame can be directed actually into a trench, and not even over it unless the trenches are less than 20 yards apart or the wind is very high and blowing from the enemy. A man crouching down on the firing step, or just inside a dug-out, should be quite safe from the flames, while any overhead cover such as is provided for a machine-gun emplacement gives perfect protection.

6th DIVISION.

NEWS SHEET. (By Wireless).

LONDON. September 15th.

Mr. ASQUITH in moving vote of credit for 250 millions in House of Commons stated, that average daily expenditure from July 18th to September 11th was £4,200,000. and net expenditure 3½ millions, Fifty millions have been repaid to the Bank of England since last Vote. The main cause of increased expenditure was the growth in advances to Allies, and provision of munitions. As to recruiting, not far short of an aggregate of three million men had enlisted. Minister of Munitions has established twenty Shell Factories and eighteen were in course of construction. Seven hundred and fifteen controlled establishments were under department, and 900.000 workmen were now employed in three factories.

French Official Communique reports, grenade fighting and artillery duels in the sectors of NIEUVILLE and BRETENCOURT. Bomb fighting took place in the region of LEHONS and the BOIS DE ST. HARD.

General POLIVANOL, Russian Minister of War, declares himself satisfied with improvement that has taken place in the provision of munitions, enormous increases of which during the last fifteen days is fully maintained. The supply of rifles has also been increased in considerable numbers. The Russian Official Communique states. German pressure continues West of JACOBSTADT - DVINSK line. Northeast of ROVNO Russians crossed the GORVS near ZVIZDYE, and captured whole Austrian Battalion. Enemy offensive in DREAZXNO and KLEVIAN districts failed, and Russians captured over 1300 prisoners near OLESZVA. Enemy were driven from RYDONEL and ROSTOKI south of WISZNICA, and lost 2000 prisoners. In districts of GONTOW and DITKOWEC Russians captured about 140 officers and 7300 rank and file, one heavy and six light guns, four limbers and twentysix machine guns, and much booty. We are pursuing retreating enemy in a Westerly direction from the front of River SERETH. From August 30th to September 11th the number of Austrian and German prisoners taken by us exceeded 40.000.

In order to devote himself among our soldiers at the front, Reverend R.J.CAMPBELL has decided to resign his pastorate at City Temple, which he has held since 1903. This indicates way in which Nonconformist normally oppose, but were supporting this war for righteousness.

Message from NEW YORK states, last night two bottles believed to contain high explosives were discovered on the liner LAPLAND, due to sail for LIVERPOOL today.

Although Wall Street gossip asserts that pro-German bankers in CHICAGO, CINCINNATI, ST.LOUIS, MILWAUKEE, and other middle western States, and some of Eastern cities, bitterly oppose any action whatever in financing Anglo-French loan, not a single banking house with even the remotest connection with German financial interests, has been invited to send representatives to gatherings at which scores of NEW YORK financiers and those of other centres have discussed the Loan. Policy excluded some of the largest financial institutions, including KUHN LOEB and Company, which is second only to J.P.MORGAN and Company. It is stated that overtures with the object of possible participation of KUHN LOEB are in progress, and that the Company would not look unkindly on the invitation to participate in the Loan.

A.B.LAWSON,

Major, General Staff.

6. FROM "Frankfurter Zeitung", Sunday, August 15th.

ENGLAND IN WARTIME - By a Neutral.

The feeling among the English people against Germany has become much more bitter since the beginning of the year.

After the excitement over the so-called destruction of Belgium had decreased to the usual indifference to all "Foreigners", came the bombardment of Scarborough and West Hartlepool through German warships, the sinking of the "Lusitania", and, finally, the use of "Poisonous Gases" by German troops.

Each of these events increased the bitterness to an enormous extent.

The Jingo Press, which was unable to "hammer" anything more out of the so-called "Destruction of Belgium", the Government and the Recruiting Agents immediately took the opportunity of making as much capital as possible out of these events; and the lower classes - the workmen particularly - who usually are not in love with the ways of the Government, were very much impressed with these "new proofs of German barbarity".

The people were brought nearer to the reality of war than by a hundred Government manifestoes, and it is a fact that recruiting for the Army received a great stimulus after each of the above-mentioned events.

R.J. Ingham.
Major, G.S.

15/9/15.

1st Div Coy R.E.   1. Summary
                    1. News Sheet

SUMMARY OF INFORMATION NO 102.

15th September, 1915.

1. OPERATIONS. Sept. 14th/15th.

   Near BELLEWAARDE FARM our snipers claim to have killed four Germans who were out mending their wire. Machine guns on this portion of the front drove off 3 enemy aeroplanes early on the morning of the 14th.

   Toby secured a good hit on the MOUND which was afterwards rifle grenaded hourly, the enemy being prevented from repairing the damage. A working party just N. of ODER HOUSES was seen and fired at by sudden bursts of machine gun fire.

   A pink rocket is reported to have been fired by the enemy during the night near the Canal.

   During the 14th the enemy shelled BELLE ALLIANCE, BURNT FARM, CONEY STREET and IRISH FARM.

2. MARCONI WIRELESS PRESS; London, Sept. 14th.

   ENGLAND. - The English Coast was visited by a Zeppelin again last night. Bombs were dropped, and anti-aircraft guns, both fixed and mobile, were in action. So far as at present known there were no casualties, and no damage has been done. As the result of an air raid by a German aeroplane on the coast of Kent yesterday 7 people have been injured, 6 of them being women.

   The House of Commons met to-day after seven weeks recess. A vote of credit for financing the war will be moved to-morrow, and a short discussion took place on the subject of National Service.

   ITALY. - Reports from Italy state that General Joffre during his three days visit to the Italian Army visited all the points of the front and was greeted with great enthusiasm by the Italian troops. He had interviews with the King, the Commander-in-Chief, the President of the War Council and members of the Government.

   DARDANELLES. - It is reported from the Dardanelles that the Turks are preparing for the forcing of the straits. Fire from batteries on the Asiatic side has slackened enormously, and enemy forces are beginning to retire into the interior. The Rumanian Government is reported to have ordered partial mobilisation.

   A telegram from ATHENS states a squadron of French torpedo boats while on patrol work torpedoed and sunk a German submarine between Tenedos and Mytilene.

   RUSSIA. - Hindenburg's new great effort in the North has resulted in cutting the Petrograd Railway between Vilna and Dvinsk. His more Northerly offensive to the West and South-West of Dvinsk is being vigorously proceeded with. On other parts of the front the Russians are fighting successful rearguard actions. They have made further progress in Galicia and have captured more prisoners and guns. The Russian Communique contains a significant statement that in the centre of their front "our artillery succeeded in developing a powerful fire".

   Monsieur Goremykin, the Russian Premier, has returned from a visit to the Imperial Headquarters. According to the best available information the Duma will be prorogued until the end of October.

   DENMARK. - A Christiania telegram states the Captain of the steamer Helsheim reports his ship was hailed by a German submarine and a British subject was taken off as prisoner. The Norwegian

P.T.O.

Legation in Berlin has been ordered to protest to the German Government, which has been done.

UNITED STATES - It is reported from New York that the present plan of the Anglo-French Financial Commission is to borrow a billion dollars there on straight British and French bonds without collateral security. If the money is obtainable it is stated all of it will be spent in the United States.

Lord Crew announced in the House of Commons this afternoon that Lord Kitchener would make a statement to-morrow with regard to the military situation.

3. GERMAN WIRELESS.

The German wireless claims further advances by the Armies of Hindenburg, Prince Leopold of Bavaria and Mackensen, and the latter is said to have taken 700 prisoners. The only mention of the Southern Galician front is, "We repel attacks by the enemy with bloody losses".

4. FRENCH OFFICIAL COMMUNIQUE.

A lively artillery action continues round ARRAS in the regions of ROYE and NOUVRON and on the CHAMPAGNE front, particularly near SOUAIN and PERTHES. A fairly heavy cannonade was also reported in the forest of APREMONT and in LORRAINE in the region of EMBERMENIL.

5. EXTRACTS FROM OTHER CORPS SUMMARIES.

(i). At 6.30 p.m. on the 9th, a hostile aeroplane was hit by one of our machine guns near BETHUNE. The left bottom plane, being hit, slanted upwards and the machine listed to the right. Apparently a stay was broken. Twice the machine nearly turned over, and then the observer was seen to climb out on the lower plane to counteract the list. He stood up, and finally lay down on the plane. The machine was then seen to descend in normal fashion.

(ii). The searchlight reported as signalling continuously the letters "S.I.T.E" is a signal on a church tower in LILLE, apparently used a lighthouse for Zeppelins. It was again working last night (13th September).

(iii). An Officer's patrol from a Division brought back a copy of the "Gazette des Ardennes" from near the enemy's trenches. On the newspaper was scrawled the following message:-
"Dear Tommy !
Old England don't like to tell you all what happened around you, so we friends send you this newspaper hopping you have learned enough by the sweet little "Mariannas" all the time long you are in France to translate the "Gazette". We would be awfully enjoyed to have in short time a good fight with you so remain with the best wishes for "Old Germany" yours trulies
friends and neighbours".
If our "friends and neighbours", the Saxons, are asking for trouble they may get it some day.

6TH. DIVISION.

NEWS SHEET (BY WIRELESS)

LONDON. September 16th.

Vigorous artillery attacks continue to be made on German positions round ARRAS, and the bombardment is also taking place in Southern and Eastern Parts of the line.

It is reported that considerable damage was done to GERMAN submarine yards, aerodromes, and other works by the recent BRITISH bombardment of OSTEND.

The Admiralty announces the loss of the Submarine E.7. in the DARDENELLES. The crew have been taken prisoners by the enemy. This submarine has done very distinguished service, and its officers and men appeared in the last Naval Honours List.

GERMAN papers are publishing telegrams foreshadowing the immediate entry of ROUMANIA into the war.

The UNITED STATES Government has no intention of forbidding participation of AMERICAN Bankers in the loan which BRITISH Commissions in NEW YORK hope to float for the purpose of restoring normal exchange between the two countries.

The Russian successes in GALICIA are making their effect felt all along the line, and the German armies have ceased for the moment to make progress in the North. The CZAR has called out the RUSSIAN Reserve by which 8 million men will be called to the forces.

Apart from the generally cheerful tone of his review of the general military situation, perhaps the most important part of LORD KITCHENER's speech in the House of Lords yesterday, was his reference to the recruiting question. The War Minister's remarks have led many people to believe that we are on the verge of conscription, but there is an equally strong body of opinion that this view is incorrect. Other important points of speech were - LORD KITCHENER's reference to the FRENCH line as being almost impregnable. He eulogised our new Divisions as being worthy of the Army's best traditions, referred to the demoralization among the TURKS, described the ITALIANS as occupying positions of first rate strategical importance, and dismissed Germany's achievements against RUSSIA as a strategic failure with nothing more than barren territory and evacuated fortresses as tangible results. He added regarding RUSSIA :- "The GERMANS appear almost to have shot their bolt".

The ANGLO-FRENCH financial commissioners and AMERICAN financiers met yesterday evening at the HOTEL BALTIMORE, the meeting lasting from four until nearly mid-night. Following the meeting there was general optimism. As far as could be learned from the BANKERS, the situation is about as follows - Pledges have already been secured for a considerable fraction of the big loan, and other pledges are in prospect. So called Pro-German Bankers in NEW YORK will be invited to participate if commissions can be persuaded they are sincere in their expressions and that they will willingly do so.
The loan will probably be divided into two parts, and possibly into four separate series of equal amounts. Bonds will bear not less than 5 per cent interest, and will be payable in dollars. The opposition to the floatation of the loan on the part of GERMAN Propagandists has strengthened friendly Bankers in the determination to float the loan, and has not seriously impeded their task.

A conference of far reaching importance in the history of Nonconformity was opened today at the MEMORIAL HALL. The object of the meeting was to consider the question of removing the barriers that divide various sections of Nonconformity. The proceedings were private.

17th September, 1915.

A.B.LAWSON, Major,
General Staff, 6th Division.

1st Lu Coy 990

SUMMARY OF INFORMATION NO 104.

17th September, 1915.

1. OPERATIONS - 16th/17th Sept.

On the afternoon of the 16th some of our field artillery bombarded the enemy's trenches near BELLEWAARDE FARM. The parapets were considerably damaged several large holes being made. Dug-outs were hit and timber and debris were thrown in the air. The bombardment appeared to be effective. The enemy retaliated on RAILWAY WOOD.

During the day the enemy shelled ST. JEAN with field guns, and also some of the communication trenches in this vicinity. Several of the shells did not explode. A considerable amount of faulty ammunition appears to be used by the enemy on this front.

Towards the Canal there was a good deal of sniping and machine gun fire by both sides during the night. EOLIAN FARM was shelled by our guns as a machine gun was located there.

The impression that a relief has taken place near ODER HOUSES is strengthened by reports that single wagons have been observed moving by day along the FREZENBURG - FORTUIN ROAD, D 25 a - C 24, which is most unusual. Also a party of officers was observed viewing our trenches from the new strong work at the FREZENBURG CROSS-ROADS, C 30 d 10.7. It is reported that two rounds were fired at this party, apparently with good effect.

2. MARCONI WIRELESS NEWS - London, 16th Sept.

LORD KITCHENER'S SPEECH, HOUSE OF LORDS, Sept. 15th.

Apart from the generally cheerful tone of his review of the general military situation, perhaps the most important part of Lord Kitchener's speech in the House of Lords yesterday was his reference to recruiting. The War Minister's remarks have led many people to believe that we are on the verge of conscription, but there is an equally strong body of opinion that this view is incorrect. Another important point of the speech was a reference to the French line as almost impregnable. He eulogised our new divisions as worthy of the army's best traditions, referred to the Italians as occupying a position of first rate strategical importance, and dismissed Germany's achievements against Russia as a strategic failure with nothing more than barren territory and evacuated fortresses as tangible results. He added regarding Russia, "The Germans appear almost to have shot their bolt".

ANGLO-FRENCH LOAN. - The United States Government has no intention of forbidding participation of American bankers in the Loan which the British Commissioners in New York hope to float for the purpose of restoring normal exchange between the two countries. The Anglo-French Financial Commissioners and American financiers met yesterday evening at the Hotel Baltimore, the meeting lasting from four until nearly midnight. Following the meeting there was general optimism. As far as could be learned from bankers, the situation is as follows:- Pledges have already been secured for a considerable fraction of a big loan, and other pledges are in prospect. So called pro-German banks in New York will be invited to participate if the Commission can be persuaded that they are sincere in their expressions, and that they will willingly do so. The Loan will probably be divided into two parts and possibly into four separate series of equal amounts. Bonds will bear not less than 5% interest and will be payable in dollars.

P.T.O.

2.

Opposition to the flotation of the Loan on the part of German propagandists has strengthened friendly bankers in their determination to float the Loan and has not seriously impeded their task.

BELGIUM. - It is reported that considerable damage was done to German submarine yards, aerodromes and other works by the recent British bombardment of OSTEND.

DARDANELLES AND THE BALKANS. - In the Dardanelles the British Admiralty announces the loss of submarine E.7, the crew of which have been taken prisoners by the enemy. This submarine has done very distinguished service, and its officers and men appeared in last Naval Honours list.

The German papers are forshadowing the immediate entry of ROUMANIA into the war.

RUSSIA. - The Russian successes in Galicia are making their effect felt all along the line, and the German armies have ceased for the moment to make progress in the North. The Tsar has called out the Russian reserve by which 8,000,000 men will be called to the forces.

3. FRENCH OFFICIAL COMMUNIQUE.

This Communique recounts vigourous artillery actions along almost the whole French front,

4. GERMAN WIRELESS - 16th Sept.

Von HINDENBURG is still advancing towards JACOBSTADT. On the rest of the front there is little change. In the South-Eastern theatre "as on preceding days, Russian attacks continue to shatter themselves against the German lines".

5. EXTRACTS FROM OTHER CORPS SUMMARIES.

(i). TURKEY IN TROUBLE.
Increasing anxiety is being felt in Constantinople for the safety of the city.
The friction between the Turks and the German Military Authorities has in some instances become acute. The following is said to have been overheard in a cafe in STAMBOUL:-
"Confound all these German Commanders,
And especially LIMAN VON SANDERS,
May Allah expel
All the beggars to hell,
Or send them to perish in Flanders".

(ii). ESPIONAGE.
A German soldier has surrendered to a French Lines of Communication unit. This man was wearing the uniform of a tirailleur algerian and stated that he had been sent into the French lines, dressed in this uniform, to act as a spy. Precautions should be taken accordingly.

B.J. Ingham
Major, G.S.

17/9/15.

SUMMARY OF INFORMATION NO 103.

16th September, 1915.

1. **OPERATIONS - 15th/16th Sept.**

    Near ODER HOUSES the enemy is believed to have carried out a relief during the night of the 14th/15th, as he was suspiciously quiet, and the following morning several men were seen exposing themselves unusually, looking over the parapet and pointing.

    The MOUND just South of ODER HOUSES was damaged by Toby and the enemy was prevented from repairing it by a continued machine gun and rifle grenade fire.

    Nearer the Canal a German working party was dispersed near KRUPP FARM in the early morning of the 15th, and one man was killed. Another working party near FORTIN 17 was stopped about the same time by artillery fire. The enemy shelled some of the farms East of the Canal during the morning but several shells failed to burst. During the afternoon a sentry who observed a Bosch at work shot him. The incident was witnessed by an officer.

    The enemy's observation balloon which rises behind POLYGON WOOD is reported to be again in action. No trace of the POELCAPPELLE balloon can be observed by our aviators.

    On September 14th one of our field batteries sniped the road passing through D.21 Centre and damaged a wagon moving on the road. On September 15th a round fired by another battery into the enemy's front line trench at I 12 c 8.6 caused an explosion which sent up a column of grey smoke.

2. **MARCONI WIRELESS NEWS - London, 15th Sept.**

    ENGLAND. - Mr Asquith in moving a vote of credit for 250 millions in the House of Commons stated the average daily expenditure from July 18th to September 11th was £4,200,000 and net expenditure 3½ millions. Fifty millions have been repaid to the Bank of England since last vote. The main cause of increased expenditure was growth in advances to Allies and provision of munitions. As to recruiting not far short of an aggregate of three million men had enlisted. The Minister of Munitions had established twenty shell factories and 16 were in course of construction. 715 controlled establishments were under the Department and 800,000 workmen were now employed in these factories.

    RUSSIA. - General Polivanov the Russian Minister of War declares himself satisfied with the improvements that have taken place in the provision of munitions, the enormous increase of which during the last 15 days is fully maintained. The supply of rifles has also been increase in considerable numbers.

    The Russian Official Communique states that German pressure continues West of the JACOBSTADT - DWINSK line. North-East of ROVNO the Russians crossed the GORYN near ZUIZDYE and captured a whole Austrian battalion. The enemy's offensive in DERAZNO and KLIVAN districts failed and the Russians captured over 1300 prisoners near OLESZUD. The enemy were driven from RYDOMEL and ROSTCKI South of WISZNICA and lost 2000 prisoners. In the districts of GONIOW and DITKOWEC the Russians captured about 140 officers and 7300 rank and file, one heavy and 6 light guns, 4 limbers, 26 machine guns and much booty. We are pursuing retreating enemy in a Westerly direction from the front of the River SERETH. From August 30th to September 11th the number of Austrian and German prisoners taken by us exceeds 40,000.

    UNITED STATES. - A message from New York states last night that two bottles believed to contain high explosive were discovered on the liner Lapland due to sail for Liverpool to-day.

    Although Wall Street gossip asserts the pro-German bankers of Chicago, Cincinatti, St. Louis, Milwaukee and other middle Western states and some of the Eastern cities bitterly oppose any action whatever in

P.T.O.

2.

financing the Anglo-French loan, no banks with even the remotest connection with German financial interests has been invited to send representatives to the gatherings at which scores of New York financiers and those of other centres have discussed the loans. This policy has excluded some of the largest financial institutions including Kuhn Loib and Company which is second only to J.P. Morgan and Company. It is stated that overtures with the object of the possible participation of Kuhn Loib are in progress, and that the Company would not look unkindly on an invitation to participate in the loan.

3. FRENCH OFFICIAL COMMUNIQUE.

To the North and South of ARRAS as well as in the region of ROYE artillery actions continue, with intensity.

At NEUVILLE the enemy has for some time been trying to dislodge us from our bridge-head at SAPIGNEUL. On the heights of the MEUSE our observers report the destruction of one of the enemy's batteries. We maintain the advantage in the artillery action in the BOIS le PRETRE and near ST. DIE.

4. NEWS FROM VARIOUS SOURCES.

CONSTANTINOPLE. - Dardanelles: On the night of the 13th September our reconnoitring detachments successfully attacked several points in the enemy's trenches. In the region of ARIBURNU we demolished an enemy's gun position and 2 well-organised observation posts.

AMSTERDAM. - Travellers arrived from England announce that on the night of the 12th September the Zeppelins damaged Chiswick in the extreme South-West suburbs of London. Contrary to the official announcements the damage is said to have been important.

Colonel Gaedke writes in the Vorwaerts as follows:-
"The Russian army has without doubt suffered losses out of all comparison with the past, but its power of resistance is in no way definitely broken; no more is that of the Government or of the directing classes. We must not delude ourselves by thinking that Russia from a military point of view is at the end of her resources".

B.J. Ingham.
Major, G.S.

16/9/15.

6th DIVISION.

NEWS SHEET. (By Wireless).

LONDON. 17th September, 1915.

PETROGRAD announces a severe struggle raging along the whole line. The RUSSIANS gained successes at the GALICIA end, but retired somewhat before the enemy's thrusts in the North and Centre. Between the DVINSK road and LATE SAMAVA, the Germans repeatedly reached the RUSSIAN wire entanglements where they were repulsed. North East of VIBNA they succeeded, however, in crossing the VELIA.

FRENCH gunners continue to make most effective practice against the enemy's works along the whole front. Some districts, says tonight's official PARIS report, GERMAN supply stores were violently bombarded.
Details of the FRENCH air raid on TRAVERS are published today. Some 20 FRENCH airmen threw 30 bombs at the Station, one bomb hitting the platform. FRENCH airmen flew up so high that anti-aircraft guns could not reach them.

The SERBIAN Premier has expressed absolute confidence in the reorganized SERBIAN Army, and says it would now be very difficult for any force to break through to CONSTANTINOPLE.

Sir Robert Borden, in the course of an address at the Canadian Club luncheon yesterday, paid tribute to the work of the Navy, which he described as wonderful. The splendid measures adopted against submarines showed more resourcefulness than people were aware of. The Navy had done vastly more to achieve victory than the Germans had on land.

A man serving in GALLIPOLI writes that the first person he met on landing was a man in dirty shirt and trousers and no coat, carrying sacks of corn. It was Lord Howard de Walden, one of London's wealthiest landlords.

The SERBIAN Premier exposes the big GERMAN bluff in the BALKANS, giving positive proof no Austro-German army is concentrating on the DANUBE, as has often been reported from enemy and neutral sources. He announces SERBIA has consented to concessions to BULGARIA, but it remains to be seen whether BULGARIA will throw in her lot with the entente or not.

What is described as a political crisis is threatened over the question of conscription. Referring to conscription question, 'Gaulois' says, "In our opinion, there is no doubt but that GREAT BRITIAN will resign her self to it. She is passing through one of the most grandiose and sublime hours of her history with remarkable suppleness, and she has transformed herself, overthrowing many of her old principles and traditions in order to rise to the height of events. Now that impulse has been given, one may be assured that there will be no slackening".

NEW YORK rumour has it that the loan to the Allies will be two hundred millions sterling, which is considered will be sufficient. Expert opinion is that success of loan of that amount is assured.

Mr. Vilhjolmer Stefensson, leader of the Canadian Polar Expedition, is safe. The Expedition left ALASKA in 1913, with equipment for two years. Last news was received last november in OTTAWA, and stated that he and two companions were making their way northwards from MARTIN POINT in April, 1914.

'Idea Nationale', ROME, states that the following decree was published by the Governor on Thursday:- All women, children and old men are leaving TRENTE and district, employes having already departed.

18th September 1915.

A.B. LAWSON. Major,
General Staff, 6th Division.

1st Lon Coy R.E.

136

SUMMARY OF INFORMATION NO. 105.

18th September 1915.

1. OPERATIONS - 17th/18th September.

As usual, RAILWAY WOOD was shelled during the day. Our guns retaliated. Otherwise this portion of the front was quiet. Near WIELTJE the enemy's snipers were reported as being more active than usual. TURCO FARM and vicinity were shelled with 4.2" howitzers and heavy trench mortars during the morning. Our retaliation with light and heavy guns and mortars was effective.

Two projectiles resembling aerial torpedoes was reported to have been fired near LA BELLE ALLIANCE. They burst high in the air making a big cloud of pink smoke from which a heavy ball of fire dropped straight to the earth, trailing heavy white smoke which remained for a long time.

Near the CANAL the farms on the BOESINGHE ROAD were shelled during the afternoon. Two Germans were hit by one of our snipers. The working parties in endeavouring to repair the trenches damaged by French artillery fire, were worried and stopped by our rifle and machine gun fire during the night.

2. MARCONI WIRELESS NEWS - London, September 17th.

Russia.

PETROGRAD announces a severe struggle is raging along the whole line. The Russians gained successes at GALICIA end, but are retiring somewhat before the enemy's thrusts in the North and centre. Between DVINSK ROAD and LAKE SAMAVA, the Germans repeatedly reached the Russian wire entanglements, where they were repulsed. North East of VILNA they succeeded, however, in crossing the VILIA.

Balkans.

The SERBIAN Premier has expressed absolute confidence in the re-organised Serbian Army and says it would now be very difficult for an enemy force to break through to CONSTANTINOPLE.

The SERBIAN Premier exposes the big German bluff in the Balkans, giving positive proof that no Austro-German army is concentrating on the DANUBE as has so often been reported from enemy and neutral sources. He announces SERBIA has consented to concessions to BULGARIA but it remains to be seen whether BULGARIA will throw in her lot with the Entente Powers or not.

England.

Sir Robert BORDEN in the course of an address at the Canadian Club luncheon yesterday, paid a tribute to the work of the navy which he described as wonderful. The splendid measures adopted against submarines showed more resourcefulness than people were aware of. The Navy had done vastly more to achieve victory than the Germans on land.

What is described as a political crisis is threatened over the question of conscription. Referring to conscription the "GAULOIS" says :- "In our opinion there is no doubt but that Great Britain will resign herself to it. She is passing through one of the grandest hours of her history with remarkable suppleness, and she has transformed herself, overthrowing many of her old principles and traditions in order to rise to the height of events. Now that the impulse has been given one may assume there will be no slackening".

United States.

NEW YORK rumour has it that the Loan of the Allies will be two hundred million sterling, which it is considered will be sufficient. Expert opinion is that the success of the Loan to that amount is assured.

3. **FRENCH OFFICIAL COMMUNIQUE.**

The French Official Communique details continued bombardment along the French front. To the South of STEINBACH the French artillery successfully destroyed the electricity works at TURCKHEIM.

4. **GERMAN OFFICIAL WIRELESS COMMUNIQUE.**

In the CHAMPAGNE a portion of the French trenches was captured by a bomb attack and a counter-attack was repulsed.
On the Russian front, the German Army is making slow progress. In South East GALICIA "there is nothing fresh to report with regard to the German troops".

5. **GERMAN RECRUITING** - (From French Corps Summary.)

The losses sustained by Germany so far has compelled her to call upon all the resources in men which she can legally command. Dire necessity has forced the recruiting authorities to enlist men who had already been set aside as medically unfit.

A study of Germany's methods of recruitment combined with the statements made by German prisoners in examination points to the following conclusions :-

Reinforcements taken from the 1915 class were sent to the front in July and August, and incorporated in units of the XIV Corps and XIV Reserve Corps, about 40 being sent per Company to the former, and 20 per Company to the latter.

The age of men of the 1st Ban Landsturm (untrained) was up to 37 years in the case of the most recent reinforcements.

From the latest information received it appears that the 1916 Class is now being trained. The last classes of untrained Landsturm up till the age of 45 have almost entirely been incorporated.

Thus, Germany's resources have not permitted the formation of large units since February, but have enabled her to maintain at their full strength the existing units. It is estimated that on the Western Front a strength of 225 men per Company has been rendered possible.

It may be noted that reinforcements, irrespective of the age or class of the men, are indiscriminately thrown into active or reserve regiments according to need.

18/9/15.

Major, G.S.

6th. DIVISION.

NEWS SHEET. (BY WIRELESS).

LONDON. September 18th, 1915.

Hurricanes of fire are reported this afternoon from PARIS by several sectors on the Western Front.

The FRENCH communique records the first instance of mine operations by the TURKS in GALLIPOLI.

A PETROGRAD telegram states that the fate of VILNA is evidently in the balance, adding that evacuation is now far advanced. The RUSSIAN communique received today shows that enemy detachments in some places have reached the railway line between NOVO VILEISK and MOLODSTOCHNO. To the North East near SVIENTSIANY where the GERMANS cut the PETROGRAD railway, strong enemy cavalry detachments are reported, while towards MEISHOGOLA North West of VILNA, the enemy is developing vigorous attacks. DVINSK which is about 80 miles North East of VILNA is also half encircled. North of SVIENTSIANY towards VIDZY, directly South of DVINSK, (the furthest point last reached by HINDENBURG's wedge between DVINSK and VILNA), PETROGRAD reports that the DAUGELISHKI village has been taken by the enemy. About 40,000 of the enemy's cavalry are said to be taking part in these operations.

In the fighting near ROVNO in VOLHYNIA just over the GALICIAN frontier, the RUSSIANS have re-occupied DERAZNO, and stormed a village, capturing 2,000 prisoners. In the attacks further South, the Russians took over 1,300 prisoners and continue successfully to check the enemy's local counter-attacks.

A new note from the ENTENTE has been handed to the BULGARIAN Premier. Its contents are being kept secret.

A Lloyds message from the AZORES states, that the fire on the SANTA ANNA is attributed to GERMAN Propagandists. Many explosions occurred, and 18 unexploded fuzes were found on board. The lives of at least 1196 passengers were imperiled.

Mr. John D. Rockefeller denies the statement attributed to him in a NEW YORK paper that he would not subscribe to the forthcoming ANGLO-FRENCH loan.

A UNITED STATES Note to GREAT BRITAIN with regard to the confiscation of cargoes has been prepared, but is being withheld by Mr. Lansing, who is going on a fortnights holiday.

19/9/1915.

A.B. LAWSON, Major,
General Staff, 6th Division.

1st Ln Coy   384

6th Division.

POLDHU PRESS. (By Wireless).

LONDON, September 20th.

The taking of VILNA announced in German Communique seems to have created some anxiety in certain minds, but today's PETROGRAD bulletin should dispel this feeling. Loss of VILNA may be presumed although it is not mentioned in the Russian Communique. It was not the fall of the Fortress which created perilous position, but the enveloping movements east and south. Germans claimed to have got on the Railway running east to MOLEDCHNO: cutting off retreat in this direction and leaving only VILNA - LIDA - ROVNO Line, running south for Russians to escape by. This line is also threatened. PETROGRAD announces, however, that enemy detachment which tried to sieze the Station of MOLEDCHNO was repulsed. On the LIDA Line also Germans were thrown back with great losses. Fierce fighting is proceeding for the passage of the CHARA, where the Russians are holding their own. In VOLHYNIA region Russians are advancing; while along the SERETH in GALACIA our Ally's troops are also meeting with successes.

In Western theatre artillery war continues. Yesterday the BRITISH FLEET bombarded the enemy's defences on the Belgian Coast.

Italian Communique states that by alternating surprise attacks and assaults in full force, an entire wood - Ferro di Cavallo - in the zone MONT SAN MICHELE in the CARSO district, has been taken in spite of persistent resistance by the enemy.

New York reports,... Washington Administrators are apparently completely ignoring so called explanation furnished by Dr. DUMBA, and it is now understood that no order for his recall having been received from VIENNA, Ambassador will be given his passports.

According to telegram from STAVANGER, German submarine has been destroyed about fourteen miles off UTSIRE. Three German hydroplanes are reported destroyed in the BALTIC.

Message from FRANKFURT to Lausanne Gazette gives gist of interview with Enver Pasha, who is reported has stated that all men under 45 years, including Christians, will be called under arms. Turkish War Minister thus hopes to be able to recruit an army of two millions. Enver Pasha also said that he did not believe Grand Duke Nicholas would make general offensive in CAUCASIA. Asked whether BULGARIA would take part in the War, he said he did not know.

Monsieur BARK, Russian Minister of Finance, arrived in PARIS this morning, being received by Ministers of Finance and Foreign Affairs.

                          A.B. LAWSON,   Major,

                                 General Staff.

1st Ln Coy

SUMMARY OF INFORMATION NO 107.

20th September, 1915.

1. OPERATIONS - 19th/20th Sept.

A quiet day is reported on most of the front. A German working party was located in a sap opposite WARWICK FARM. The guns were turned on to them and two shells had an excellent effect. There was less hostile gun-fire about POTIJZE, but more rifle fire. LA BRIQUE was shelled in the afternoon with heavy shells, but not much damage was done. One of our tobies fired several shells with good effect against the enemy's front line near NO MAN'S COTTAGE. On the left of the front enemy working parties were dispersed by rifle grenades. Three German snipers are reported to have been accounted for on the Corps front.

One of our batteries, while retaliating, hit what was apparently a bomb store. An armour-piercing shell caused a big explosion, throwing a large number of sandbags into the air.

Three of our batteries opened rapid fire on a 15 cm. howitzer battery, which was reported as active by French and British airmen. The effect was reported to be excellent, and the German No. 1 gun was destroyed. The enemy replied with a fairly violent shelling of some unoccupied positions.

2. MARCONI WIRELESS NEWS - LONDON, 19th Sept.

RUSSIA. - The official report from PETROGRAD received this morning states that the battle for VILNA is proceeding with extreme violence. The Germans are putting forward most desperate efforts to surround the position and compel the Russians to fall back or risk a heavy defeat. Our gallant Allies, however, are maintaining the battle with the utmost stubbornness. Terrific losses have been inflicted on the enemy who are described as lying in heaps before the barbed wire entanglements. From careful examination of the map however it would appear that the Germans have made some progress, though whether progress is commensurate with the price paid is extremely doubtful. South-East of ORANY the Germans have pressed back the Russians towards RADUN which is about 45 miles from VILNA and not less than 20 miles from the VILNA-LIDA railway, which is the section of the Great Transverse system which the Germans are straining every nerve to secure. It is stated that in the general action between ROVO and KOVEL on the front of about 60 miles the enemy were beaten and retreated in disorder. In this region the driving power of the Germans has clearly exhausted itself, no progress having been made here for more than a fortnight. It is manifest that the German effort is now being concentrated in the VILNA sector, and the acquisition of the transverse system railways would enable them to move their troops North and South with comparative ease, and to concentrate their forces at any point as dictated by necessities, either offensive or defensive.

BALKANS - The Balkan situation is still vague. The Bulgarian Minister in London professes to know nothing about the signing of a Turko-Bulgarian agreement. It is not to be expected that he would have received the Official Communique on the subject even if such a compact had been completed. The omens generally bearing upon King Ferdinand's Government are not propitious. The most that can be said is that the Balkan drama has not yet run it's course and that the climax may still be a master stroke of diplomacy.

ENGLAND - After a prolonged conference and discussion of points at issue with Mr Lloyd George the Union representatives have

P.T.O.

1st London Co. R.E.

at STOKE divested themselves of all their hard won privileges and agreed to all the concessions asked from them by the Government. The main points in the agreement are an advisory committee to be appointed to assist the Minister of Munitions, restrictive trade union rules to be suspended, investigation to be made to enable machinery to run 24 hours daily, and male and female labour to be employed on a more extensive scale. This offers one more proof of the absolute unanimity of the nation with regard to the war, and the determination of all classes to win.

2. FRENCH WIRELESS NEWS - PARIS, 19th Sept.

BELGIUM - The British fleet combined with the French heavy artillery found NIEUPORT in bombarding the German works and batteries on the Belgian coast.

FRANCE - In ARTOIS the German artillery fire has slackened. On the AISNE - MARNE canal the French have kept the bridge-head at SAPIGNEUL in spite of three German attacks.
In the forest of APREMONT, North of FLIREY, in LORRAINE, and in the VOSGES, the French artillery fire has been very effective. Four German ammunition depots were blown up.
Near ST. MIHIEL a German aeroplane fired on by the French guns and by a machine gun in a French aeroplane fell headlong into the German lines.

3. FROM OTHER CORPS SUMMARIES.

Some titles from the "Bayerische Zeitung".

Among others the following have received the Iron Cross:-
Fireinsurance   inspector   Ingolstadt.
Boerexporter Reichart.
Fieldspiritual and Linesofcommunicationparson Ginlielminotto.
Vicewatchman Heinrich Geissler.
Bookbinderssen von Barnberg.

4. PRESS EXTRACTS.

(The Sunday Times, Sept. 19th)

Telegrams from Switzerland describe the daring raid made by two French aviators on the railway going from Donaueschingen to Villingen in the Grand Duchy of Baden.
Eye-witnesses relate that the airmen sighted a troop train while they were manoevring at a very low altitude, and swooped down to within twelve to fifteen feet of the ground. One flew on the right of the line and the other on the left alongside the train and opened fire with machine-guns through the windows of the carriages upon the Germans, who were powerless to defend themselves. The German authorities evidently considered that there was no risk of a raid at a point so far from the frontier, for there was not a single cartridge among the troops.
Again and again the aviators flew up and down the train, killing the stoker and many soldiers. Others jumped from the train while in motion and sought for shelter.
The attack ended at Marbach Junction where the raiders fired into the ranks of the German soldiers drawn up on the platform, causing heavy loss.

20.9.15.

SUMMARY OF INFORMATION NO 108.

21st September, 1915.

1. OPERATIONS - 20th/21st Sept.

There was a good deal of hostile shelling of the right sector of our line. Our artillery bombarded the enemy's trenches round BELLEWAARDE FARM.

Snipers near OLER HOUSES were quieter after Toby had made 3 hits on their trenches.

On the left of the line it is reported that cries and groans were heard from a German working party on which our machine guns had fired.

In the evening the enemy bombarded VLAMERTINGHE with 17 inch shells.

Our artillery report that their early morning bombardment considerably damaged the enemy's wire in places, and knocked their front parapet about. Many sandbags and much timber and material were displaced, and two German shirts were seen in the air - whether occupied or not is uncertain.

A German battery was engaged with wireless observation in collaboration with the French. The airman reported excellent effect on the target, and a small wood near by was set on fire, causing an explosion.

Hostile aircraft have not for the last 3 days attempted to come far over our lines, and from cross-bearings taken, it is clear that our firing on enemy balloons has inspired respect.

On the 17th, 18th and 19th of this month it is calculated that about 650 shells were fired by the enemy into YPRES. The high explosive shells varied from 6 to 12 inches in size, and there was a considerable amount of 5.7" shrapnel and some gas shells. The majority appeared to come from the direction of HILL 60 or ZONNEBEKE.

2. MARCONI WIRELESS PRESS - LONDON, Sept. 20th.

RUSSIA - The taking of VILNA announced in the German communique seems to have created some anxiety in certain minds, but to-day's Petrograd bulletin should dispel this feeling. The loss of VILNA may be presumed although it is not mentioned in the Russian communique. It was not the fall of the fortress, however, which created the perilous position, but the enveloping movements East and South. The Germans claimed to have got on the railway running East to Molodehno, cutting off retreat in this direction and leaving only the Vilna - Lida - Rovno line running South for the Russians to escape by. This line is also threatened. Petrograd also announces that the enemy detachments which tried to seize the station of Molodehno were repulsed. On the Lida line also the Germans were thrown back with great losses. Fierce fighting is proceeding for the passage of the Chard where the Russians are holding their own. In the Volhyria region the Russians are advancing, while along the Soroth in Galicia our Ally's troops are also meeting with successes.

ITALY - The Italian communique states that by alternating surprise attacks and assaults in full force an entire wood, Ferro de Cavallo, in the zone of Monte San Michele in the CARSO district has been taken in spite of persistent resistance by the enemy.

AMERICA - New York reports the loan to Great Britain

P.T.O.

and France will be between six and eight hundred million dollars. It will be underwritten by a large syndicate of financiers and bankers who will receive a small commission, possibly half or 1%. Security will be British and French Government bonds and the price to investors will be par.

The Washington administration is apparently ignoring completely the so-called explanation furnished by Dr. Dumba, and it is now understood that no order for his recall having been received from Vienna, the ambassador will be given his passports.

NORWAY - According to a telegram from Stavanger, a German submarine has been destroyed about 14 miles off UTSINE.

3. **FRENCH OFFICIAL COMMUNIQUE.**

The German artillery has been very active and has heavily bombarded the suburbs of ARRAS with big shell.
In the Western ARGONNE the Germans have exploded a mine close to the French trenches.
In the WOEVRE a German column of infantry was dispersed by artillery fire.

4. **NEWS FROM GERMAN SOURCES.**

FRANKFORT - It is reported from Constantinople that the activity of German submarines is causing alarm and despondency among the Allies. A German submarine torpedoed an English transport carrying 15,000 men from Egypt to the Dardanelles.
(This was some transport!)

AMSTERDAM - The Wolff Agency has learned from travellers arriving from London, that as a result of the last Zeppelin raids, the Bank of England has been hit, also that a single factory, hit by a bomb, has suffered damage to the extent of £150,000 sterling.
(This is German news via Amsterdam).

5. **FROM OTHER CORPS SUMMARIES.**

The casualties reported in the heavy bombardment by heavy shell of the trenches in the Northern sector of the 2nd Corps front 2 days ago were only two.
The bombardment was certainly accurate as 8 bays of the parapet were blown in and other parts of the trenches blocked. The fortunately few casualties to personnel appear to be entirely due to the presence of good "slits", men going to ground on the signal being given.

21/9/15.

Major, G.S.

6th DIVISION.

POLDHU PRESS. (By Wireless).

LONDON, September 21st.

The Russian Army in the Northern Section is undergoing a severe ordeal. Following the fall of VILNA, desperate efforts are being made by the Germans to cut off their opponents successful retreat. The result is not definitely known yet, but an optimistic report comes today from PARIS. This statement, which is sent by a newspaper correspondent at the Russian Headquarters declares that the Army at VILNA has escaped encirclement, that the position which has been disquieting is now good, and the retreat is being carried out under normal and even very favourable conditions. Against the Austrians further South, the Russians maintain their successes and have captured a considerable number of men and a large amount of supplies.

The ITALIAN communique emphasises the importance of the success gained on Saturday to the North West of ARZIERO. The enemy was defeated and repulsed after four hours fierce fighting.

Through ODESSA comes a report not officially confirmed, that what is described as a TURCO-GERMAN submarine, was recently caught in the BLACK SEA and destroyed by Russian ships.

Tonights FRENCH despatch reports further effective work by the Allied big guns at many points along the front. The FRENCH troops have gained a footing on the right bank of the AISNE-MARNE Canal, and a German counter-attack on both sides of the SAPEGNEUL post was driven back. The FRENCH have also by means of grenade fighting made marked progress on the HARTMANN - WEILERKOPF in the VOSGES.

In the House of Commons this afternoon, Mr. McKenna, the Chancellor of the Exchequer, introduced the Budget. In the course of the speech, Mr. McKenna said, that on the existing basis of taxation, the revenue for the current year might be put at £273,000,000, and expenditure at £1,590,000,000 Great as was the present expenditure, he was sure the country was prepared to face it with courage and confidence. Every section of the nation must be called upon to contribute and make great sacrifices. The taxes he had now to propose must be upon a scale never before imposed. It was estimated that at the end of this year the dead weight of debt would be £2,200,000,000 This would by no means cripple our resources. We had to contemplate a Navy costing £190,000,000, an Army costing £715,000,000, and external advances amounting to £423,000,000. Grave as was the warning of his predecessor last May, his words had far weightier significance today. The best estimate that could be formed of the total daily rate of expenditure on all services from now to the end of the financial year was upwards of £4,500,000, and in the later weeks of the financial year, it might rise to more than £5,000,000. In the expenditure during the current year there was a charge of £66,000,000 on pre- and post-moratorium bills, and £170,000,000 on ordinary national services excluding Army and Navy, in all £1,590,000,000. There is no record of any nation ever having voluntarily accepted a bearing with so high a proportion to the national income which had to be made within a single year. The question of new taxation was largely involved with the question of machinery. He would only make such proposals as he was advised were practicable, so that he could assure the House that if they were accepted, the departments would be able to give effect to them promptly and efficiently. Revenues were now and always the

P.T.O.

2.

first object of the taxation, but there were other objects which must not be left out of view. What he was going to say would satisfy neither strict free trader nor scientific tariff reformer. Both must for the time being put fiscal theories on one side. We must look to the state of foreign exchanges and discourage imports. They had to have strict regard to the necessity also of reducing consumption. He proposed to add 40% to Income Tax rates. This would be combined with approved machinery for assessing employers and special relief where income had fallen more than 10%. The 40% rate of increase would be for the full year, making 20% for the remaining 6 months of the year. The exemption limit would be reduced from £160 to £130, and the abatement from £160 to £120. The super-tax scale would be raised to 2/10d between £8,000 and £9,000, 3/2d between £9,000 and £10,000, and 3/6d on surplus above £10,000. A man with no children earning £2-15-0 a week would pay 12/1d quarterly, £3 would pay 19/11d quarterly, £4 would pay £6 quarterly, £5,000 would pay £1,029. Excess profits tax, 50% of surplus above £100 to be taken. Adjustable on appeal. This would give £30,000,000 on a full year. Sugar duty increased from 1/10d a hundredweight to 9/4d. The Royal Commission on sugar reduced the prices by 2/6d to 3/6d per cent. Sugar would rise in price to 1/2d a lb. An all round increase of 50% on tea, tobacco, coffee, chicory, and dried fruits. No alteration on beer and spirit duties. Heavy import duties have been imposed on all foreign countries. The halfpeeny postage has been abolished and press telegrams must be self supporting.

A.B.LAWSON. Major,

General Staff.

6th DIVISION.

POLDHU PRESS. (By Wireless).

LONDON. September 22nd.

Important news comes today from BULGARIA, where a general Mobilisation is now taking place. Mobilisation of the railways is complete, and several cavalry regiments have left the Capital for unknown destinations. Bulgarian Minister in London has explained this development to mean an armed neutrality.

French and English aeroplanes have bombarded German positions in Belgium.

There have been violent artillery engagements in the neighbourhood of ARRAS and other parts of the French front.

The Russian army is now fighting east of VILNA; while to southern end of line Austrians are retiring before General IVANOFF.

English papers today are mainly concerned with the BUDGET, which has been very favourably received. The new taxes, though considerable, have not been criticised unfavourably by any responsible newspapers or section of community.

It is expected that announcement will be very shortly made that negotiations for a Franco-British Loan in New York has been concluded. Note expressing surprise of the United States Government at the action of British Prize Courts regarding confiscation of cargoes of food, will be sent to London as soon as reports on subject and views from exports arrive at Washington.

Officially announced that SERBIAN Legation in London has received instructions from its Government requesting all Serbian subjects between ages of sixteen and fifty, residing in the United Kingdom to communicate with Serbian Consuls for purpose of making necessary arrangements to rejoin Serbian Colours if called upon.

Liner KONINGIN EMMA, 9181 tons, belonging to NEDERLAND Steamship Company has struck a mine. All passengers and crew were saved.

LISBON newspapers announce default of over eighty thousand pounds in Accounts Department, Lisbon Custom House; some well known people being implicated.

Final jute forecast from CALCUTTA shews decrease of thirtyone lakhs bales or 29.4 percent as compared with last year.

It was stated at General Post Office today that new Post Office rate will probably not become operative until November 1st. To avoid dislocation of trade as much as possible, notice will be given in advance by Postmaster General as to when new charges will come into force.

A.B.LAWSON, Major,
General Staff.

1st Lin Coy 954

1st London bde
R.E.

SUMMARY OF INFORMATION NO. 109.
22nd September, 1915.

1. **OPERATIONS - 21st/22nd September.**

   A fairly quiet day is reported.
   Early in the morning the right sector of our line near RAILWAY WOOD was heavily bombarded, and our artillery replied. YPRES was shelled about mid-day. In the centre sector of our line Toby still keeps the enemy tame.
   The left sector was shelled considerably during the last 24 hours.
   A German aeroplane was fired at by our Anti-Aircraft guns and apparently hit, as it fell rapidly for about 400 feet, and then righted itself and flew over the German lines.

2. **MARCONI WIRELESS NEWS - LONDON, September 21st.**

   RUSSIA - The Russian army in the Northern section of the war is undergoing a severe ordeal. Following the fall of VILNA desperate efforts are being made by the Germans to cut off their opponents successful retreat. The result is not yet definitely known. A newspaper correspondent at the Russian headquarters declares that the   army at VILNA has escaped encirclement, that the position which had been disquieting is now good, and that the retreat is being carried out under normal and even favourable conditions. Against the Austrians further South the Russians maintain their successes, and have captured a considerable number of men and a large amount of supplies.

   ITALY - The Italian Communique emphasises the importance of the successes gained on Saturday to the North West of ARZIERRO. The enemy was defeated and repulsed after 4 hours fierce fighting and then sent forward another force which was similarly repelled, some prisoners being taken.

   FRANCE - To-night's French despatch reports further effective work by the Allied big guns at many points along the front. French troops have gained a footing on the Aisne - Marne Canal, and a German counter-attack on both sides of the Sapigneul post was driven back. The French have also by means of grenade fighting made marked progress on the Hartmanns Veilerkopf in the VOSGES.

   ENGLAND - In the House of Commons this afternoon Mr. McKenna, Chancellor of the Exchequer, introduced the Budget. In the course of the speech Mr. McKenna said that on the existing basis of taxation the revenue for the current year might be put at £272,000,000 and expenditure was estimated at £1,590,000,000. Great as was the present expenditure, he was sure the country was prepared to face it with courage and confidence. Every section of the nation must be called upon to contribute and make great sacrifices. The taxes he had now to propose must be upon a scale never before imposed. It was estimated that at the end of this year the dead weight of debt would be £2,200,000,000. This would by no means cripple our resources. We had to contemplate a navy costing £190,000,000, an army costing £750,000,000, and external advances to the amount of £423,000,000. The best estimate that could be formed of

P.T.O.

the daily rate of expenditure on all services from now to the end of the financial year was upwards of £4,500,000 and in the later weeks of the financial year it might rise to more than £5,000,000 a day. He proposed to add 40% to income tax rates. This would be combined with improved machinery for assessing employees and special relief where income had fallen more than 10%. The 40% rate of increase would be for the full year making 80% for the remaining 6 months of the year. Exemption limit would be reduced from £160 to £130 and the abatement from £150 to £120. Super-tax scale raised to 2/10d. between £8,000 and £9,000, 3/2d. between £9,000 and £10,000, 3/6d. on surplus above £10,000. A man with no children earning £2.5/ would pay 12/1d. quarterly; £3. would pay 18/11d. quarterly; £4. would pay 26/2d quarterly.

3. <u>FRENCH WIRELESS NEWS - PARIS.</u>

Violent artillery actions are reported in LORRAINE. The French have destroyed the emplacements prepared near HAMPONT for heavy long range guns to fire on NANCY and LUNEVILLE.
19 aeroplanes bombarded the railway junction at BENSDORF. About 100 bombs were dropped in buildings and stationary trains which were seriously damaged.

4. <u>FRENCH COMMUNIQUE.</u>

RUSSIA - In spite of Austrian denials, G.H.Q. declares that during the operations on the Western front between the end of August and the beginning of September, 70,000 prisoners were counted. This number will be considerably increased when all the small bands of prisoners are brought in. Many prisoners are so done up that they are quite unable to march.

<u>EXTRACT FROM THE "HAMBURGER NACHRICHTEN."</u>

<u>Utilization of fruit which has fallen from the trees.</u>

In order to make the most of every article of consumption produced by our country, no single fruit must be lost, which can be consumed by man or beast. This applies particularly to fallen fruit, and to certain wild fruit which is allowed in certain districts to be wasted. These fruits are very valuable, as, if they are spread on bread, they take the place of butter, dripping, etc. which are becoming more and more scarce. Depots will be formed all over the Empire to collect fallen and wild fruit.

22/9/15.

B.J. Ingham
Major, G.S.

SUMMARY OF INFORMATION NO 110.

23rd September, 1915.

1. OPERATIONS - Sept. 22nd/23rd.

    A quiet day is reported on the whole front.
    About RAILWAY WOOD there was continuous artillery fire from North and South during most of the day. The enemy damaged some of our trenches near ODER HOUSES with a trench mortar, and Toby retaliated with effect. Eight Germans are reported to have been accounted for by snipers and machine-gun fire.
    A German aeroplane dropped a bomb near ABEELE, but no damage was done.
    On September 20th, 21st and 22nd over 600 shells are reported to have fallen in YPRES, of which 400 fell on the 22nd., when there was a continuous bombardment from 4 a.m. The majority of the shells were high explosive from 6" to 12" and 5,7 shrapnel. Three 17" shells fell on the 22nd.
    The enemy are reported to be working hard and carrying timber near HILL 60. Our artillery damaged some of the new work and loopholes there.

2. MARCONI WIRELESS NEWS - LONDON, Sept. 22nd.

    BALKANS. - Important news comes from Bulgaria to-day where a general mobilisation is now taking place. Mobilisation of the railways is complete, and several cavalry regiments have left for unknown destination. The Bulgarian Minister in London has explained this developement to mean an armed neutrality.

    BELGIUM. - French and English aeroplanes have bombarded German positions in Belgium.

    FRANCE - There have been violent artillery engagements in the neighbourhood of ARRAS and other parts of the French front.

    RUSSIA - The Russian army is now fighting East of VIJNA, while to the Southern end of the line the Austrians are retiring before General Ivanoff.

    ENGLAND - The budget has been very favourably received and the new taxes, though considerable, have not been criticised unfavourably by any responsible newspaper or section of the community. It is expected that the announcement will be very shortly made that negotiations for a Franco-British loan in New York have been concluded.

    SERVIA - It is officially announced that the Serbian Legation in London has received instructions from it's Government requesting all Serbian subjects between sixteen and fifty residing in the United Kingdom to communicate with Serbian Consuls for the purpose of making the necessary arrangements to rejoin the Serbian colours if called upon.

    HOLLAND - The liner Koni gin Emma, 9181 tons, belong-

P.T.O.

2.

belonging to the Nederland Steamship Company has struck a mine. All the passengers and crew have been saved.

PORTUGAL. - The Lisbon newspapers announce an important financial default of over £80,000 in the accounts department of the Lisbon Customs House, some well known people being implicated.

3. FRENCH WIRELESS NEWS - PARIS.

The same artillery activity continues N. and S. of ARRAS and in the ARGONNE.

A violent bombardment near VILLE-aux-BOIS has forced the enemy to evacuate a fortified post, which the French have occupied.

In CHAMPAGNE, a German patrol which tried to penetrate the French lines was entirely wiped out.

As a reprisal for the bombardment by the Germans of open towns in France and England, a squadron of French aeroplanes bombarded STUTTGART, the capital of Wartemberg. About 30 bombs were dropped on the Royal Palace and the railway-station. All the aeroplanes returned safely.

4. NEWS FROM GERMAN SOURCES.

The Turks have satisfied themselves that we use our hospital ships to transport troops, and that we have observation posts on the masts. They also claim that their cavalry, reinforced by volunteers, made a successful raid on the back of one of our camps, and put our men to flight.

23/9/15.

R.J. Ingham
Major, J.S.

6th DIVISION.

POLDHU PRESS. (By Wireless).

LONDON, September 23rd.

Violent reciprocal Bombardments along line in France are recorded in tonights official report. In ARTOIS the German artillery is active, while to the South of the AVRE, the French directed an intense and efficious fire on the enemy's trenches. Several German munition depots were blown up in CHAMPAGNE. Trench to trench combats have been fought round NEUVILLE. Between the MEUSE and MOSELLE fighting with bombs, aerial torpedoes and grenades has taken place.

The purpose of the order of mobilisation of the BULGARIAN Army is not yet known. 4 Divisions, each of 30,000 men, have been called up. A Division of cavalry has left SOFIA for an unknown destination. ATHENS is greatly excited at the news, and there is much diplomatic activity in the GREEK Capital. Meanwhile SERBIA calmly awaits the developments of a German attack on the North-East Frontier. The bombardment across the DANUBE and SAVE continues.

Doubt no longer exists that the RUSSIAN Army in the VILNA district has escaped encirclement, thanks to heroic rearguard actions of the Russian Troops. Having failed to destroy the VILNA Army, the enemy is now making a formidable encircling movement against DVINSK. PETROGRAD announces that desperate and increasing actions are being fought. Enemy is developing hurricane fire on this front. In the meantime movements are taking place at the extremities of the line which should influence the VILNA-DVINSK district where the Russians are beset. In the extreme North, General RUSKY is delivering a counterstroke which is meeting with success in the FRIEDRICHSTADT region, while in VOLHYNIA and GALACIA General IVANOFF has achieved further successes.

Aeroplanes yesterday dropped bombs on STUTTGART, Capital of WURTEMBERG. 30 shells fell on the Royal Palace and Station, and the aviators although often cannonaded, returned without a scratch. The BERLIN version of the raid declares that 4 persons were killed and that soldiers and civilians were wounded, but that the material damage was not important. Meantime a German airman was fired upon by Germans.

The ITALIAN communique shows the admirable results that followed daring and carefully concealed plans in the mountainous region North West of CORTINA D'AMPEZZO. In the CRISTALLO zone especially, many small detachments of the enemy were dislodged and ultimately driven down and back in the direction of the valleys of FELCZON (BOITE) and SELLAND (PIENZ)

A.B.LAWSON, Major,

General Staff.

1st Ln Coy

6th Division.

NEWS SHEET BY WIRELESS.

LONDON. September 24th.

The GREEK Army has been mobilized as a result of the mobilization by BULGARIA, but this measure, however, must be regarded for the present as a defensive one in view of the uncertainty which exists as to the attitude of BULGARIA.

GERMAN attacks have been repulsed in LORRAINE by the FRENCH Army. On all points of the Western front the Allied artillery continues to hold mastery over the enemy, and in some areas, particularly in the ARRAS sector, the enemy's defences have been seriously damaged.

The RUSSIAN offensive in GALICIA continues with great success, and a telegram to a FRENCH newspaper, which is confirmed by AUSTRIAN admissions, states that LYCK has been recaptured.

The LONDON correspondent of the AMSTERDAM TELEGRAAF visited the Institution in which GERMAN civilians are kept at ISLINGTON, LONDON, and describes the camp as being perfectly managed and the prisoners fairly treated without any harshness.

A telegram from BERLIN states the subscriptions to the third GERMAN War Loan amount to twelve milliards and thirty million marks (£601,500,000). The result of small subscriptions is still unknown.

A BUCHAREST paper gives the following losses suffered by the AUSTRIAN ARMY up to August 1915:- 551,000 killed, 1,915,300 wounded, and 863,500 prisoners.

The HARRISON of LIVERPOOL, homeward bound, has been sunk; part of the crew have been rescued and are being brought to land by steamer.

Sd. A.B.LAWSON, Major,

General Staff.

1st Lin Coy 308.

SUMMARY OF INFORMATION NO. 111.

24th September 1915.

1. OPERATIONS - September 23rd/24th.

    The right sector of the line was again shelled heavily round RAILWAY WOOD, while our artillery bombarded the enemy's trenches about BELLEWAARDE FARM.
    A German heavy howitzer, firing from the direction of PILKEM, put about six shells into the German trenches near VERLOREN-HOEK, doing considerable damage.
    There was more shelling than usual on the CANAL bank, and YPRES was shelled at intervals during the afternoon.

2. MARCONI WIRELESS NEWS - London, September 23rd.

    France.

    Violent reciprocal bombardments along the line in France are recorded in tonight's official reports. In ARTOIS the German artillery is active, while to the South of the AVRE the French directed an intense and efficacious fire on the enemy's trenches. Several German munition depots were blown up in CHAMPAGNE. Trench to trench combats have been fought round NEUVILLE. Between the MEUSE and the MOSELLE fighting with bombs, aerial torpedoes, and grenades has taken place.

    Balkans.

    The purpose of the order for the mobilisation of the Bulgarian army is not yet known. Four Divisions, each of 30,000 men, have been called up. A Division of Cavalry has left SOFIA for an unknown destination. ATHENS is greatly excited at the news and there is much diplomatic activity in the Greek capital. Meanwhile SERBIA is calmly awaiting the development of the German attack on the North-east frontier. The bombardment across the DANUBE and the SAVE continues.

    Russia.

    Doubt no longer exists that the Russian Army has escaped encirclement, thanks to heroic rearguard actions of the Russian troops. Having failed at   VILNA, the enemy's army is now making a formidable encircling movement against DVINSK. PETROGRAD announces that desperate and unceasing actions are being fought. The enemy is developing a hurricane of fire on this front. In the meantime movements are taking place on the extremities of the line which should influence VILNA - DVINSK district where the Russians are beset. In the extreme North, General RUSKY is delivering a counter-attack which is meeting with success in the FRIEDRICHSTADT region, while in VOLKYMA and GALACIA, General IVANOFF has achieved further successes.

    Italy.

    The Italian communique shows the admirable results that followed the daring and carefully conceived plans in the mountainous region North-west of CORTINA D'AMPEZZO. In the CRISTALLO zone especially, many small detachments of the enemy were dislodged and ultimately driven down and back in the direction of the VALLEYS OF FELEZON (BOITE) and SEELAND (RIENZ).

3. FRENCH WIRELESS NEWS.

A French dirigible bombarded last night several railway stations where German movements have been reported.
French aeroplanes compelled several captive balloons to make a rapid descent. Aeroplanes bombarded the railway stations of OFFENBURG, CONFLAUS, and VOUZIERS, and the rest billets at LANGEMARCK and MIDDELKERKE.
(NOTE: It is certain the enemy will declare that the first of these places is an open town).

4. FRENCH OFFICIAL COMMUNIQUE.

A telegram from COLOGNE asserts that the French aeroplanes which bombarded STUTTGART bore the German marks. This is absolutely untrue. The aeroplanes bore quite clearly the cockade with the French colours. In addition they were frequently fired on while going and returning over the German lines

On the night of the 22nd/23rd BELGIAN aeroplanes bombarded CORTEMARCK Station and German rest billets.
It is reported that one of the Allies' aeroplanes dropped bombs on a troop train between DOUAI and VALENCIENNES, and derailed it.

5. FROM OTHER CORPS SUMMARIES.

The 330th Prussian casualty list includes several names of the Headquarters Staff at FREIBURG in BADEN.
Apparently this is the result of one of the recent bombings of FREIBURG by French airmen, so that the damage done was not entirely "without military significance" as the German communique asserts. The casualty list gives the names of a Major-General and several regimental commanders as killed.

24/9/15.

B. J. Ingham
Major, G.S.

SUMMARY OF INFORMATION.

Wire from G.H.Q. 9.25 p.m. 26/9/15.

"There has been severe fighting today on the ground won by us yesterday. The enemy made determined counter-attacks East and North East of LOOS. The result of this fighting is that, except just North of LOOS, we hold all the ground gained yesterday, including the whole of LOOS itself. This evening we retook the Quarries North West of HULLUCH which were won and lost yesterday. We have, in this fighting, drawn in the enemy's reserves, thus enabling the French on our right to make further progress. The number of prisoners collected after yesterday's fighting amounts to 26,000 nine Field Guns, and a considerable number of machine guns have been taken. Our aeroplanes today bombed and derailed a train near LOFFRE, East of DOUAI, and another which was full of troops at ROSULT near St.AMAND. VALENCIENNES station was also burnt."

Wire from G.H.Q. 10.10 p.m. 26/9/15.

"The French attack yesterday in CHAMPAGNE captured the whole of the German first and second line trenches on a front of 21 kilometres. Mist, this morning, prevented an attack on the third line before 2 p.m., and the attack started at that hour. Result not yet known. Amended figures of French captures yesterday in CHAMPAGNE are 18,000 prisoners and 31 guns."

First Army wires 7.30 a.m. 27/9/15.

"The attack on the QUARRIES yesterday reported successful after prolonged fighting. The Germans still hold one point on which a bombing attack was ordered for 2.30 p.m. Elsewhere no change".

FRENCH OFFICIAL COMMUNIQUE - 7 p.m. - 27/9/15.

In the ARRAS District we have occupied the whole of SOUCHEZ village and are advancing towards GIVENCHY.
Further South we have taken LA FOLIE and pushed forward North of THELUS. In the course of this fighting about 1,000 prisoners were made.
In CHAMPAGNE the advance continues. After having captured the strong system of trenches between AUBERIVE and VILLE-SUR-TOURBE, our troops pushed forward towards the North and forced the Germans to retire on their Second Line, 3 or 4 kilometres further back. Fighting continues on the whole front. We have reached L'EPINE DE VEDEGRANGE and passed the cottage on the SOUAIN - SOMME PY road, and the hut on the SOUAIN - TAHURE road; to the East we hold the MAISON DE CHAMPAGNE farm. The enemy have suffered very severe losses from our fire and in the hand-to-hand fighting. A large quantity of stores, which up to the present it has not been possible to count, were left in the abandoned trenches.
Up to now 24 Field guns have been captured; the number of prisoners is increasing and at present exceeds 16,000 unwounded men, including at least 200 officers.
Altogether on the whole front the Allies have made in two days more than 20,000 prisoners.

A.B.L.

General Staff.

SUMMARY OF INFORMATION NO 114.

27th September, 1915.

1. OPERATIONS - September 26th/27th.

    There was a little shelling along the Corps front, but the situation is reported generally to be quiet.
    One of our aeroplanes was brought down near PILCKEM by three enemy aeroplanes fitted with machine-guns.

    FRENCH FRONT - The French have captured SOUCHEZ and LES TILLEULS.
    In CHAMPAGNE the French captured the whole of the German first and second line trenches on a front of 21 kilometers, also 18,000 prisoners and 31 guns.

    FIRST ARMY FRONT.
    Sunday - There was severe fighting on the ground won by us on Saturday, and the enemy made determined counter-attacks East and North-East of LOOS. The result is that, except just North of LOOS, we hold all the ground gained yesterday, including the whole of LOOS itself. In the evening we retook the quarries N.W. of HULLUCH, which were won and lost yesterday. We have in this fighting drawn in the enemy's reserves, thus enabling the French on our right to make further progress. The number of prisoners collected after yesterday's fighting was 2,600, and 9 field guns and a considerable number of machine guns were taken.
    Monday. - There is no change in the situation.
    The night was spent in consolidating the ground gained.

2. MARCONI WIRELESS NEWS - LONDON, Sept. 26th.

    RUSSIA - Last night's PETROGRAD communique states that near DUBNO the Russians made over 1,600 prisoners and repulsed attacks on the Galician front making over 3,500 prisoners.
    In the fighting at LUTZK 6,000 prisoners were taken.

    BALKANS - A message from Marseilles to the Petit Parisien states that Greece is recalling ships, and the captains of Greek ships have received instructions to-day to get under way with the least possible delay for their different ports, where they will hold themselves at the disposition of the Government. A semi-official statement issued in Sofia yesterday says the declaration of armed neutrality by Bulgaria is, according to the views expressed in Government circles, to be explained by the changes which have recently occurred in the political and military situation. Bulgaria has not the slightest aggressive intentions but is firmly resolved to defend fully-armed her rights and independence. Following the example of Holland and Switzerland who did not hesitate to resort to such an action at the beginning of the present war. Bulgaria is obliged, in view of the movement of troops effected by her neighbours, and in view of the danger which threatens her from the fact of the Austro-German offensive against SERBIA, to proclaim her armed neutrality, while at the same time continuing her conversations and pourparlers with representatives of the two belligerent groups. A message from ATHENS states the military commander at Demotika and

P.T.O.

DADEAGATCH have signed at DEMOTIKA a treaty regarding the cession of territory by TURKEY to BULGARIA.

3. NEWS FROM GERMAN SOURCES.

The Germans claim that as a consequence of the bombardment of ZEEBRUGGE by the English Fleet one ship was sunk and two others damaged. There does not appear to be any truth in this statement.

The Germans admit that one of their Divisions was driven out of the first line into the second line near LOOS and that they suffered considerable loss. They also state that they voluntarily evacuated the ruins of what was once the village of SOUCHEZ.

H C Jackson
Major, G.S.

27/9/15.

NEWS SHEET. (BY WIRELESS).

LONDON. September, 27th, 1915.

Two fine successes have been registered by the BRITISH and FRENCH on the Western battle front. South of LA BASSEE, the BRITISH have advanced for a distance of 2½ miles on a five mile front, and in CHAMPAGNE the FRENCH thrust on a 17 mile front took them some 2½ miles into the German lines. So far as is known to date, no fewer than 20,000 GERMANS including 300 officers have been taken prisoners by the Allies, and 33 field guns have been captured, 9 by the BRITISH and 24 by the FRENCH. The BELGIAN Army also reports success. On the evening of September 25th, troops captured a GERMAN listening post on the right bank of the YSER making prisoners of the whole garrison. This occupation of the post has forced the GERMANS to evacuate 100 metres of trenches along the YSER. According to this afternoon's official message, these gains have all been maintained, and the record of officers taken prisoners has been increased from 200 to 300. Altogether along the whole front, some 23,000 prisoners have been taken during the weekend, the greatest success on the Western front since the GERMAN retreat from the MARNE a year ago. No further message has been received from Sir John French since yesterday apparently, but the usual communique outlining the result of the operations to date was issued in PARIS this afternoon. This, although naturally it does not contain another catapogue of advances such as that published yesterday, indicates that however strenuously the GERMANS may have attempted to re-capture the ground they lost in the last 2 days, they have not succeeded. In ARTOIS the positions won have been maintained, and in CHAMPAGNE the fighting continues with tenacity on the whole front. Scrupulously accurate FRENCH officials now correct the report contained in yesterdays communique. The advance reported at first as having reached the destroyed telograph station North of THELUS to the East of SOUCHES, has not passed the Orchard of LA FORELIE and the road from ARRAS to LILLE. It has, however, been entirely maintained. On the front South of the SOMME there has been bomb and torpedoo fighting in the direction of ANDECHY. The GERMAN batteries bombarding the FRENCH position at QUENNEVIERES were vigorously countered. Between the MEUSE and MOSELLE in LORRAINE, there was intense cannonading on both sides, but in the VOSGES a violent storm temporarily suspended all warlike operations.

According to a message published in the ECHO DE PARIS, General IVANHOFF gained yesterday in the South Eastern theatre, a victory over the Austrians and Germans, capturing thousands of prisoners. No official confirmation of this has yet been received.

Commenting in the PETIT PARISIEN on the FRENCH success in ARTOIS and CHAMPAGNE, Colonel ROUSSET says the battle was fought in abominable weather and deluge of rain which must have greatly hampered assailants.

A.B.L.

General Staff.

1st Ln Coy 823

NEWS SHEET. (BY WIRELESS).

FRENCH COMMUNIQUE. 3 p.m. 29th September 1915.

The accounts which arrive allow one to measure more completely each day the importance of the success gained by the FRENCH offensive in CHAMPAGNE, combined with that of the Allied troops in ARTOIS. The Germans have not only been obliged to abandon on a broad front positions strongly entrenched, on which they had orders to resist to the end. They have suffered losses of which the total killed wounded and prisoners exceeds the effective of three Army Corps. The total number of prisoners is now more than 23,000. The number of guns brought back to the rear is 79. 17,055 prisoners and 316 officers have passed through CHALONS to go on towards their destination for internment. During the day and night the FRENCH have reached after a severe fight HILL 140, the culminating point of the crests of VIMY, and the Orchards to the South. The total number of prisoners taken in this single sector reached a thousand. The GERMANS have violently bombarded the trenches to the North and South of the AISNE, in the regions of BOIS-SAINT-MARD, of TROYON, and of VAILLY. The FRENCH replied energetically.

LONDON. September 29th.

The BRITISH forces operating in MESOPOTAMIA routed the TURKISH forces on both banks of the TIGRIS. In the House this afternoon, the Secretary for INDIA read telegrams announcing that the enemy is in full flight to BAGHDAD, that the BRITISH are in pursuit, and that many prisoners and guns and much ammunition have been captured; a smashing blow at the TURKS in this region.

The Italian battleship BENEDETTO BRIN has been accidentally blown up in the harbour at BRINDISI, and it is feared with heavy loss of life. Amongst the killed were Admiral Rubin De Cervin, and most of the officers of the ship, which although built 14 years ago, and thus not one of ITALY'S strongest naval units, was nevertheless a powerful vessel mounting four 12-inch, four 8-inch, and twelve 6-inch guns.

The struggle for DVINSK still continues/unabated fierceness, but the RUSSIANS are keeping the enemy in check, and the pressure has been relieved by the transfer of GERMAN troops from this quarter to the Western area.

On the GALICIAN front, developments are important, but up to the present the telegrams do not give any clear result though it seems evident that heavy fighting is in progress.

The watchful and determined ITALIAN troops have defeated another attack in the CEVEDALE zone, and our Ally has been also successful in driving back an enemy advance on the CARSO.

The BALKAN outlook is brighter. It is significant as indicating an improvement that the RUSSIAN Minister has had an interview with King Ferdinand, the result of which is believed to be satisfactory. ROUMANIA, says one correspondent, has 160,000 men under arms while not mobilized. The GREEK mobilization is proceeding smoothly.

If the report from ATHENS is to be believed, some 300,000 AUSTRO-GERMAN troops have been ordered to advance on the AUSTRO-SERBIAN frontier in the direction of ORSOVA.

It is now officially announced that the UNITED STATES loan to the ALLIES for the purpose of steadying the exchange is to be £100,000,000, at 5 per cent. It will be issued at 98 in 100 dollar bonds and instalments will be accepted.

Mr. GAFFNEY, the American Consul General at MUNICH, has been asked to resign on account of his Pro-German utterances, and if he refuses, he will be dismissed. Indicative of the distress existing amongst the working classes in MUNICH is the fact that over 3,000 women applied personally for positions as tramway conductors when only 300 were required. Besides these, several hundreds sent written applications.

It is semi-officially stated that the DUTCH Government has made a serious protest to the GERMAN Government concerning GERMAN airships sailing over DUTCH territory, and declares it expects adequate measures to be taken to avoid repetition of such violation of neutral territory.

RECEIVED FROM 1st ARMY. 10.5 p.m. 29th September.

"Enemy has made several attacks in the neighbourhood of FOSSE No.8. All these have been repulsed, and the latest report states that severe fighting is going on in the neighbourhood of HOHENZOLLERN* and FOSSE No.8. Heavy shelling on the rest of the 1st and 4th Corps. Nothing to report North of the Canal."

* An important German work.

RECEIVED 7.40 a.m. FROM 6TH.CORPS.

"The FRENCH have made further progress in CHAMPAGNE. In the LA MAIN position 1,000 prisoners were taken belonging to 21 battalions of 18 different regiments.
The total captures by the FRENCH up to date are reckoned at 100 guns and 25,000 prisoners. There is, as yet, no further news of the three Divisions which broke through the German second line."

A.B.L.
General Staff.

SUMMARY OF INFORMATION No 116.
29th September, 1915.

1. OPERATIONS - Sept., 28th/29th.

    On our own front there is little to report. YPRES was shelled during the early morning of the 28th with 17 inch shells. The enemy's artillery was active during the day, particularly against the centre of our section where the communication trenches behind CROSS ROADS FARM were damaged. Near the Canal a German wearing a cap similar to one of our winter caps, shouted across in English. He was promptly sniped and conversation ceased.

2. FRENCH OFFICIAL COMMUNIQUE.

    On the morning of the 28th September the French continued to gain ground foot by foot towards the crest East of SOUCHEZ. 100 prisoners were made, among which were men of the Guard Corps which had been brought back a few days ago from the Russian front. In CHAMPAGNE there has also been fresh progress, particularly near to MESSIGES where the French have made another 800 prisoners. In the ARGONNE the enemy violently bombarded the French trenches but made no infantry attack. Some bombing attacks have enabled the French to regain some portions of their first line, where the enemy had established himself yesterday.

3. MARCONI WIRELESS NEWS - LONDON, Sept., 28th.

    RUSSIA - PETROGRAD announces that in the DVINSK region, where there has been a lull, violent fighting is again taking place. Elsewhere on the 1,000 mile front, the Russians have met with further successes.

    BALKANS. - In the House of Commons this afternoon Sir Edward Grey made an important statement on the situation in the BALKANS. He stated that the BULGARIAN Government declared they had taken up a position of armed neutrality in defence of their rights and independence, and without any aggressive intentions whatever. Our view of the BALKANS situation, he stated, is that not only is there no hostility in this country to BULGARIA, but there is a traditional warm feeling of sympathy with the BULGARIAN people. So long, therefore, as BULGARIA did not side with the enemies of GREAT BRITAIN there could be no question of BRITAIN'S influence being used against BULGARIA'S interests. If, on the other hand, BULGARIA assumed an aggressive attitude we should give our friends in the BALKANS all the support in our power. Our policy had been to obtain an agreement between the BALKAN STATES, based on the general principle of territorial and political union of kindred nationalities. The policy of Germany on the other hand had been to create dissension. TURKEY, like AUSTRIA, was now subordinate to and dependent on GERMANY in order to realise GERMAN aspirations from BERLIN to BAGDAD. Germany's aim is to use the BALKAN NATIONS in the same way. The policy of the Allies is to further the aspirations of the BALKAN STATES without sacrificing their independence.

4. GERMAN WIRELESS NEWS.

    Western Theatre - The enemy continued yesterday his efforts to break through our front, suffering severe losses without attaining any success. At LOOS, following a fruitless gas attack by the

P.T.O.

English, we countered, capturing important ground and 770 prisoners including 20 officers. This brings the total for this zone up to 3,397 including officers. Five additional machine-guns were taken in the SOUCHEZ district.

Along the whole front in CHAMPAGNE up to the foot of the ARGONNE, French assaults were incessantly repulsed. Near LORRAIN the enemy so far misjudged the situation as to push ahead cavalry which was, of course, swept with fire, soon taking to flight. In the ARGONNE we, in turn, engaged on a slight advance by "LA FILLE MORTE" taking 4 officers and 250 men. On the heights of LOMBRES the enemy's position was shattered by mines along a considerable line.

Eastern Theatre - Army Group of Field Marshal von Hindenburg - The enemy forces on the S.W. front pressed back yesterday on Hindenburg and attempted to make a stand, but were again thrown back. In throwing back the enemy's VILNA forces to the line NAROEZ - SEE - SMORGON - WISCHREW, the army of Lieut-General von Lichorn captured 70 officers, 21,908 men, 3 guns, 72 machine guns and much transport. On account of the speed of our pursuit it has only now been possible to give attention to the booty mentioned. None of these captures have been reported previously.

General von Linsingen has forced the passage of the Styr below LUTSCH, the Russians North of Rovno being in full retreat along the whole front.

5. LATE NEWS.

The situation about LENS, morning Sept. 29th. - On the 1st Army front there is no material change. The chief feature of yesterday was the advance of the 10th French Army to the S. of LENS. Here they took the second German line on a front of about 1,200 yards and have thus gained a footing on the North end of the VIMY road. Their line now runs approximately as follows:-

From the original line W. of ANGRES by the West edge of the GIVENCHY WOOD to about 1,500 yards E. of NEUVILLE ST. VAAST.

6. EXTRACTS FROM GERMAN DOCUMENTS.

Extracts from letters found on prisoners taken at HOOGE 25th September:-

"The Trenches"
25th Sept., 1915.

"This morning we have to leave our trenches as the Artillery are going to bombard the English front line; it is because they cannot shoot very accurately that we have to go out. However, 10 of our company have to remain at their posts".

"In the Trenches".
24th Sept.

"We are going into rest billets again soon, perhaps to-morrow morning. Thank God for it! it is terrible in these trenches, as the English shell us very often with large calibre shells, and as they are good shots it becomes very unpleasant for us. A great number of the shells come right into the trenches and the rest break and upset all the work we do at night, which means work again all night long, Ugh! There is another shell! That means they have begun again. Why we have not all been killed, God alone knows. Really we have not lost as many as we might have done, considering how often and how heavily we are shelled, but still

3.

still/ our losses have not been very heavy lately".

29/9/15.

[signature] Lieut.
for Major, G.S.

STOP PRESS NEWS

A report just received states that three French Divisions have broken through the last German line in CHAMPAGNE.

1st Ln Coy

-:NEWS SHEET (by wireless):-

LONDON. 30th September.

This afternoon's French Communiqué again contains cheerful news. In CHAMPAGNE the Allies gained footings at several points in the trenches of the second position of the German defence to the West of the BITTE DE TAHARE and to the West of NAVARRIN FARM. At this last point some troops crossed the German lines and resolutely advanced beyond, but their progress was not maintained on account of artillery curtain fire and very violent flank fire. To the South of REPONT the Allies have enlarged and completed conquest of first German position by carrying a portion of a very important supporting work. Despite unfavourable atmospheric conditions, air squadrons bombarded lines of communications behind the German front. Shells were thrown on several railway stations, as well as on a column on the march.

Two new Russian successes are reported today. In the IKVA they have penetrated into trenches of Austro-Hungarians and the battle is now proceeding, while in the North of VILEIKA Russian cavalry have defeated forces supporting General EICHHORN. Round DVINSK the cannonade continues without a moment's respite. It is reported that the Germans are bringing up reinforcements but so far rushes are being stopped.

GREECE appears for the moment to bulk most largely in the BALKAN situation. The Chamber has a credit of £6,000,000 for mobilisation purposes and proclaiming state of siege through MACEDONIA. It is added in ATHENS report giving this information that VENIZELOS, who met with enthusiastic reception, stated the reasons which compelled GREECE to mobilise, and insisted upon the gravity of the situation

Many leading ROUMANIAN senators and deputies have called for mobilisation in their country also; another equally significant message regarding BUCHAREST is that parts of four German submarines, which were intended for TURKEY, are held up by ROUMANIAN Government.

LONDON. September 30th.

The following order of the day was issued by General JOFFRE before the assault on Saturday:-
"Offensive is to be carried out without truce and without respite. Remember the MARNE - Conquer or die."

PARIS newspapers state that Prince de Polignac, Captain of Infantry, has succumbed to wounds sustained fighting in CHAMPAGNE. He was wounded some time ago, but left again for the front.

In the House of Commons this afternoon Motor import duties were carried by 174 votes to 8.

A NEW YORK telegram states that all the morning papers predict the greatest success for the Anglo-French Bond Issue, declaring that three hundred million dollars will be taken by NEW YORK alone, while CHICAGO will probably subscribe one hundred million. Some papers express the opinion that the loan will be over-subscribed.

The STRASSBURGER POST, one of the most optimistic of the German organs, of the ALSACE-LORRAINE Press, admits importance of present Allies successes and acknowledges that GERMANY must have suffered very heavily. The same Journal, speaking of British offensive says:-
"Many of those adversary gains are immeasurable."

An AMSTERDAM telegram states that Zeppelins have been sighted going in a Westerly direction.

1st London Field Coy RE   275

Mr. Lloyd George has accepted invitation to address Congress on Munitions in relation to war profits and labour.

General verdict of British Peers concerning DUMBA incident today summarised situation by pointing out that it makes no difference to Great Britain whether Austria is represented at Washington by DUMBA, or any other diplomatist, all are much alike and all tarred with the same brush. It is for the Government and people of United States to appraise the crafty gang of unscrupulous German and Austrian diplomatists at Washington, and to let them stay or pack them off, as seems best to themselves.

News from ROTTERDAM states that three airships yesterday performed inexplicable evolutions over DUTCH Territory, one flying low over forts on outskirts of ROTTERDAM.

A.B. LAWSON, Major,

General Staff, 6th Division.

1st Fn Fd Coy 20.
R.E.

CALENDAR FOR SEPTEMBER 1915.

DATE	DAY	SUN Rises a.m.	SUN Sets p.m.	MOON Rises	MOON Sets	REMARKS.
1	Wed	4.57	6.32	9. 3p	1.58p	
2	Th.	4.59	6.29	9.50p	2.50p	THE PROGNOSTICATIONS OF
3	Fri	5. 1	6.27	10.47p	3.47p	COLONEL HARRISON, U.S.A.
4	Sat	5. 2	6.24	11.21p	4.24p	
5	Sun	5. 3	6.22	11.55p	4.50p	AUGUST:
6	Mon	5. 5	6.20	1.9a	5.12p	West. No change: an increased expenditure of ammunition. Reinforcement and extension of the English line.
7	Tu.	5. 6	6.18	2.27a	5.29p	
8	Wed	5. 8	6.16	3.46a	5.43p	
9	Th.	5.10	6.14	5.46a	5.58p	Italy. Investment of TRIESTE and ISTRIA.
10	Fri	5.11	6.12	6.26a	6.9 p	Russia. End of the German offensive through lack of men. Local Serbian offensive. Organisation of a BALKAN Union.
11	Sat	5.13	6.10	7.48a	6.24p	
12	Sun	5.14	6. 8	9.13a	6.42p	
13	Mon	5.15	6. 6	10.43a	7. 5p	East. ROUMANIA declares war. BULGARIA declares war.
14	Tu.	5.17	6.3	12. 6p	7.37p	
15	Wed	5.19	6. 1	1.32p	8.21p	SEPTEMBER:
16	Th.	5.20	5.58	2.37p	9.25p	West. General German offensive; tremendous expenditure of ammunition.
17	Fri	5.22	5.56	3.27p	10.41p	
18	Sat	5.23	5.52	4. 0p	11.24p	Italy and Russia. Junction of the Southern fronts: ITALY - SERBIA - ROUMANIA. Advance by both Russian wings.
19	Sun	5.25	5.51	4.25p	12. 7a	
20	Mon	5.27	5.49	4.44p	1.33a	East. Collapse of TURKEY. Fall of CONSTANTINOPLE. Opening of the DARDANELLES.
21	Tu.	5.28	5.46	4.58p	2.54a	
22	Wed	5.30	5.44	5.10p	4.16a	
23	Th.	5.32	5.42	5.22p	5.33a	
24	Fri	5.33	5.39	5.37p	6.49a	
25	Sat	5.35	5.37	5.50p	8. 4a	
26	Sun	5.36	5.35	6. 8p	9.20a	
27	Mon	5.38	5.32	6.31p	10.33a	
28	Tu.	5.39	5.30	7. 1p	11.43a	
29	Wed	5.41	5.28	7.43p	12.41p	
30	Th.	5.43	5.25	8.35p	1.39p	

The above tables are approximately correct for VI Corps front, the sun and moon rising and setting about 5 minutes later than times given.

1st London boy
R. 6

2/4

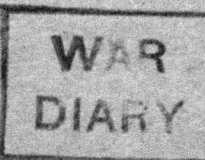

GENERAL STAFF

6th DIVISION

OCTOBER

1915

Attached:
Div. Operation Orders.

Confidential

121/7384

War Diary
of
General Staff – 6th Division

From 1st October 1915

To 31st October 1915

Vol XIV

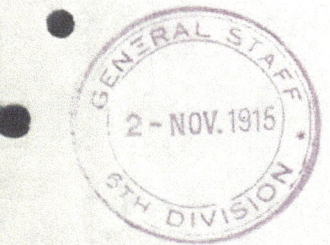

WAR DIARY
INTELLIGENCE SUMMARY
(Erase heading not required.)

Army Form C. 2118.

Instructions regarding War Diaries and Intelligence Summaries are contained in F.S. Regs., Part II. and the Staff Manual respectively. Title pages will be prepared in manuscript.

Hour, Date, Place	Summary of Events and Information	Remarks and references to Appendices
Oct 1st	Heavy shelling in vicinity of ST JEAN. Movement of heavy transport from N. to S. High velocity naval gun shelled the Canal bank	
Oct 2nd	Percentage of German "dud" shells rapidly increasing in most classes of shells. A German Sniper donned by a Westminster. A Zeppelin cruised on us at 11:15 pm.	
Oct 3rd	Heavy transport heard going from Melin to South. Normal day.	
Oct 4th	Quiet day except for a few shells in POPERINGHE	
Oct 5th	Nothing to report.	O.O. 38 Issued

Army Form C. 2118.

WAR DIARY
or
INTELLIGENCE SUMMARY.
(Erase heading not required.)

Instructions regarding War Diaries and Intelligence Summaries are contained in F.S. Regs., Part II. and the Staff Manual respectively. Title pages will be prepared in manuscript.

Hour, Date, Place	Summary of Events and Information	Remarks and references to Appendices
Oct 6th	Probable that (2) Germans about FORWARD COTTAGE were relieved. A good deal of sniping	O.O. 39 issued
Oct 7th	Men of the 73rd Bde, 24th Division in trenches under training. Heavy sniping. WILSONS FM heavily shelled	
Oct 8th	ODER HOUSES sniped all night and a good deal of whizbang & trench mortars	
Oct 9th	Normal day	
Oct 10th	Shelling at MORTALDJE ESTAMINET	O.O. 40 issued
Oct 11th	17th Bde withdrawn from line preparatory to departure from Divi'ion. Normal Day.	

WAR DIARY
or
INTELLIGENCE SUMMARY.
(Erase heading not required.)

Army Form C. 2118.

Instructions regarding War Diaries and Intelligence Summaries are contained in F.S. Regs., Part II. and the Staff Manual respectively. Title pages will be prepared in manuscript.

Hour, Date, Place	Summary of Events and Information	Remarks and references to Appendices
12th Oct	Distribution 18th Bde. Front line W. Yorks. D.L.I + E. Yorks Close Support including St JEAN and POTIJZE defences WESTMINSTERS + One Co. Frontiers Canal Bank Toronto bns 1 Co. 16th Bde Mhposm Left Section 2/WYL, KSLI. 2 Cos Lndrs. Right Section Buffs. 14th Bde in bttlo. Quiet night. Nothing to report.	
13th Oct		
14th Oct	Exchange of 17th and 71st Bdes took place in accordance with O.O. 41. Intermittent shelling during night of roads. Light wind and fine weather	O.O. 41 in rear.
15th Oct	Nothing to report.	

WAR DIARY or INTELLIGENCE SUMMARY.

(Erase heading not required.)

Army Form C. 2118.

Hour, Date, Place	Summary of Events and Information	Remarks and references to Appendices
16th Oct	Line again divided into 3 sections on right 16th by the entrance into line of 7th Bde in the centre section. Normal day, nothing to report.	
17th Oct	Distribution **Right Section** 18th Bde. D.L.I & W. Yorks in front line. Canal and POTIJZE defences. WESTMINSTERS. Camp B. FORESTERS Poperinghe. E. YORKS. **Centre Section** 7th Bde. 8th Bedfords & 2 Cos & 2 platoons Suffolks in front line. 1 Co & Platoon Suffolks in X line. 1 Platoon Suffolks 3rd Team defences. Remainder A.30 Wood & Poperinghe. **Left Section** 16th Bde. K.S.L.I. Buffs in front line. 1.Siwalis in Camp C and 1 Co at Maedline from Ypres Poperinghe. Nothing to report.	

Army Form C. 2118.

WAR DIARY
or
INTELLIGENCE SUMMARY.
(*Erase heading not required.*)

Instructions regarding War Diaries and Intelligence Summaries are contained in F.S. Regs., Part II. and the Staff Manual respectively. Title pages will be prepared in manuscript.

Hour, Date, Place	Summary of Events and Information	Remarks and references to Appendices
18th Oct	A few shells in left Section. Heavy transport heard behind German lines. A good deal of sniping.	
19th Oct	Situation during night normal. Heavy bursts of fire at 7pm & 11pm. 18" from German lines. Heavy Shelling in the Centre Section. Aeroplanes active. Several working parties dispersed by our fire.	
20th Oct	St Jean dump shelled at 9.15pm. 19½". a few Grenades thrown at "NO MANS COTTAGE". No damage. Six Commanding Officers paid a visit to the N.C.O's school at ZUTHPEN. Noise of pile driving heard E. of PRATT Street. Shelling heavy along line line.	O.O. 42 issued.
21st Oct	Nothing to report.	

WAR DIARY
or
INTELLIGENCE SUMMARY.
(Erase heading not required.)

Army Form C. 2118.

Hour, Date, Place	Summary of Events and Information	Remarks and references to Appendices
Oct 22nd	Reliefs successfully carried out. Shelling heavy along the line.	
Oct 23rd	German grenadiers attempted to bomb listening patrol in left horn of CRATER in 167th Bde line but were driven off. Large number of heavy trench mortar shells fired at 164th Bde.	O.O. 43 instead
Oct 24th	Visit of Munster workers. Much trench mortaring of Rly wood. Active shelling along the line.	
Oct 25th	A good deal of movement from line during night opposite Cawler Bastion	
Oct 26th	Bellewarde feet wire 4 ft deep. Germans letting water into lake. Germans working at wire opposite right section	

WAR DIARY
or
INTELLIGENCE SUMMARY.
(Erase heading not required.)

Army Form C. 2118.

Instructions regarding War Diaries and Intelligence Summaries are contained in F.S. Regs., Part II. and the Staff Manual respectively. Title pages will be prepared in manuscript.

Hour, Date, Place	Summary of Events and Information	Remarks and references to Appendices
Oct 27th	Some heavy shelling of YPRES Salient	
Oct 28th	Essex transferred to 78th Bde in relief of Sherwoods to 7/8 Bde. Nothing to report	
Oct 29th	Heavy shelling right section in latter retaliation ordered. Effective result.	
Oct 30th	Quiet. Back such with a little nite whiz-bangs. Weather very bad	
Oct 31st	Weather very bad, Continuous rain. Enemy quiet	

Gris.

E. Ironside
Major ft.

DIVISIONAL OPERATION ORDERS NOS. 38, 39, 40, 41, 42 & 43.

Secret.

War Diary

Copy No. 12

—: 6th DIVISION OPERATION ORDER No. 38 :—

5th October, 1915.

Reference :— Map Sheet 28, 1/40,000.

1. On the night of the 6th/7th October, the Right Sector will be extended to I.5.d.5.1.

   G.O.C. 18th Infantry Brigade will arrange relief with 41st Infantry Brigade, 14th Division.

2. 41st Infantry Brigade hand over all trench stores and grenades.

3. Machine-Gun detachments will be relieved on the morning of 7th, under arrangements to be made between Brigadiers concerned.

4. G.O.C. 17th Infantry Brigade will place 1 battalion at the disposal of G.O.C. Right Sector for the purpose of holding the new line.

5. The KAAIE salient, and the Brigade Headquarters in I.2.c.1.8 will be retained by 14th Division.

   The billets on the BRIELEN road in I.7.a. will be handed over to 6th Division.

6. Acknowledge.

E. Ironside
Major,
General Staff. 6th Division.

Issued at 4 pm.

```
Copy No. 1 to 16th Inf. Bde.      Copy No. 7 to "Q".
  ..   .. 2 .. 17th Inf. Bde.       ..   .. 8 .. A.D.M.S.
  ..   .. 3 .. 18th Inf. Bde.       ..   .. 9 .. 14th Division.
  ..   .. 4 .. G.O.C. R.A.          ..   .. 10 .. 6th Corps.
  ..   .. 5 .. C.R.E.               ..   .. 11 .. Office.
  ..   .. 6 .. Signals.             ..   .. 12 .. Office.
```

Secret

6th Division Operation Order No 39   Copy No 12

~~FIFTH DIVISION OPERATION ORDER No. 39~~

6th October, 1915.

Reference:- Map, sheet 28, 1/40,000.

1. Under orders received from 6th Corps, the 17th Infantry Brigade will be withdrawn from the line for attachment to the 2nd Corps for an indefinite but temporary period.
The 2nd London Regt will remain attached to the 16th Infantry Brigade.
The 2nd Leinster Regt will be relieved by the 14th Division.
The 17th Infantry Brigade will assemble 3 battalions in POPERINGHE, and 1 battalion in the huts in A.30.

2. The line will be divided into 2 sectors:-
   Right Sector:- from CRUMP FARM to LIVERPOOL STREET, inclusive, under G.O.C. 18th Infantry Brigade.
   Left Sector:- Remainder of present line, under G.O.C. 16th Infantry Brigade.
   No dates can yet be fixed, but all arrangements will be made for carrying out the reliefs at shortest notice on the order being given, which will be within the next 3 or 4 days.

3. When the 17th Infantry Brigade has been relieved, one battalion from each of the 16th and 18th Infantry Brigades can be billeted in the huts in A.30; remainder must be East of VLAMERTINGHE.

4. Each of the 3 Brigades will leave 1 N.C.O. and 4 men to look after billets in POPERINGHE, and the 17th in addition will leave a similar party to look after their camp in Wood A.30.

5. Trench stores will be left in the line duly handed over.

6. Acknowledge.

Issued at 6.45 pm.

Ironside
Major,
General Staff. 6th Division.

Copy No. 1 to 16th Inf. Bde.   Copy No. 7 to "Q".
"   " 2 .. 17th Inf. Bde.   "   " 8 .. A.D.M.S.
"   " 3 .. 18th Inf. Bde.   "   " 9 .. 14th Division
"   " 4 .. G.O.C. R.A.   "   " 10 .. 49th Division.
"   " 5 .. C.R.E.   "   " 11 .. 6th Corps.
"   " 6 .. Signals.   "   " 12 & 13 Office

War Diary

Copy No. 13

6TH. DIVISION OPERATION ORDER No.40.

Reference:- Map Sheet 28, 1/40,000.   9th October '15.

1. The 17th Infantry Brigade (including 2nd London Regt) will be relieved by troops of the 16th and 18th Infantry Brigades before daylight on Tuesday 12th instant, and go into rest billets in POPERINGHE and A.30.

2. From that date the line will be divided into two sectors as laid down in 6th Division Defence Scheme (G.25/55/5).

3. For the present the 18th Infantry Brigade will hold the line on the right taken over from the 14th Division, and will relieve the troops of the 17th Infantry Brigade now holding this section.

4. Arrangements for the relief and adjustment of the line will be made between Brigadiers concerned.

5. Troops of the 73rd Infantry Brigade now under instruction will return to billets to-morrow night the 10th/11th. Arrangements re lorries will be notified later, but will probably be as before.

6. Completion of relief and adjustment, also any previous relief before night 11th/12th to be reported.

7. Acknowledge.

G.F. Boyd
Lt.Colonel,
General Staff, 6th Division.

Issued at 7 p.m.

Copy No. 1 to 16th Inf.Bde.
 "   " 2   17th Inf.Bde.
 "   " 3   18th Inf.Bde.
 "   " 4   G.O.C.,R.A.
 "   " 5   C.R.E.
 "   " 6   Signals.
 "   " 7   "Q".
 "   " 8   A.D.M.S.

Copy No. 9 to 14th Division.
 "   " 10   19th Division.
 "   " 11   6th Corps.
Copies No.12 & 13 - Office.
 "   " 14 to 73rd Inf Bde

Copy No..........

8TH. DIVISION OPERATION ORDER No.40.

Reference:- Map Sheet 28. 1/40,000.   6th October, '15.

Copy No..........

8TH. DIVISION OPERATION ORDER No.40.

Reference:- Map Sheet 28. 1/40,000.   6th October, '15.

Copy No. 14

6TH. DIVISION OPERATION ORDER NO. 41.

Reference Map Sheet 28, 1/40,000.   12th October 1915.

1. On the 14th instant, the 17th Infantry Brigade will come under the orders of the 24th Division, and will leave the 6th Division area in accordance with instructions already issued, two Battalions being temporarily attached to the 3rd Division, remainder marching to RENINGHELST, being clear of POPERINGHE by 12 noon.
The two battalions from WOOD A.30 will march via the HOSPITAL FARM and VLAMERTINGHE road, and be clear of the wood by 5 p.m.

2. On the same day, the 71st Infantry Brigade will move three battalions into the huts in WOOD A.30, and one battalion into POPERINGHE.
The three battalions moving into huts A.30 will march via main POPERINGHE-YPRES road at ½ hour intervals, and turn North at G.5.d.1.2., the leading battalion reaching the wood at 4.30 p.m.

Precautions must be taken against hostile aeroplanes.

The battalion moving to POPERINGHE will pass the Square at 12.30 p.m., and go into billets under arrangements to be made by "Q" Staff 6th Division.

3. On the night of 16th/17th the 71st Infantry Brigade will take over the Centre Sector of the 6th Division line, i.e. from GARDEN STREET (inclusive) to the junction of LOMBARD STREET (inclusive) with B.16. (See G.25/55/7).
The G.O.C. 71st Infantry Brigade will relieve the G.O.C. 18th Infantry Brigade and assume command of Right and Centre Sectors. Command to pass at 6 p.m. 16th.
All arrangements for readjustment of the line to be made between Brigadiers, and completion of relief reported by 71st Brigade.

4. Accommodation of Battalions of the 16th and 18th Brigades on readjustment of the line to be arranged by "Q".

5. The six resting Battalions will be in 6th Corps Reserve and under the command of G.O.C. 18th Infantry Brigade for Tactical purposes.

6. The Machine Guns of the 16th and 18th Brigades, with suitable detachments, now in the Centre Sector will remain in their present positions until further orders.

7. ACKNOWLEDGE.

N.B.. The 71st Brigade will hold the Centre Sector with two Battalions, and have two Bns: resting - one in Wood A 30. and one in POPERINGHE.

Issued at 6.30 p.m.

G.F. Boyd
Lt.Colonel,
General Staff, 6th Division.

Copy No. 1 to 16th I.B.
"   "   2 .. 17th I.B.
"   "   3 .. 18th I.B.
"   "   4 .. 71st I.B.
"   "   5 .. G.O.C.,R.A.
"   "   6 .. C.R.E.
"   "   7 .. A.D.M.S.

Copy No. 8 to Signals.
"   "   9 .. "Q".
"   " 10 .. 14th Division.
"   " 11 .. 49th Division.
"   " 12 .. 6th Corps.
"   " 13 .. Office
"   " 14 .. Office.
"   " 15 .. 24th Division.

SECRET.   Copy No. 13

6th DIVISION OPERATION ORDER No. 42:-

Reference:- Map, sheet 28, 1/40,000.

20th October, 1915.

1. The 6th Division is to take over the line now held by the 14th Division, and the 49th Division to take over our Left Sector. The 14th Division (less Artillery) will be in 6th Corps Reserve.

2. On the night 21st/22nd October, the 49th Division will take over our Left Sector from the 16th Infantry Brigade, and on the same night the 16th Infantry Brigade will take over the Left and Centre Sectors of the 14th Division line with two battalions, reserve troops of the 14th Division remaining in position.

3. On the night 22nd/23rd October, the 16th Infantry Brigade will take over the Right Sector of the 14th Division line, and Reserve Troops 14th Division will be withdrawn.

4. Arrangements for reliefs to be made between the Brigadiers concerned.
   Hd. Qrs. 16th Infantry Brigade:- RUE des POTS, POPERINGHE.

5. On the night 23rd/24th October, the 18th Infantry Brigade will place a permanent garrison of one company in the KAAIE SALIENT, who will be responsible for defence and upkeep.

6. Artillery 6th Division and Artillery 14th Division are to remain in present positions and cover their present zones.

7. The 26th Trench Mortar Battery is allotted to the 16th Infantry Brigade. Arrangements for relief of the 14th Division Trench Mortars to be made between Brigadiers. O.C. 26th Trench Mortar Battery has been ordered to reconnoitre the positions today.

8. Machine guns in our Left Sector will be relieved by the 49th Division by the night 22nd/23rd October, guns of the rear battalion being relieved on night 21st/22nd.
   Relief of Machine Guns of 14th Division will be completed by the night 23rd/24th October under arrangements to be made by Brigadiers.

9. The 12th Field Company R.E. is allotted to the 16th Infantry Brigade. The C.R.E. will arrange for the work required in our present Right and Centre Sectors to be carried on by the London and West Riding Field Companies.

10. The 49th Division will occupy 17th Infantry Brigade Headquarters. O.C. Signals to arrange that communication is complete to Artillery, and battalions in Left Sector.

11. Under arrangements with 14th and 49th Divisions, G.Os.C. 71st and 42nd Infantry Brigades will remain in command of their present sectors until the reliefs are completed, the two battalions 16th Infantry Brigade being temporarily under G.O.C. 42nd Infantry Brigade from the night 21st/22nd October until completion of relief.

12. All trench stores to be handed over, but NOT 1st class bombs or gum boots.

P.T.O.

13. G.O.C. 16th and 71st Infantry Brigades to report completion of reliefs to 6th Division Headquarters

14. Resting battalions 18th and 71st Infantry Brigades will be in Divisional Reserve.

15. Acknowledge.

                                            Lieut. Colonel,
                             General Staff. 6th Division.

Issued at 10 am.

```
Copy No. 1 to 16th Infantry Brigade.
  "    "  2 "  18th       "        "
  "    "  3 "  71st       "        "
  "    "  4 "  G.O.C. R.A.
  "    "  5 "  C.R.E.
  "    "  6 "  Signals.
  "    "  7 "  "Q".
  "    "  8 "  A.D.M.S.
  "    "  9 "  6th Corps.
  "    " 10 "  14th Division.
  "    " 11 "  49th Division.
  "    " 12 "  Office.
  "    " 13 "  Office.
  "    " 14 "  Divisional Mounted Troops.
```

War Diary

SECRET.

Copy No. 11

6th Division Operation Order No. 43.

23rd October 1915.

Reference map Sheet 28, 1/40,000.

DEFENCE and UPKEEP. 1. On the 24th instant, the G.O.C. 18th Infantry Bde will place one battalion at the disposal of the G.O.C. 16th Infantry Brigade.

The 16th Infantry Brigade will be responsible for the defence and upkeep of the KAAIE Salient, the permanent garrison of which is one company and two machine guns.

The 16th Infantry Brigade is also responsible for the upkeep of the RAMPARTS of YPRES, as far south as the SALLYPORT (inclusive) where the 6th Division joins the 3rd Division.

BRIDGES. 2. The 18th Infantry Brigade is responsible for Guards on the Canal bridges (1), (1a), and (1b), the C.R.E. making any necessary arrangements with regard to their destruction.

POSITIONS TO BE RECONNOITRED. 3. Brigadiers will ensure that Battalion and Company Commanders who are not already acquainted with the defences of the KAAIE Salient and the RAMPARTS of YPRES as far south as the SALLYPORT, reconnoitre these positions as opportunity offers.

ACCOMMODATION. 4. (a) Besides the RAMPARTS as far south as the SALLYPORT, the 16th Infantry Brigade is allotted the dug-outs along the disused CANAL which runs through I.7. and I.1. (with the exception of those occupied by the advanced sections of the West Riding Field Company), and the houses in the BRIELEN ROAD.

(b) BRIELEN may be used by the 71st Infantry Bde if required, but troops must keep quiet there in day time, and good air guards must be kept.

(c) BURGOMASTER FARM and MACHINE GUN FARM are allotted to the 18th Infantry Brigade, but any mutual arrangements may be made between Brigadiers.

DIVISIONAL RESERVE. 5. Resting Battalions (Divisional Reserve) must be accommodated in the WOOD A.30, from the 25th instant.

6. ACKNOWLEDGE.

Lieut.Colonel,
General Staff, 6th Division.

Issued at 6 a.m.

Copy No. 1. to 16th Inf:Bde.   Copy No. 5. to C.R.E.
Copy No. 2. to 18th Inf:Bde.   Copy No. 6. to Mounted Troops.
Copy No. 3. to 71st Inf:Bde.   Copy No. 7. A.D.M.S.
Copy No. 4. to G.O.C.,R.A.   Copy No. 8. "Q".
                                Copy No. 9. Signals
                                Copy No.10. Office.

GENERAL STAFF

6th DIVISION

NOVEMBER

1915

Attached:

Div. Operation Orders.

— Confidential —

121/7637

War Diary

of

General Staff 6th Division

From 1.11.15 To 30.11.15

Vol XVI

Army Form C. 2118.

WAR DIARY
or
INTELLIGENCE SUMMARY.
(Erase heading not required.)

Instructions regarding War Diaries and Intelligence Summaries are contained in F. S. Regs., Part II. and the Staff Manual respectively. Title pages will be prepared in manuscript.

Hour, Date, Place	Summary of Events and Information	Remarks and references to Appendices
Nov 1st	Distribution 16th Bde Right Sector K.S.L. 1&4 Yth and Leicesters Buffs 2 Cos 2nd line. 1 Co in h farm, 1 Co in Ramparts. 3 Cos E Yorks disused Canal 1 Co in KAME Salient 18th Bde Centre Sector. Westminsters and West Yorks Front line. Essex on Canal Bank and Potinze. D.L.I in A 30. 71st Bde Left Sector. Suffolks and 2 Co Bedfords Front line. 1 Co Beds support. 1/2 Co Beds St Jean 1/2 Co Beds Canal. 2 Co Norfolks French Dugouts 2 Cos Canal. Very rainy weather. Very quiet except for a little sniping	

WAR DIARY
or
INTELLIGENCE SUMMARY.
(*Erase heading not required.*)

Army Form C. 2118.

Hour, Date, Place	Summary of Events and Information	Remarks and references to Appendices
Nov. 2nd	Weather very wet. Trenches in a dreadful state. Situation very quiet, only sniping in the right sector (and a little shelling of B.14.	
Nov. 3rd	Very heavy rain. Trenches very wet. Enemy shewing German sappers to be mining against our right Coy in day.	
Nov. 4th	Very wet. Both Germans and ourselves indulging in bailing. Very little fring rifle or gun.	
Nov. 5th	We have the 17th Div in our right and the 4Qu Div on our left. Right MENIN ROAD the left just short of MORTELDJE ESTAMINET. Weather very wet and bad. Trenches full of water. Nothing to report.	
Nov. 6th	Nothing to report. Weather clearing.	

Army Form C. 2118.

WAR DIARY
or
INTELLIGENCE SUMMARY.
(Erase heading not required.)

Instructions regarding War Diaries and Intelligence Summaries are contained in F. S. Regs., Part II. and the Staff Manual respectively. Title pages will be prepared in manuscript.

Hour, Date, Place	Summary of Events and Information	Remarks and references to Appendices
Nov 7th	Weather fine. Enemy very quiet. Both sides repairing parapets	O.O. 44 inclosed.
Nov. 8th	Weather fine. Sentries active. Nothing to report.	
Nov 9th	Very wet. Shuns going down. Mine up in the Right Sector. German Trench successfully enveloped and thrown throught a few Germans destroyed. Heavy shelling of the YPRES Salient and Canal. Enemys trench mortars very Powders Rly. engaged artilleries. A good deal of Shiz-Changing on Menin Road.	O.O. 45 inclosed
Nov 10th	Very wet and heavier. Very muddy. Very quiet in Ciuarance: Relief in 30.4 & completed 17th Bn. now go up to supports north of ROULERS railway.	
Nov 11th	Very wet. heavier. Snow falling in flakes. Very quiet. Except for naval shelling of YPRES. 16th Bde in reserve.	

WAR DIARY
or
INTELLIGENCE SUMMARY.

(Erase heading not required.)

Army Form C. 2118.

Hour, Date, Place	Summary of Events and Information	Remarks and references to Appendices
Nov. 12th	Very wet. Usual shelling of YPRES. 16th Bde in reserve.	
Nov. 13th	Very wet. Trenches [flooded] in. Relief on in 00.45. Completed. Trenches in MORTALDJE sector taken over by 16th Bde from 4 & 9 Div in a dreadful state	
Nov. 14th	Rain has ceased for the finning day.	
Nov. 15th	Fine day. Glass rising. Two shells on Canal and KAAIE Salient. Bombs from aeroplane dropped POTIJZE	
Nov. 16th	Rain again after short frost during night.	
Nov. 17th	Very wet morning. A good deal of shelling over the whole of our area, mill very little effect.	O.O. 46 issued

Army Form C. 2118.

WAR DIARY
or
INTELLIGENCE SUMMARY.
(Erase heading not required.)

Instructions regarding War Diaries and Intelligence Summaries are contained in F. S. Regs., Part II. and the Staff Manual respectively. Title pages will be prepared in manuscript.

Hour, Date, Place	Summary of Events and Information	Remarks and references to Appendices
Nov. 18th	Great aeroplane activity. Bombs dropped on POPERINGHE. Very wet and stormy from about 11 a.m. onwards.	
Nov. 19th	Relief of 18th I.B. by 42nd Bde 14th Div took place during night & 16th I.B. by 41st I.B. Both successfully completed.	
Nov. 20th	Relief of 41st I.B. by 43rd Bde completed during night. The whole of the Infantry of 6th Div now withdrawn from the line. the Artillery still in position.	
Nov. 21st	The relief of the Artillery of the Division ordered and the Artillery to go to WATTEN camp near ST OMER	

Army Form C. 2118.

WAR DIARY
or
INTELLIGENCE SUMMARY.
(Erase heading not required.)

Instructions regarding War Diaries and Intelligence Summaries are contained in F. S. Regs., Part II. and the Staff Manual respectively. Title pages will be prepared in manuscript.

Hour, Date, Place	Summary of Events and Information	Remarks and references to Appendices
Nov 22nd	Divs. in located as follows:- 1st de xxxx HOUTKERQUE 2 Bdes in xxxx A 30 and POPERINGHE Supplying 4 Coys of Patrols Platoon for wiring parties for 1st and 49th Divisions respectively. In Line. Artillery by Nov. 27 Leaving Guards/WATTEN in training under order of C.R.A. Training proceeding rapidly.	
Nov 27th		
Nov 28th	No Change in disposition of Nov. 22nd	
Nov 30th		

E. Ironside
Maj Gl

DIVISIONAL OPERATION ORDERS NOS. 44, 45 & 46.

War Diary

Copy No........ 13.

6th Division Operation Order No.44.

Reference Map - Sheet 28, 1/20,000.

7th November, 1915.

RELIEF.
1. The 51st Infantry Brigade, 17th Division, will relieve the 16th Infantry Brigade up to and inclusive of Trench A.1. A.2.

2. Under arrangement with the 17th Division, the relief will take place as follows, all details to be arranged between the Brigadiers concerned:-

(a) All machine guns, and the working battalion of the 14th Division, will be relieved by the morning of the 10th November.

(b) The remainder of the Infantry will be relieved on night 10th/11th November.

(c) Command will pass to the G.O.C. 51st Infantry Brigade on completion of relief, and handing over reported to 6th Division Head Quarters.

ACCOMMODATION.
3. On relief on night 9th/10th, the working battalion of the 14th Division, attached to the 16th Infantry Brigade, will come under orders of the G.O.C. 18th Infantry Brigade, and be accommodated in an area selected by him.

On relief on night 10th/11th, 16th Brigade Head Quarters and 2 battalions will go into rest in POPERINGHE and WOOD A.30, under arrangements to be made by "Q" 6th Division.

BOUNDARY.
4. After relief the boundary between the Vth and VIth Corps will be :-

The junction of trenches A.1. and A.2., I.5.d.3.2. - South of trench P.S.1. - I.10.b.10.5. - North of House I.10.a.9.3. - I.9.b.10.0. - I.9.d.4.5, thence along the MENIN ROAD to MENIN GATE, inclusive to Vth Corps - South side of YPRES SQUARE - RUE ELVERDINGHE.

The communication trench I.10.a.2.0. to the "X" line inclusive to the Vth Corps, but available for use by VIth Corps in case of emergency.

The MENIN GATE and MENIN ROAD to cross roads I.8.b.6.4. available for use by the VIth Corps.

Boundary West of YPRES will be notified later.

ARTILLERY.
5. The relief of the Artillery covering the front taken over by the 17th Division is to be completed by the morning of 12th November.
Arrangements to be made between C.R.A's concerned, as also arrangements for relief of the Trench Mortar

P.T.O.

ARTILLERY (Continued).

Mortar Battery, which may go into rest until required by the G.O.C. 16th Infantry Brigade later.

The O.C. Trench Mortar Battery will bring out all beds etc, taken over from the 14th Division, unless suitable exchanges can be made.

TUNNELLING COMPANY RE.
6. The Tunnelling Company, and those men of the 6th Division at present attached, will come under orders of Vth Corps on completion of relief.

TRENCH STORES.
7. Bombs and other trench stores, with the exception of gum boots, will be handed over, and a receipt obtained.

R.E. MATERIAL.
8. The C.R.E. will hand over to 17th Division any R.E. material possible.

HEAD QRS, SIGNALS.
9. 51st Infantry Brigade Head Quarters is to be established in the RAMPARTS.

O.C. 6th Divisional Signal Company will give 17th Division any assistance possible with regard to lines in the vicinity.

MEDICAL.
10. Details with regard to Medical arrangements will be arranged between A.D.M.S's concerned.

11. The G.O.C. 16th Infantry Brigade will be prepared to take over a part of the line now held by the 49th Division, with two battalions, on or about the night 12th/13th instant. Details later.

12. ACKNOWLEDGE.

Issued at 7 p.m.

G. F. Boyd
Lt.Colonel,
General Staff, 6th Division.

Copy No. 1 to 16th I.B.
" " 2 " 18th I.B.
" " 3 " 71st I.B.
" " 4 " G.O.C.,R.A.
" " 5 " C.R.E.
" " 6 " A.D.M.S.
" " 7 " Signals.
Copy No. 8. to "Q".
" " 9 " 6th Corps.
" " 10 " 14th Divn:
" " 11 " 17th Divn:
" " 12 " Office.
" " 13 " Office.

Copy No. 11

6th Division Operation Order No. 45.

Reference 1/10,000 Trench Map.   9th ~~8th~~ November, 1915.

RELIEF.   1. On night 13th/14th November, the 16th Infantry Bde will take over part of the line now held by the 146th Infantry Brigade, 49th Division, (H.Q. at old 17th Bde. CANAL BANK), and part of the line now held by our 71st Infantry Brigade.

2. Arrangements for relief to be made between Brigadiers concerned.

BOUNDARIES.   3. Boundaries will be as follows:-

Between 16th and 71st Infantry Brigades:-

Junction of B.15. and B.16. at C.21.b.3.4. - junction of CORNHILL B. and LOMBARD STREET - S.13.d. S. of B in BUFFS ROAD - junction of CORNHILL and THREADNEEDLE STREET - CANAL BANK at LARGE BRIDGE.

Between 16th and 146th Infantry Brigades:-

C.15.c.7.6. (M.G. emplacement to 6th Division) - West end of S.18. - S.18.a. to junction with HOPE DRY CUT - SOUTH to junction of GOWTHORPE ROAD and S.16.c. - North end of S.15.b. - X.10. at C.26.b.7.8. - West end of FRASCATIS - CANAL at point 150 yards South of Bridge No.4.

GOWTHORPE ROAD to 49th Division (6th Division right of passage).

MACHINE GUNS.   4. Machine Guns will be relieved by the morning of 15th November.

TRENCH STORES.   5. Trench stores will be taken over, with the exception of gum boots, and a list obtained.

COMMAND.   6. Command will pass to G.O.C. 16th Infantry Brigade on completion of relief, and notified to 6th Division Head Quarters.

R.E.   7. Between the 10th and 13th instant, thorough R.E. reconnaissance will be made, and all arrangements prepared for commencing work on the night of 13th.
Between the 10th and 13th, 12th Field Company R.E. will concentrate on dugouts in the 16th Brigade CANAL BANK area.

TRENCH MORTAR BTTY.   9. The 26th Trench Mortar Battery will be available for the 16th Infantry Brigade, if required, on taking over the new line.

10. ACKNOWLEDGE.

Issued at 6 am. ~~p.m.~~

G P Byd
Lt.Colonel,
General Staff 6th Division.

Copy No.1 to 16th I.B.
" " 2 " 18th I.B.   Copy No.8 to "Q"
" " 3 " 71st I.B.   " " 9 " 6th Corps.
" " 4 " G.O.C.,R.A.   " " 10 " 49th Divn.
" " 5 " C.R.E.   " " 11 & 12 - Office
" " 6 " Signals.
" " 7 " A.D.M.S.

•SECRET

War Diary

Copy No. 14

6th Division Operation Order No.46.

16th November, 1915.

RELIEFS. (1) The 14th Division is to take over the line now held by the 6th Division on nights 18th/19th and 19th/20th instant, and the 6th Division will go into rest.

Artillery. (2) The Artillery of the 6th Division will remain at present in the line, and come under the orders of the G.O.C. 14th Division on completion of relief.

Trench Mortars. (3) The 38th Trench Mortar Battery, now in action, will remain until further orders.

If not in action by the night 18th/19th, the 26th Trench Mortar Battery may go into rest.

R.E. (4) All arrangements for relief of Advanced Sections of R.E. Field Companies will be made between the C.R.E's. concerned.

Infantry, and machine guns. (5) On the night of 18th/19th the following moves will take place:-

(a) 18th Infantry Brigade will be relieved by the 42nd Infantry Brigade (with one Battalion of 43rd Infantry Brigade attached), and will march out via YPRES and SALVATION CORNER.

(b) 16th Infantry Brigade will be relieved by the 41st Infantry Brigade, and will march out via BRIELEN - VLAMERTINGHE.

Machine guns of the 16th and 18th Infantry Brigades will be relieved on night 19th/20th.

(6) On the night of 19th/20th, the 71st Infantry Brigade will be relieved by 2 battalions of the 43rd Infantry Brigade (with one battalion of 41st Infantry Bde attached).

Machine guns of the 71st Infantry Brigade will be relieved on the night 20th/21st.

P.T.O.

2.

(7) All arrangements for above reliefs to be made between Brigadiers concerned.

Trench Stores. (8) All trench stores, including trench boots (thigh only), will be handed over, (except a fair proportion of those belonging to the 16th Inf: Bde: for their working Battalion and Company attached to the 49th Division) and a receipt obtained.

Platoon bombs will be brought out by arrangement.

Reconnaissance. (9) Representatives of Brigades and Battalions will come to 16th and 18th Infantry Brigade Head Quarters to-morrow the 17th instant, at 4 p.m. and 11 a.m. respectively, and to 71st Infantry Brigade Head Quarters on the 18th instant at 10 a.m., for purposes of reconnaissance.

Working Bn: (10) The G.O.C. 16th Infantry Brigade will place one Battalion and one Company at the disposal of the 49th Division for work from the 18th instant. (see para 8) The battalion will be located at ELVERDINGHE, and the company on the CANAL BANK. (Details re Battalion later). Arrangements regarding the company will be made through G.O.C. 148th Infantry Brigade – Head Quarters near Bridge No.4.

Billets, & transport. (11) Billeting orders will be issued by "Q" Staff, 6th Division, as soon as definitely settled, and any arrangements possible regarding transport notified.

Command. (12) Completion of reliefs to be reported.

G.O.C. 6th Division will remain in command of the line until the relief is completed.

(13) Acknowledge.

Lt.Colonel,
General Staff, 6th Division.

Issued at 4.30 p.m.

Copy No. 1 to 16th I.B.   Copy No. 7 to "Q"
 "   " 2 .. 18th I.B.   "   " 8 .. A.D.M.S.
 "   " 3 .. 71st I.B.   "   " 9 .. Mtd.Troops.
 "   " 4 .. C.R.A.   "   " 10 .. 6th Corps.
 "   " 5 .. C.R.E.   "   " 11 .. 14th Divn:
 "   " 6 .. Signals.   "   " 12 .. 17th Divn:
                              "   " 13 .. 49th Divn:
           Copies No.14 & 15 – Office.

WAR DIARY

GENERAL STAFF

6th DIVISION

DECEMBER

1915

Attached:

Paper G/44/7.
Div. Operation Order.

__Confidential.__

War Diary of General Staff 6th Division

From 1-12-15 to 31-12-15

Vol XVI

Army Form C. 2118.

WAR DIARY
of
INTELLIGENCE SUMMARY.
(Erase heading not required.)

Instructions regarding War Diaries and Intelligence Summaries are contained in F.S. Regs., Part II. and the Staff Manual respectively. Title pages will be prepared in manuscript.

Hour, Date, Place	Summary of Events and Information	Remarks and references to Appendices
Dec - 1st	Divn in still at rest. Working parties from font Renn found for 49th and 14th Divn.	9/4/17 moved 5th Dec OO. No 47 moved in Dec 12th
Dec - 12 - 13th	Machine-guns of the two other Bdes, 18th and 71st relieved 15 mg's 14th Div.	
Dec 15th	The 18th and 71st Bdes relieved the 42nd & 3rd Bdes respectively of the 14th Div in the feeler from the gully not north of the ROMLERS Rly to gnd Short of TWIETTE SALIENT. Relief had no incidents	
Dec 16th	16th Bde relieved the 41st Bde during night. Weather good though misty. Quiet day. Intermittent shelling by both sides.	
Dec 17th	Quiet day. Rain twice.	

Army Form C. 2118.

WAR DIARY
or
INTELLIGENCE SUMMARY.
(Erase heading not required.)

Instructions regarding War Diaries and Intelligence Summaries are contained in F.S. Regs., Part II. and the Staff Manual respectively. Title pages will be prepared in manuscript.

Hour, Date, Place	Summary of Events and Information	Remarks and references to Appendices
Dec 18th	Rain during day, fine towards evening. Very quiet day.	
Dec 19th	The Germans delivered a gas-attack. Right Bde (18th Bde). Right resting on gully near Renters Ry and left just south of WIELTJE SALIENT. At 5.30 am the 14th D.L.I. the left Battalion, reported gas and the 2nd Bn D.L.I. on the right at 5.35 am. The enemy then commenced a violent bombardment of our front line and communications. Gas helmets were adjusted and proved efficient. No serious Infantry attack was made, but six dead Germans were counted opposite the left of the 14th D.L.I. Most of these were floated down from the north and was not discharged from opposite this Bde front. Wire was cut by the evening fire in several places. Our barrage was very successful and was brought on quickly.	

Army Form C. 2118.

WAR DIARY
or
INTELLIGENCE SUMMARY.
(Erase heading not required.)

Hour, Date, Place	Summary of Events and Information	Remarks and references to Appendices
19th Dec	**Centre Bde** (7th Inf. Bde)	
	At 5.25 am one red light went up opposite WIELTJE and the gas was reported to be coming from cylinders among the trees C.29.a.3.3. with a hissing noise. Seven or eight red lights went up afterwards.	
	At about 5.50 am the Germans opened a heavy bombardment against the X line and communication. No Infantry attack was developed at any time.	
	Left Bde (16th Inf Bde)	
	At 6.15 am the enemy fired several coloured lights and began emitting gas with a simultaneous rifle fire. At the same time a bombardment of flux line and communication commenced.	
	By 6.35 am. WIPERS was practically clear from the front of this sector. Towards (obsc.) Soillet received little attention.	

WAR DIARY or INTELLIGENCE SUMMARY

Army Form C. 2118.

Hour, Date, Place	Summary of Events and Information	Remarks and references to Appendices

19 Dec — General

After Germans left their trenches and entered its notably northern horn, but were killed or driven out by R.S.L.I. the left Bn.

The Germans reported to have left their trenches were probably patrols sent forward to ascertain the effects of the gas. No attack appears to have been intended, but the hostile trenches were manned probably with a view to taking full advantage of a successful effect from the gas.

(1) It is doubtful whether their wire was prepared and they did not cut ours deliberately with gun-fire. If they intended to attack they must have relied solely on the effect of the gas. Possibly the heavy rifle fire from our trenches & the F.A. barrage was too much for them.

(2) A sudden change in the wind (which veered much to the north) may have caused them to cancel their orders for an attack, whilst they were unable to cancel orders to the gas. Gas was apparently let out from the left of V¹⁵e⁹/¹⁰/¹¹ to the left of V¹⁵⁴/¹⁵/¹⁶ to V¹⁶ 49ᵗʰ Div at their junction with 1ˢᵗ French white soldiers in our line, a front of about 2¾ miles WIGHTIE

WAR DIARY or INTELLIGENCE SUMMARY.

Army Form C. 2118.

Hour, Date, Place	Summary of Events and Information	Remarks and references to Appendices

19th Dec

apparently from gas batteries about 200 yds apart & lasting 30—40 minutes.

(3) The Germans may have decided that our-syptiomatic bombardment of their front trenches, which had been going on for over a week, with orders to searching out to these gas batteries, was too accurate, and that it was better to make use of them before they were destroyed. The sq'n was certainly luck first favourable day that they had, as the day was very fine and still with about 2½ miles an hour (a little too slow for gas).

(4) Therefore attack may have been intended as a big retaliation for our constant ever increasing shelling of the German trenches.

(5) The whole affair may have been a demonstration to distract attention from an attack elsewhere.

(6) It may have been a lot of new gas Patrols being used. So is believed the Chlorine + Prussic Acid

WAR DIARY
or
INTELLIGENCE SUMMARY.
(Erase heading not required.)

Army Form C. 2118.

Hour, Date, Place	Summary of Events and Information	Remarks and references to Appendices
19th Dec	The gas was felt as far back as VLAMERTINGHE CHATEAU being especially bad about the KRUIS SALIENT and the Southern end of the Canal. It travelled into & past Vlamertinghe village was heavily shelled by 9" Howrs. Effect on the back areas being poor into regard to the amount of shells expended.	
20th Dec	Numerous alarms of gas caused by the wind clearing out the affected dug outs and Shell-holes. The ventilator sprayers into Hyposolution not disipating lte gas at all. About the night of the 19th/20th during lte 20th there was a heavy bombardment with lachrymatory shells into Ypres, but none into Vlamertinghe.	
21st Dec	Rain which cleaned upas a light about time towards evening.	

Army Form C. 2118.

WAR DIARY
or
INTELLIGENCE SUMMARY.
(Erase heading not required.)

Instructions regarding War Diaries and Intelligence Summaries are contained in F.S. Regs., Part II. and the Staff Manual respectively. Title pages will be prepared in manuscript.

Hour, Date, Place	Summary of Events and Information	Remarks and references to Appendices
Dec 22nd	Weather foggy and inaccurate for artillery observation. Quiet day in consequence. A few hostile working parties engaged with success as the mist rose. Snipers active.	
Dec 23rd	The weather bad and trying. A few shrapnel over 18"/13. Guns in this sector undertook a little wire cutting 16"/13. report that areas given as of a furnace were seen about C.15.d.15.8. No ex Denunciation of this.	
Dec 24th	16 th Bde had a bombing attack against them near MORSELEDE. We drove it off with rifle and machine gun fire. Lewd communication trenches alternated during the	
Dec 25th	Very quiet day. No movement experiences	
Dec 26th	Q.2.ii How did a shoot against Moorsland near OOSTER Houses.	

WAR DIARY
or
INTELLIGENCE SUMMARY.
(Erase heading not required.)

Army Form C. 2118.

Hour, Date, Place	Summary of Events and Information	Remarks and references to Appendices
27th Dec	18th Bde quiet night. Situation normal and wind safe. 16th & 17th Bdes. Nothing to report. A good deal of shelling of back areas, with little damage.	14th Div. relieved the 49th Div on our left.
28th Dec	A lot of gassed animals picked up and sent in to the V.O. 6 cats. Poperinghe shelled, and back areas persistently during the day. Wind safe. Situation normal. Weather fine.	
29th Dec	Wind SE. But not dangerous. Shelling of back areas continuous during the day. Weather fine, but windy.	
30th Dec	Weather fine, mud drying up. Situation normal. Wind safe.	
31st Dec	Situation normal. Nothing to report.	E J Ronaldehay CS.

PAPER G/44/7.

SECRET.

G/44/7.

16th Infantry Brigade.
18th Infantry Brigade.
71st Infantry Brigade.
G.O.C. R.A.
C.R.E.
A.D.M.S.
"Q".
14th Division.
49th Divsn Signals

---

1. No date has yet been assigned for the relief of the 14th by the 6th Division, but there is likely to be very short notice.

2. The following will be the arrangements:-

   1st night - Right Sector - 18th Brigade relieves 42nd Bde.
   -do-   - Left Sector - 16th Brigade relieves 41st Bde.
   2nd Night - Centre Sector - 71st Brigade relieves 43rd Bde.

   Brigades will take over the sectors exactly as now held by the 14th Division. A sketch map with the boundaries is attached.

3. Brigadiers relieving on the 1st night will get into communication with the Brigadiers they relieve during today. A motor car will be placed at their disposal to do so.

4. Artillery relief will be carried out direct between C.R.A.s on the 2nd and 3rd nights, unless the 14th Division require to relieve one Brigade of Artillery on the 1st night.

5. Trench Mortars. The 38th Trench Mortar Battery will be allotted to the 18th Infantry Brigade, and the 26th Trench Mortar Battery to the 71st Infantry Brigade, except two guns which will be allotted to the 16th Infantry Brigade.

6. All gum boots thigh are being handed over by the 14th to the 6th Division.

7. Brigadiers will report the names of the battalions they propose to move into the line, as early as possible, in order that transport arrangements may be made for them.

8. Acknowledge.

H.Q. 6th Divn.
5th Decr, 1915.

Ironside
Major,
General Staff.

DIVISIONAL OPERATION ORDER NO. 47.

SECRET

War Diary

Copy No. 15

6th DIVISION OPERATION ORDER No. 47:-

Reference Map Sheet 28, 1/40,000.

Reference G/44/7, dated 5th December 1915, of which para. 2 is amended:-

1. On night 15th/16th December, the 18th Infantry Brigade will relieve the 42nd Infantry Brigade in the Right Sector, and the 71st Infantry Brigade will relieve the 43rd Infantry Brigade in the Centre Sector of the 14th Division line.

    Machine Guns will be relieved on the night 14th/15th.

2. On the night 16th/17th December, the 16th Infantry Brigade will relieve the 41st Infantry Brigade in the Left Sector of the 14th Division line.

    Machine Guns will be relieved on the night 15th/16th.

3. All arrangements for the above reliefs to be made between the Brigadiers concerned.

ARTILLERY. 4. The 6th Division Artillery will relieve the 14th Division Artillery on the 16th and 17th December, relief being completed by the morning of the 18th.

   All details to be arranged between C.R.A.s concerned.

AMMUNITION, STORES, etc. 5. All ammunition, grenades, tools, and trench stores are to be handed over by the 14th Division.

   These must be carefully checked and receipts given.

DOCUMENTS, MAPS, etc. 6. Copies of Defence Schemes, programmes of work in hand and proposed, and trench maps will be taken over by incoming Brigadiers.

FIELD COYS. 7. Field Companies will be attached as follows:-

   16th Infantry Brigade........London Field Company.
   18th Infantry Brigade........12th Field Company.
   71st Infantry Brigade........West Riding Field Company.

   Relief of the Field Companies 14th Division will take place on the same night as those of the Brigades to which they are attached, arrangements being made between the C.R.E.s concerned.

ACCOMMODATION. 8. BURGOMASTER FARM (H.5.a.5.7) is allotted to the 16th Infantry Brigade.

   MACHINE GUN FARM (H.5.centre) and KAT FARM (H.10.a.) are allotted to the 71st Infantry Brigade.

MOVEMENTS. 9. Movements in connection with the reliefs of the Infantry will take place as shown on attached Table, further arrangements for movements by train and bus being made by "Q".

2.

THIGH BOOTS. 10. All thigh boots are to be taken over from the 14th Division and receipts given. Special instructions will be issued.

COMMAND. 11. Brigadiers 6th Division will assume command of their Sectors on completion of reliefs, and report completion to 6th and 14th Divisions.

G.O.C. 6th Division will assume command of the line at 10 am on December 16th, C.R.A. 6th Division assuming command of the Artillery at the same hour.

12. Please acknowledge.

Lt. Colonel,
General Staff.

Issued at   pm.

```
Copy No.  1 to 16th Infantry Brigade.
  ..  ..  2 .. 18th Infantry Brigade.
  ..  ..  3 .. 71st Infantry Brigade.
  ..  ..  4 .. C.R.A.
  ..  ..  5 .. C.R.E.
  ..  ..  6 .. Signals.
  ..  ..  7 .. "Q".
  ..  ..  8 .. A.D.M.S.
  ..  ..  9 .. Mounted Troops.
  ..  .. 10 .. 6th Corps.
  ..  .. 11 .. 14th Division.
  ..  .. 12 .. 17th Division.
  ..  .. 13 .. 49th Division.
  ..  .. 14 .. Office.
  ..  .. 15 .. War Diary.
```

Brigade.	Unit.	Present Position.	14th/15th Decr.	15th/16th Decr.	16th/17th Decr.
15th	1.Grs.	Houtkerk.	Houtkerk	Houtkerk.	Canal.
	1st Buffs.	Houtkerk.	Houtkerk.	Houtkerk.	16th I.B.Billets, Poperinghe. By march route not to arrive before 4.30 p.m.
		H.Q.E.2.b.			
	8th Bedfords.	Watou.	Watou.	Camp "C". By march route Not to arrive before 5 p.m.	Trenches. Entrain G 5.45.p.m.
	1st K.S.L.I.	H.Q. Watou. Houtkerk. H.Q.E.20.a.	Houtkerk.	71st I.B.Billets. Pop. By march route not to arrive Station 3.45. before 7.30 p.m.	Trenches. Entrain Po Station 3.45.
	2nd Y.& Lancs.	Herzeele. H.Q. Herzeele.	Herzeele.	16th I.B.Billets. Pop: By march route not to arrive Pop. before 5.30 p.m.	½ bn. Trenches. E ½ bn. Cam Station 3.15 ½ bn. Camp march route arrive befor Trenches.
	M.Gun. Co.	Houtkerk.	Houtkerk.	Canal. Embark on 3 buses from Houtkerk Ch: 2.30 p.m.	
18th.	H.Q.	Rue des Pots. Poperinghe.	Rue des Pots. Poperinghe.	Canal.	Canal.
	1st W.Yorks.	Elverdinghe.	49th Div: Area.	Trenches. By bus if possible.Details to be arranged later.	Trenches.
	11th Essex.	Canal.	18 I.B.Billets. Pop. Entrain Asylum 5.15.p.m.	18 I.B.Billets. Poperinghe.	18 I.B.Billets. P
	2nd D.L.I.	Camp A. "C".	Camp "C".	Trenches. Entrain G.6.d. 5.45.p.m.	Trenches.
	14th D.L.I.	18 I.B.Billets. Poperinghe.	Canal. Entrain Pop. Station 4.15.p.m.	Canal.	Canal.
	1st Q.W.R.	Canal.	Canal.	Canal.	Canal.
	M.Gun. Co.	Poperinghe.	Canal. Entrain Pop. Station 4.15.p.m.	Trenches.	Trenches.

NOTE:- Trains will leave stations 15 minutes after the times given above.

Brigade.	Unit.	Present Position.	14th/15th Decr.	15th/16th Decr.	16th/17th Decr.
71st	Headquarters.	43.Rue de L'Hopital. Poperinghe.	43.Rue de L'Hopital. Poperinghe.	Canal.	Canal.
"	9th Norfolks.	16 I.B.Billets. Poperinghe.	16 I.B.Billets.Pop.	Trenches. Entrain Pop. Station. 3.45.p.m.	Trenches.
"	9th Suffolks.	Camp "A".	Camp "A".	Camp "A".	Camp "A".
"	1st Leics.	Houtkerk. H.Q. Houtkerk.	Houtkerk.	Houtkerk.	71 I.B.Billets.Pop. By march route not to arrive before 3.30.p.m.
"	2nd N. & D's.	71 I.B.Billets. Poperinghe.	71 I.B.Billets. Poperinghe.	Trenches. Entrain Pop. Station 7.45.p.m.	Trenches.
"	M.Gun. Co.	Poperinghe.	Canal. Entrain Pop. Station 4.15.p.m.	Trenches.	Trenches.

NOTE:- Train will leave Stations 15 minutes after the times given above.

R. S. MAY,

Lieut.-Colonel,

A.A. & Q.M.G., 6th Divn.

14th December, 1915.

www.ingramcontent.com/pod-product-compliance
Lightning Source LLC
Chambersburg PA
CBHW080816010526
44111CB00015B/2567